PROPHETS IN THEIR
OWN COUNTRY

Prophets in Their Own Country

Living Saints and the Making of Sainthood in the Later Middle Ages

AVIAD M. KLEINBERG

WITHDRAWN

The University of Chicago Press
Chicago and London

The University of Chicago Press, Chicago 60637
The University of Chicago Press, Ltd., London
© 1992 by The University of Chicago
All rights reserved. Published 1992
Paperback edition 1997
Printed in the United States of America

01 00 99 98 97   5 4 3 2

ISBN: 0–226–43971–2 (cloth)
ISBN: 0–226–43972–0 (paperback)

Library of Congress Cataloging-in-Publication Data

Kleinberg, Aviad M.
    Prophets in their own country: Living saints and the making of
sainthood in the later middle ages / Aviad M. Kleinberg.
        p. cm.
    Includes bibliographical references and index.
    1. Christian saints—Europe—History.   2. Church history—
Middle Ages, 600–1500.   I. Title.
BX4659.E85K54   1992
235'.2'0902—dc20   91–38561
                                                              CIP

IN MEMORY OF MY GRANDPARENTS,
MOSHE MORDECHAI AND RIVKA RACHEL,
MY AUNTS, ESTHER AND YOSEPHA,
AND MY UNCLE, CHAIM YOSL, WHO
WERE MURDERED BY THE NAZIS

"And when the Sabbath had come, He began to teach in the synagogue. And many hearing Him were astonished, saying, 'Where did this man get these things? And what wisdom is this which is given to him, that such mighty works are performed by his hands? Is this not the carpenter, the son of Mary and brother of James, Joses, Judas, and Simon? And are not his sisters here with us?' And they were offended at Him. But Jesus said to them: 'A prophet is not without honor, but in his own country, among his own relatives, and in his own house.' And He could do no mighty work there, except that He laid His hands upon a few sick people, and healed them. And He marvelled because of their unbelief."

(Mark 6:2–6)

"'And Noah was a just man, perfect in his generations.' *In his generations:* Some of our rabbis interpret it in his praise: had he lived in a generation of just men, he would have been even more just. Some interpret it to his blame: in his generation he was considered just; had he lived in the generation of Abraham, he would have been considered of no significance at all."

(Rashi, gloss to Gen. 6:9)

CONTENTS

CONTENTS

PREFACE

Prophets in Their Own Country is a preliminary discussion of the role living saints played in medieval society and of the social processes by which a community came to recognize one of its members as a saint. Strangely (at least for me—we always find it strange that others do not share our interests), this problem has never been discussed systematically. Like all preliminary discussions, the book runs the risk of either saying too many things or of saying the same thing too many times. It was my goal to ask the sources a new set of questions; the answers I suggest can only be partial. I write in what follows that we need to explore the full spectrum of patterns of saintly interaction. I could only suggest certain possibilities. Others, I hope, will complete the picture and make it richer in tone and nuance.

In a study that seeks to uncover the process of making medieval holy men and women it seemed only natural to wish to tell readers about the process of producing my own analysis. I cannot accept the role historians often assume of impartial observers, totally absent from their texts. The partial observers referred to in the title of chapter 3 are both medieval onlookers and modern historians. All historians engage in a dialogue with their texts. They bring with them their methodological and personal creeds and, if they are honest, they do not try to conceal them from the reader. I told readers why I have made certain choices, even when I knew that those choices would not be easy to defend. In doing so, however, I also tried to avoid the tendency to turn historical writing into an excuse for autobiographical ruminations or theoretical bravado. My book is neither about the things that motivate me as a historian, nor about pure theoretical problems, nor a political essay in disguise. My main interest is medieval people. All other discussions are meant to improve our understanding of their world.

To the best of my ability, I tried to avoid the use of jargon, be it literary jargon, social-science jargon, feminist jargon, psychoanalytical jargon, and even—if such a thing really exists—historiographical jargon. I resent both the sacred obscurity it brings into our writing and its use to keep away the uninitiated and make it easier for the elect to recognize one another. Readers will realize very quickly, I believe, that while I found many theoretical "systems" useful, and have used them in my work, I have not become a devotee of any of them.

Finally, I gave some thought to the issue of gender in my writing. I was unhappy with the apologetic use of the masculine ("whenever I say he it means he or she"), and I did not want to always use the plural as a substitute for the missing neuter. I decided to use "he or she" when appropriate and simply switch from the masculine to the feminine in talking about the medieval saint or the modern historian. This might be a bit confusing at first, but I think it is more natural than the alternatives.

It is a pleasant duty to thank the people who read various versions of this work and offered me their comments and their advice. Sally McKee read the very first draft of what eventually became this book. She submitted my work to the most penetrating critique and suggested thoughtful ways for improvement. It is thanks to her that a group of vague ideas became a coherent argument.

I had the privilege of having Brian Stock as my supervisor at the University of Toronto. He broadened my intellectual horizons in ways I will always be grateful for, encouraging me to find my own way, even when that meant disagreeing with him. My debt to him goes beyond his many helpful suggestions concerning this book.

Maruja Jackman and Roy Aarons graciously volunteered to give my book the knowledgeable layperson's reading. They asked many insightful, and at times unexpected, questions—questions that made me rethink and rephrase whole sections of the manuscript. Phyllis Pobst read the manuscript with typical thoroughness and saved me from many an infelicity. I would also like to thank the readers of the University of Chicago Press for their suggestions and their encouragement and the Social Sciences and Humanities Research Council of Canada for its financial support.

1

SAINTS AND SAINTLY
SITUATIONS

THIS book is about lived sainthood in the later Middle Ages. It does not deal with the abstract notions of sanctity developed by theologians, nor with the veneration of relics or the role the saints played in the liturgy. It is a study of sainthood as it was "practiced" in day-to-day encounters between living individuals considered saints by their contemporaries and other members of their communities. The chapters that follow examine the relation between official and unofficial sainthood (chapter 2), saints' *Lives* as a literary genre and their reception by the modern reader (chapter 3), the careers of four medieval saints (chapters 4–6), and the role played by miracles in the rise and fall of a saintly reputation (chapter 7). The present chapter offers, in its first part, some preliminary observations about sainthood as a social phenomenon and, in the second part, an examination of the quantitative and sociological-anthropological approaches to sainthood.

As the saint began to fade from the memory of the community, her image underwent a series of changes. The saint of everyday life with her ambiguous and contradictory messages, with her warts and wrinkles, was gradually replaced by a more coherent creation. The oral tradition simplified the saint; it turned her into a mnemonic unit. Many of the trivialities that make a living person were removed in order to get to the saintly core—that which made this saint holy. Among other things, society's role in making the saint was forgotten. The saint's contemporaries could tell about discord and skepticism, about collaboration and collusion, but with time little but the saint's victories remained. The saint of posterity was presented in her Sunday clothes, with the other persons in the picture almost disappearing into the hazy background.

The fuller image of the saint passed into the sphere of bookish culture, predominantly clerical. Only the literati had access to the written eyewitness accounts—canonization proceedings, mem-

1

oirs, and the early *Lives*—where much of the potentially dangerous or "irrelevant" aspects of the saints' lives were retained. But in the simplified adaptations of earlier works that the literati produced for the unlettered or barely lettered, the saint was similarly stripped of most of her contradictions and eccentricities and presented to the public in an ideal form.

Early biographies of a new saint—one not yet universally considered a saint—were rarely the smooth stereotypical product they could turn into with time. The biographer of a living or recently deceased individual had to reach a compromise between conflicting drives. On the one hand, the biographer was familiar with the canonical models of his trade, *Lives* considered classics, and wanted his own work to resemble them, just as he hoped to demonstrate that his saint resembled the great saints of the past. On the other hand, he was under considerable pressure to deviate from the canonical models. People who met the saint wanted the story of their encounter told, even if it did not convey a clear moral message. A mention in the *Life* of a saint guaranteed a modest measure of immortality. Contemporaries were also curious about details which future generations might consider irrelevant.

Thus, the writer of a *Life* written before or shortly after the saint's death was quite likely to produce a surplus of information that blurred the fine contours of the ideal. This is not an infallible rule; some early *Lives* are in fact quite stereotypical and some later versions retain the freshness of the original, but the tendency was, with very few exceptions, for early eyewitness accounts to be richer and less conventional than later versions.[1]

The idealized *Lives* of later generations and of purely fictional saints have led many scholars to a mechanistic approach toward the genre in general. Instead of examining the way in which each hagiographer adapted the conventions to his saint, most studies have stressed the elements common to all *Lives*. Historians have charted the typology of the different possible "plots" available to the saints and dismissed the peculiarities of each reenactment as trivial. As a result, saints' *Lives* appear to be much more regular in scholarly literature than they are in reality (I will return to this subject in chapter 3).

1. Cf. Leon de Kerval, ed., *Sancti Antonii de Padua vitae duae* (Paris, 1904).

The eyewitness/biographer usually repeated many of the clichés of the hagiographical genre, but by proclaiming his loyalty to standard representations, he could interpret their meaning in such a way as to give them an entirely new content. The hagiographer could affirm, for example, that his saint lived an ascetic life or was completely orthodox, but relate actions and words that could not easily be interpreted as ascetic or orthodox.[2] Furthermore, similar elements can have different meanings in different *Lives*. Actions and words acquire their meaning from their role within the *Life;* only later can we relate them to the broader context of the genre. Even the most basic cultural symbols could be changed when it was felt that such idiosyncratic use was necessary. Thus, the lamb or the sheep is the symbol of Christ and the elect par excellence. Goats, on the other hand, symbolized the wicked. Yet Raymond of Capua does not hesitate to liken Christ to a goat (*hircus*) to make a metaphor work better.[3] Similar miracles, similar phrases, similar gestures could mean different things in different contexts.[4]

The dismissal of all saints' *Lives* as untrustworthy and stereotypical is partly to blame for the neglect of the sociology of medieval sainthood. It is simpler and less risky to treat all *Lives* as literary products—which of course they are—and not get entangled in an effort to tell social reality from literary invention. But this is not the only reason. The notorious inaccuracies of medieval sources do not deter scholars from writing the history of medieval economy. It seems that another reason is responsible for the dearth of scholarly work on the interaction between living saints and their communities.

That reason is the notion, implicit in most scholarly works on medieval sainthood, that a saintly reputation is a natural, indeed instinctive, reaction to the saint's charisma. The Weberian notion of charisma still prevails among students of sainthood (whether they actually derive it from Weber or not): charisma is a quality of certain individuals that causes people to be "carried away" and submit themselves unquestioningly to the person possessing it. According to this view, both success and failure of a charismatic can be

---

2. Pierre Delooz, "Pour une étude sociologique de la sainteté canonisée dans l'Eglise catholique," *Archives de sociologie des religions* 13 (1962); 17–43.

3. Raymond of Capua, *Vita S. Catharinae Senensis* 1.7, *AA.SS.* 30 Apr., p. 891.

4. Cf. Dan Sperber, *Le symbolisme en général* (Paris, 1974), pp. 148–49.

explained solely in terms of the performer, his self-assurance and sense of mission, and not in terms of his audience. Even when a charismatic leader is deserted by his followers, it does not indicate that they exercise any significant influence over him. It is to be assumed that the charismatic himself had lost his charisma and that this was realized by his followers.[5]

The audience, if we were to accept this notion of sainthood, does not determine the saintly performance, but merely reacts to it. When a person really "has it" (sainthood), others cannot but treat him according to the conventions that regulate the relationship between saints and ordinary mortals. Since it is evident, however, that not all people react in the same way to the same type of person, historians have assumed that different audiences are conditioned differently. The various ideals of sainthood operate like litmus paper: an audience remains indifferent unless exposed to the right substance. The Italian saint might not be appreciated in England, since English expectations were different, but within his own milieu the true saint would always be recognized and respected.

Studies of historical sainthood, then, have considered it sufficient to investigate the psychological processes occurring within the saint on the one hand and the culturally determined audience expectations on the other hand. Between these two spheres, it seems, there is nothing that requires explanation. The processes that actually established a person as a saint, the specific social transactions that made a saint out of a nonsaint, have been left out of this picture.[6] But sainthood was not immediately and universally acclaimed. The status of saint was conferred upon a person in a gradual process that involved disagreement and negotiation, as well as collaboration and even collusion. Without an understanding of

5. Weber's classic discussion of charismatic authority—in which category he includes Christian saints—can be found in his *The Theory of Social and Economic Organization* (1947, pp. 329–41).

6. A notable exception is William A. Christian, Jr. In an article on apparitions in twentieth-century Spain, Christian writes: "The audience, the Greek chorus, the hagiographer, the message takers and the message transmitters should be as much the focus of our attention as the charismatic figures on whom they are concentrating" ("Tapping and Defining New Power: The First Month of Visions at Ezquioga, July 1931," *American Ethnologist* 14, no. 1 [Feb, 1987]: 163). I am looking forward to Christian's forthcoming book on contemporary apparitions.

those social mechanisms, modern scholarship detaches the product (sainthood) from the labor that was needed to produce it as a social phenomenon.

By focusing either on the psychology of individual saints or on the saintly types, supposedly expressing a saintly common denominator, scholars have left the actual development of a devotion largely uncharted and often misunderstood. The distinctions between real life and literature are blurred. For while it is true that there were certain generic conventions regulating the depiction of different categories of saints, it is not at all clear that such common traits existed in actuality. People's reputations were not created in a void. The specific frame of reference within which they were seen (bishops, monks, laypersons, etc.) presented them with a finite repertoire of choices (bishops cannot get married, for example; laypersons can). This was especially important in the first stages of a saintly career, when a saint still had to prove that he or she was like other saints. But it could not have been more than a vague framework. A reputation was not created by means of a checklist; it was created in everyday encounters that often made the broader categories irrelevant.

The medieval perception of sainthood was fluid; it was personal, concrete, and of an ad hoc nature. Rather than trying to fit individuals to a clearly defined ideal, communities shaped their ideas of sainthood around specific individuals. Medieval communities venerated simultaneously very different individuals who belonged to the same external categories, indifferent to the logical contradictions such behavior entailed. Evans-Pritchard has noted that "Zande doctrines are so numerous, varied and plastic that a man [or a community] can always find in them an element to serve his interests in any given situation. He does not deny the doctrines, but he selects from them what is most to his advantage in each situation and excludes the rest" (1937, p. 133). In the absence of a consistent and universally accepted system of classification, the status of specific cases is perennially ambiguous. This ambiguity gives rise to conflicting interpretations and opens the door for social negotiation.

Sainthood is not a quality or a set of characteristics but an attribution. Although certain acts are accepted as virtuous, the sanctity of the performer is not a self-evident consequence of such acts. The

5

true nature of saintly acts and the legitimacy of using them as proof of sainthood in a particular case needs to be debated and agreed upon. In Ernest Gellner's words:

Agurramenhood [Moroccan sainthood] is in the eyes of the beholders, all of them in a sense squint to see what is in the eyes of other beholders, and if they see it there, then they see it also. Collectively, this characteristic is an ascription, but for any one man it is an objective fact, an inherent characteristic: for if all others see it in a man, then for any single beholder, that man truly has it. (1969, p. 74)

The inherent characteristic they all ascribe to the saint is moral excellence, but its presence is too uncertain to permit an enduring ascription and a general consensus. It is rarely the case that "all others see it in a man." There is more than one "it". Different beholders behold different things and so one can never stop squinting. Worse still, saints and devotees must be prepared to face beholders who simply will not see it.[7]

At least as long as the saint lived, the debate over his or her correct classification remained unsettled. Not only is the saint of group A not a saint for group B, but the saint of situation C is not considered a saint in situation D. The living saint could be given no formal (papal or other) recognition, for one could never be certain about his or her future activities. The saintly status of a living person was never established once and for all; the tacit "pact" between saint and community had to be constantly renegotiated.

Consider an incident from the *Life* of St. Margaret of Cortona. Margaret used to cry and groan loudly while she prayed to God. Her neighbors gathered around her cell and, listening to her fervent prayers and tearful sighs, felt "restored in the love of God." One day, the saint's companion with whom she shared her cell sensed that the women were distracting Margaret with their pray-

7. Cf. Howard S. Becker, *Outsiders: Studies in the Sociology of Deviance* (New York, 1963), p. 9. Reinhard Bendix notes (1962, p. 304 n.6) that Weber did not "consider the alternative possibility, namely that the disciples and the community do not wish to preserve the charisma of the leader and indeed reject him as a 'false prophet.' . . . Such an eventuality," he notes, "would be evidence in Weber's terms that the leader has lost his charism; the people reject him because he had failed to 'prove' himself, or because he has proved himself 'false.'"

ing and loud crying. She went out and tried to make them leave. One of the women responded with great rage. Margaret, who heard the voices, came out of her cell and tried to soothe the woman's anger. She sent her companion away and begged the woman to join her in her cell for the night. But the woman, still furious, refused to be placated. She heaped insults on Margaret's head, would not enter the saint's cell nor let the saint enter her own house.[8] This abrupt switch from devotion to abuse was not denounced as sacrilege by the other women. Although a short while earlier they had treated Margaret publicly with the deepest devotion, they were not horrified by their friend's behavior. If anyone, it was the saint herself who seemed eager to be reconciled. The people who treated a person as a saint in one instance could treat her quite differently the next.

The living saint's status could be called in doubt at any given moment. In every situation, depending on circumstances and audience, the saint played a somewhat different role. It is more useful, then, to regard not the saint, but the saintly situation—that situation where a person is labeled a saint and his or her behavior interpreted within the parameters of saintly performance—as the basic unit in the dynamics of sainthood. The biographical approach extends sainthood beyond its realistic contours to cover the entire personality and the full range of activity of those whose frequent participation in saintly situations makes them known as saints. Much of what the saints do, however, is unrelated to their saintly performance and should not be included in a social study of sainthood.

From a social point of view, saints exist in a Berkeleyan world— if they are not seen they do not exist. This does not mean that the saint's reputation relies only on what he or she actually did in public; a reputation relied heavily on what saints reputedly did in private. It means that, for others, saints are what they are seen and believed to be, not what they actually are. The saints' inner lives and sincerity, important though they may be in theory, are of little concern to society, because they are beyond its reach. In other words,

8. Giunta Bevegnati, *Vita Margaritae de Cortona* 92–93, *AA.SS.* 22 Feb., p. 322.

the charismatic need not believe in the authenticity of his powers to succeed in his role.[9] The sincere ecstatic and the successful imposter play exactly the same social role and belong in the same social category.

But how can we know which living individuals were labeled saints? This is a more difficult question than it may seem at first sight. Simply being referred to as a "saint" is insufficient. The term was used very loosely in the Middle Ages to refer to anyone who lived a pious life. The most important "symptom" of sainthood, one that the historian can use, is the treatment of the saint as a source of supernatural spiritual power.

The saint possessed virtue (meaning both a quality of life and power) and as such gave rise to the expectation that she would manifest her power. The individuals I shall study are those to whom both moral excellence (however vaguely defined) and supernatural power were attributed. It is important to insist on the ascription of virtue, because power was ascribed to other categories of persons who were not saints, such as magicians and demoniacs. This definition, as we shall see, is not very different from the papal requirement that candidates for canonization manifest both *virtus morum* and *virtus signorum* (a virtuous life and the power to work miracles). The difference is that whereas the papacy saw these requirements as objective and tried to prove them empirically, I am interested in them as ascriptions: it is not relevant for my purposes whether *X* was really virtuous and his or her miracles authentic, just that others considered them to be so.[10]

A historical understanding of sainthood cannot remain at the abstract level. A phenomenon that is essentially an interaction needs to be examined in the here and now of specific situations.

9. Weber doubts whether Joseph Smith, the founder of Mormonism, should be included in a discussion of charismatic authority, because "there is the possibility that he was a very sophisticated type of deliberate swindler" (Weber 1947, p. 329). But what matters is not whether or not Smith was a true prophet, but that his disciples believed him to be one.

10. A similar distinction between the saintly and saints is made in Thomas Cantelupe's process of canonization by his steward, John de Clare. Asked about his master, John states in his native French: "Verrayement, il fut bon homo et de bone vie; mes ieo ne sey pas quey miracles dussent estre fet pur luy." (The full text of the London depositions is published in André Vauchez, 1981, appendix 2, pp. 649–52. John's words are on p. 650).

"Thick descriptions," to use a term made popular by Clifford Geertz, of a small number of cases are more likely to do justice to medieval saints than a cursory survey of a great number of cases. This book offers three detailed studies of medieval saints: Christina of Stommeln (1242–1312) in chapter 4, Lukardis of Oberweimar (c. 1257–1309) and Douceline of Digne (1214–74) in chapter 5, and Francis of Assisi (1181–1226) in chapter 6.

I have selected these particular saints not because they are more representative than others—this question will be dealt with presently—but because their biographies provide rich descriptions of different levels of saint/audience interaction. My cases will not be presented in chronological order but according to the size of the saints' following, moving from the least popular saint to the most popular. Christina of Stommeln, a laywoman of peasant stock, won the admiration of few people apart from her biographer, the Swedish Dominican Peter of Dacia. Lukardis of Oberweimar was venerated as a saint by the small Cistercian community to which she belonged. Douceline of Digne, who enjoyed a reputation of sainthood in Marseilles, was used mainly as a contrast to Lukardis of Oberweimar. Francis of Assisi, possibly the most popular saint of the Middle Ages, provides a control case of sorts for the three women. I hope to show that regardless of his power, Francis was as dependent on the reaction of his spectators as his humbler counterparts.[11]

But let us return to the question of the representative saint. One common solution to the problem of valid generalizations is the quantitative approach. It guarantees that all cases included in the data base will be taken into account. Common denominators reached by careful counting and statistical analysis are more reliable, it is assumed, more representative, than would be cases selected on the basis of impressionistic observations. Saints, moreover, seem particularly appropriate for quantification. We know more about saints than about any other category of medieval people. Information of some sort regarding a great number of holy individuals exists in conveniently indexed printed collections. It seems almost natural to collect this data, arrange it in different

11. Cf. Octavio Ignacio Romano V (1965: 1151–73). The author uses the spread of the healer/saint's fame as the analytical criterion.

categories, run it through a computer, and produce the "average" medieval saint.

If, however, my earlier observations about the nature of sainthood are correct, what we need is not a typology of biographical profiles but of modes of social dynamics. We need not the "average saint" but a repertoire of interactive models. Quantification is not well suited for *this* task. I would like to proceed now to an examination of two quantitative studies, each with its distinctive problems, but also with problems common, I believe, to any application of quantification to the study of sainthood.

André Vauchez (1981) has written what is to date the most important study of medieval sainthood. His erudite book, *La sainteté en Occident aux derniers siècles du moyen âge*, describes the history of the process of canonization in the late Middle Ages and offers a typology of late medieval saints based mostly on canonization records. The author dedicates only one chapter ("Typologie de la sainteté officielle: Aspects quantitatifs," pp. 291–328) to a quantitative breakdown of his data. Vauchez uses quantification to chart changes over time in attitudes toward sainthood as reflected in papal canonizations. His study of saintly models, of the emergence of cults, and of the political power play involved in the process of canonization is rich and nuanced. But in an attempt to reach more solid generalizations, Vauchez runs into serious problems.

Vauchez analyzes persons who were either canonized or for whom a process was instigated between 1198 and 1431. He notes, for example, that between 1198 and 1304, 17.7 percent of lay candidates for canonization were Scandinavian. Between 1305 and 1431 that percentage rose to 18.2. More significantly, Vauchez calculates that between 1198 and 1304 laypersons constituted 24 percent of canonizations, while between 1305 and 1341 the number rose to 30 percent, indicating, in Vauchez's view, an increase in the importance of lay saints. It must be remembered, however, that we are dealing with very small numbers. One Scandinavian (out of a total of ten canonizations) was canonized between 1198 and 1304, and one (out of a total of eight canonizations) between 1304 and 1431. As for laypersons, six were canonized in the earlier period and three in the later.

Although Vauchez's general category (based on canonization

proceedings) is clear enough, his subcategories are not always as indisputable. Catherine of Siena, for example, though a laywoman from a strictly legal point of view, was a Dominican tertiary, wore a habit, and was generally regarded as a Dominican saint. One can also question whether Bridget of Sweden, the founder of a religious order bearing her name, should be considered a lay saint. Her saintly career began in earnest only after her husband's death in 1344, after which she led the life of a religious until her death in 1373. If she too is taken off the list, we are left with laypersons constituting only 10 percent of saints in the fourteenth century. This 10 percent stands for St. Sebald, an obscure eleventh-century hermit, who by the time of his canonization in 1429 had become a figure of legend, supposedly the son of the king of Denmark.

According to Vauchez himself, Sebald owed his canonization neither to popular demand nor to a new papal appreciation of the laity, but to the pressure applied on Pope Martin V by the city of Nuremberg, whose patron saint Sebald was. In Vauchez's words (1981, p. 98) "The city of Nuremberg extracted from Martin V the canonization of its patron St. Sebald . . . , who under different circumstances could never have aspired to such an honor." If these qualifications are accepted, there was, if anything, a decrease in the importance of the laity in papal canonizations in the later Middle Ages.

My point, however, is not that the importance of lay saints did not rise in the fourteenth century, but rather that the quantitative treatment gives a semblance of precision to data that are often very ambiguous. Vauchez's sample—thirty five canonizations and thirty six unsuccessful processes—is too small to permit meaningful quantification. The increases and decreases in percentage points convey a false sense of precision, where the margin of error is often as large as the group itself.

There are more serious problems with this type of approach. First, for the sake of "quantification," it treats all cases as equal. Second, it assumes that one can isolate single elements in a saint's dossier—for example, status or class—and treat them as meaningful in relation to similar information in other cases. The two points are very closely related. Vauchez assumes implicitly that all canonizations were the same. The canonization of St. Catherine of Siena—an immensely popular saint—is given the same weight as that of St. Sebald—a saint almost unknown outside Nuremberg. Each is considered as an equivalent reflection of papal and popular attitudes.

This is a highly questionable premise. Canonizations were the result of a variety of causes and conflicting pressures in the church. The political situation and the person of the pope could have a decisive influence on the successful termination of a cause. There is also a time lag that distorts the results, since canonization could be the culmination of a very lengthy process. The canonization of Catherine of Siena took place when it did mainly because a Sienese, Pius II, sat on the papal throne. Had it not been for that, her canonization might have been delayed for an indefinite time.

This brings us to the second point: can all elements in the saint's dossier be considered equally important? Catherine's origin was a vital element in her canonization, as was Sebald's in his. However, they were not just civic patrons; Sebald was a pilgrim and a hermit, Catherine was a mystic and a stigmatic, and so on. If we isolate the different elements in the saints' dossiers, we may come up with an impression that the papacy was more prone to canonize laypersons, or hermits, while the reality might be that it was more sensitive to civic pressure. My point is not that my interpretation of the cases of Catherine and Sebald is the only one possible, but that the quantitative analysis of the data with its need to have similar basic units for comparison oversimplifies complex material.

Consider the case of St. Louis of Toulouse. Louis was canonized by Pope John XXII, who was his personal friend and had great love for the young man. Louis was also very much under the influence of the Spiritual Franciscans. He was on his way to Rome to renounce his bishopric in order to live more faithfully the (Spiritual) Franciscan ideal of holiness when he died. It would be a mistake to see his canonization as an approval of his politics, or his spirituality, for if there is one thing of which John XXII cannot be accused, it is any special liking for Spiritual Franciscans. Likewise, St. Elzéar of Sabran was canonized by Pope Urban V, who was his nephew and his godson. One wonders whether a similar layman, not related to the pope, would have been canonized by him.

In sum, when a pope ordered a person's canonization, he did not thereby approve of every element in that person's dossier. Similarly, not every aspect of the saint had the same weight in his cult, regardless of its importance in the saint's life. St. Louis was often depicted in late medieval iconography as a young bishop, though he was neither comfortable nor competent in this role. St. Jerome, for example, is always depicted as a cardinal in late medieval art, historical anachronism notwithstanding.

The medieval papacy did not have a preconceived list of necessary conditions for canonization against which candidates were compared. Except for a number of fixed, technical minimum requirements, the papacy tolerated all kinds of saints. Popes canonized persons, not ideal profiles. Being the pope's uncle was probably never a formal requirement, but it could help, while living a pious life and working miracles were necessary, but not sufficient. Elzéar of Sabran's wife, Delphine, was in many ways her husband's alter ego. In fact, she was the driving force behind Elzéar's choice of a saintly way of life. Nor was there any shortage of miracles ascribed to her intervention, yet she was never canonized.

Saints were canonized at a particular moment in time because all the procedures had been exhausted, because the pope was sympathetic to the cause, because it was an opportune moment, and because nobody objected. A delay in canonization or even a refusal to canonize did not necessarily mean papal disapproval, nor were its consequences critical to a cult. Thus, treating papal canonizations as a sensitive seismograph of papal or popular attitudes can be a mistake. With canonization such a rare event in the Middle Ages (thirty five canonizations between 1198 and 1434), and since there were neither definite guidelines for papal approval nor a consistent policy, it would be dangerous to try to draw conclusions from the entire body of papal canonizations over the centuries. It is safer to treat each case separately within its historical context.

In *Saints and Society,* Donald Weinstein and Rudolph Bell (1982) attempt a more ambitious quantitative study. They use as their data base a list of 864 saints derived from Pierre Delooz's list in *Sociologie et canonisations* (1969). Delooz, relying for his data on the collection, *Les vies des saints et des bienheureux,*[12] divided saints into four categories: 1, 3, and 4 consist of persons who gained

---

12. Jules Baudot et al., *Les vies des saints et des bienheureux selon l'ordre du calendrier avec l'historique des fêtes,* 13 vols. (Paris, 1935–39). Delooz used this work simply because it consists of conveniently abridged *Lives* in French.

some sort of papal recognition (as saints or as blessed); 2 consists of 1,188 persons who were venerated without papal approval (Delooz 1969, pp. 125–40). Weinstein and Bell (1982, p. 278) took from Delooz's list all the names in the three groups of official saints relevant for their time range (the years 1000 through 1700) and every second name from the group of unofficial saints.

The authors counter possible objections to their choice of a list by conceding from the outset that they

make no claim that [their] sample is random in a technical statistical sense. Since no one agrees even on the 'population-at-risk,' such a sample would be impossible. Rather, we have included all the major cases and a large enough number of others to be reasonably confident about our statistical findings. Nevertheless, we are most confident about our numerical findings when they corroborate literary sources or other forms of evidence. (1982, p. 279)

Admitting a problem does not solve it. There are a number of objections one could raise about Weinstein's and Bell's strategy.[13] First, there is the question of the "population-at-risk": what are the criteria for inclusion in the sample, and what would make a useful sample? Vauchez has noted already regarding Delooz's list of names of the second category that it is heavily biased toward Latin, and more specifically Italian, saints. If one were to do a study of earlier periods, the thousands of Irish saints would have tilted the (quantitative) balance toward Irish models. The bias toward "official" saints is also questionable. There is no reason to believe that official saints were "major" for their societies compared with unofficial saints, or that in canonizing a person the pope was momentarily inspired by the Zeitgeist, marking exactly those saints that were the most important. How important, for example, were Lawrence O'Toole, Margaret of Scotland, Stanislas of Cracow, and the already mentioned Sebald—all canonized saints?

Second, one wonders why the authors chose only 50 percent of Delooz's list of unofficial saints and whether choosing every second name in an alphabetical list is a good strategy. The answer to both questions lies in the authors' implicit assumption that saints, like

13. Some of these have already been made by Vauchez in his short, but scathing, critique of *Sociologie et canonisation* (see H. Deroche, J. Maître, and A. Vauchez 1970): 109–115; Vauchez's contribution is on pp. 111–13).

any professional group, are equal qua saints. They may be different in other respects, but inasmuch as they are saints, they are the same.

This assumption would have been true had we been dealing with bakers or Franciscans, or even, to a limited degree, canonized saints. For such groups there exists a simple definition: bakers bake, Franciscans are members of the Franciscan order, and canonized saints were canonized by the pope. But all that unofficial saints have in common is that they were venerated by others. One cannot be more Franciscan, or more canonized than others, but one can enjoy a greater or lesser reputation. If the purpose of the study is to investigate Western society's ideas concerning sanctity, as its title suggests, then some saints have an enormous importance, and others have little or none whatsoever.

The authors are not unaware of the difficulty, yet they choose to dismiss it out of hand. "Is Francis of Assisi ten, one hundred, one thousand, or one million times more important than Herman the cripple when we turn to using perceptions of sanctity as an index of changes in popular piety? And would such a weighing factor change over time and across different geographic areas?" (Weinstein and Bell 1982, pp. 279–80). Excellent questions. The authors decide, however, that any system of evaluation would be misleading. Quite possible. They therefore assign equal value to Francis and to Herman. Furthermore, the authors choose not to study variations over space and time. The result is neither historical nor representative of the relative value of individual saints.

Of the 864 saints used by Weinstein and Bell in their data base, 210 are marked by the authors with letters E–Q, signifying sources ranging from one century after death (E) to about nine centuries after death (M) to "information forged" (Q). The authors state that they have deliberately not distinguished between real and legendary saints (hence their indifference to the quality of the data). They are critical of Michael Goodich, who "by excluding persons whose historicity he doubts, falls into the trap of seeming to assert the historical accuracy of the material he does include. Our concern is with perception" (Weinstein and Bell 1982, pp. 277–78).

Whose perception are we concerned with? Whose ideas of sainthood are expressed in a *Life* written nine centuries after the saint's death—those of the saints' contemporaries or those of the biographer? Moreover, the extent of each saint's reputation is recorded at

15

its zenith, blurring even further the historical contours of the saint's reputation (Weinstein and Bell 1982, p. 279).

An even more serious problem is implied in the assumption that all accounts can be treated as "perceptions." This assumes that when people write a true or partly true account and when they write a fabricated account, the end product is identical. This postulates a world where people live their "perceptions," or write their reality. It could also mean that there are no true accounts of the lives of the saints—all are fabricated—or that telling true from false accounts is impossible. These are sweeping claims which are neither necessary nor convincing.

No saint was just a collection of topoi, nor would such a product reflect people's interactions with real human beings. Still, it is not without value to study the development of the literary representations of sainthood. Alison Goddard Elliott, for example, has undertaken such a study in her *Roads to Paradise: Reading the Lives of the Early Saints*.[14] She argues persuasively that in a study of literary images of sainthood, the more removed the *Life* is from reality, the better it conveys the fictionalized ideals of the *Life's* writer. Elliott looks for the "megatext," the text consisting of the essential and recurring themes in *Lives*. If one wants to measure the importance and influence of such perceptions, it is better to examine the spread and volume of the literary product. How many manuscripts of a *Life* exist? How often is a *Life* quoted? In answering these questions we may get a more accurate (and historical) idea of the saints' literary careers.

To understand the social behavior of real people, however, we must distinguish between true accounts and idealized accounts of the saints' interaction with their societies. This is not easy. The social reality of living saints is, in the absolute sense, beyond our reach. But there are grades of proximity. Both a sworn testimony given in court and a novel have their principles of literary organization, but they reflect different positions vis-à-vis real events. It is not always possible to tell the two apart, but often it is. The stories examined in this book come, with few exceptions, from *Lives* written while the saint, or at least eyewitnesses, were still alive. Although

14. See Alison Goddard Elliott (1987) and cf. Brigitte Cazelles (1982, pp. 20–23).

16

this is not a guarantee of authenticity, it does increase its likelihood (this problem will be addressed in greater detail in chapter 3).

If we decide against the quantitative approach with its large numbers and representative samples, we find ourselves again facing the problem of deducing valid generalizations from a limited number of cases.[15] It is hard to find representative saints since we do not know of what exactly they are supposed to be representative. I have argued earlier that saints do not constitute a distinct population. All saintly individuals were to some extent exceptional. The student of sainthood must concentrate on the saints' communities.

The individuals under consideration in this book were in some situations recognized by their contemporaries as belonging to the category of saints as it was understood in that time and place. Once they entered the public arena, they were treated in culturally meaningful ways, and their behavior was interpreted within a conventional frame of reference. The shared cultural attitudes and behavioral patterns, and the interplay between them and local ways, are the basis for any valid generalization regarding sainthood. Rather than try to determine arbitrarily what is representative, we must begin by acquiring an understanding of specific situations and communities. One richly documented case can tell us more about sainthood than a hundred cases about which we have but scanty information. The cases I have chosen offer, for reasons that will be discussed later, a wealth of information that is not available for many better-known saints.

One last question still needs to be discussed: Does the emphasis on image and reputation not reflect modern preoccupations? Would a medieval saint not be surprised, even horrified, by the suggestion that he or she was "building" a reputation, or involved in "strategic interaction," to use contemporary sociological jargon? Were the saints not engaged in a pursuit of perfection, or pastoral work, or penitential activity; and should we not respect our subjects' own idea of what it was they were doing?

The temptation to see people in the past or in other cultures as basically "like us," and ascribe motivations similar to ours to their actions can be deceptive. The historian, like the anthropologist,

15. Cf. Lawrence Stone, "The Revival of Narrative: Reflections on a New Old History," in *The Past and the Present* (London, 1981), pp. 74–96.

must try to understand and respect the "native's point of view." There seems to be, however, an implicit assumption among some historians that the student must not only respect the native's point of view, but limit his or her interpretation to what would be acceptable to the "native." It is felt that a sociological or anthropological approach somehow detracts from the dignity of the saints. The student who questions the saints' official motives is accused of a patronizing attitude or of projecting his or her own cultural bias on the subjects of study.[16]

We should certainly avoid the offhand application to other cultures of the latest fad in the social sciences, but the sensitivity to the object of study's point of view can be exaggerated. Once we achieved an understanding of what our subjects said they were doing, it is necessary that we examine other possible interpretations of their activity. It is legitimate to highlight other aspects of it that they might have considered secondary or even offensive (for example, that they were moved by political interest).[17] Without this we can only achieve a partial, and often misleading, understanding of another culture.

There is no contradiction in saying that the saints and their followers were engaged in a spiritual quest for salvation and acknowledging that they were at the same time also engaged in other interactions involving power relations, nonreligious personal aspirations, and a need for recognition and status. It would be wrong to assume that such motives are mutually exclusive, nor is it necessary or helpful to rank them in order of importance. As Patrick Geary noted concerning the theft of St. Nicholas's relics: "The secular importance of the translation was not something added after

16. For Clifford Geertz's critique of this approach, see "'From the Native's Point of View': On the Nature of Anthropological Understanding," in his *Local Knowledge: Further Essays in Interpretive Anthropology* (New York, 1983), pp. 55–70.

17. See Winston Davis (1980, p. ix): "Understanding a foreign culture presupposes both empathy and genuine distance. Simply putting that culture into the categories of one's own civilization inevitably causes distortion and misunderstanding. On the other hand, all goodwill and objectivity notwithstanding, it is also impossible to understand a foreign culture simply by introducing it into our thought-world on its own terms. Introjection is not interpretation."

the fact, but rather logically and chronologically simultaneous with the religious devotion that led to the translation (Geary 1978, pp. 115–16).

But not only is it reasonable to assume a plurality of motives and of planes of reference; it is also quite unnecessary to assume for "the natives" the most "nonmodern" view imaginable. In other words, the belief that medieval people were not aware of the practical aspects of the veneration of the saints is both unfounded and anachronistic. Medieval people were quite capable of making very perceptive, mundane—often highly skeptical—observations on the saints and their followers. Of course, such observations were usually restricted to people the observer considered impostors rather than saints, but one person's saints are another's impostors and vice versa.

One might be surprised by the "modernity" of Salimbene's analysis (written c. 1283) of the reasons for the emergence of new cults. "There are many reasons," he says, "for this devotion to [new] saints: the sick crave health, the curious are looking for novelties, the clerics are motivated by their envy toward the modern religious [the Mendicant orders], and the bishops and canons are motivated by greed (Salimbene de Adam 1966, 2:736). Salimbene then mentions the wish of political exiles to use the peacemaking functions of the saints to return to their homes. This explanation would be entirely acceptable even to a modern materialist: despair, curiosity, political rivalry, greed, and the use of the sacred for the settlement of civic disputes. Salimbene attributes all these worldly motives to others. He himself is moved by nothing but true devotion to the elect of God. But the fact that he is capable of such sociological observations, albeit where others are concerned, demonstrates that modern interpretations are not necessarily so alien to the "native."

I have said that the saints were not necessarily aware of the effect their actions had on their reputation; but they were not necessarily unaware of it. How else would we interpret the following episode, for example? St. John Bonus (d. 1249) realized that people were whispering that his abstinence was not so much spiritual as physical, or, in simpler words, that he could not eat much because he suffered from a blocked bowel (*strictum budellum*). To disprove this rumor, John ate great amounts of food at great speed in public, so

19

that all would know that he could eat if he chose to.[18] Clearly John was not considering merely the inherent value of his fasting vis-à-vis God, but was also interested in the impact it made on his viewers. After all, what was the point of behaving like a saint, if it were not recognized as such by others?

Contemporaries of the saints often accused them of self-promotion and conscious planning of their reputations.[19] Doubts were not expressed solely in the occasional reference to the putative impostor, nor were they restricted to any particular segment of medieval society. Skepticism was a formative part of the dynamics of sainthood. As will be shown in more detail in chapter 2, all saints, even the most popular, were vulnerable to attacks on their sainthood, because sainthood is an inherently ambiguous phenomenon.

Some actions of the saints resulted in the spread of their reputations, while others roused doubts. The saints' contemporaries could choose from a wide repertoire of possible reactions to claims (explicit or implicit) to sainthood. Their attitudes toward the saints had a deep impact on the future development of the "candidate." The saint's audience did not simply observe and applaud (or boo), it shared the stage with the saint. Together saints and devotees were writing and rewriting the script of sainthood.

18. *AA.SS.*, 22 Oct., pp. 816, 840, 841.
19. See Salimbene's sarcastic description of Bd. John of Vicenza (Salimbene de Adam 1966, 1:110). See also *Vita prima di S. Antonio,* edited and translated by V. Gamboso (Padua, 1981), p. 296; Peter Damian, *Vita B. Romualdi* 27, edited by G. Tabacco (Rome, 1957), pp. 56–57.

11

NEGOTIATING SAINTHOOD

O NE of the prevailing misconceptions concerning the medieval veneration of saints is an exaggerated view of the role the papacy played in regulating it. The medieval papacy is portrayed as having a clear ideal of sainthood which it sought relentlessly to impose on the masses. In fact, canonization was never a major factor in the medieval veneration of saints. Between 1198 (when we begin to speak about canonization in the full sense) and 1434, seventy-one canonization processes were opened, of which thirty-five ended successfully. During the same period a great many new cults (estimated in the hundreds) appeared in Europe. There were also numerous individuals who were considered saints during their lifetime and for whom no posthumous cult developed. What was the relationship between the small group of canonized saints and the much larger number of uncanonized individuals? Did communities all over Western Europe measure their holy men and women against canonized saints? The universalist claims of the papacy must not be taken at face value. We have to look beyond the rhetoric of papal pronouncements to the actual relationship between official and unofficial sainthood.[1]

In the first three centuries only martyrs were venerated by the Christian community. During the period of persecution, the group glorified those whose loyalty to the common ideal was uncondi-

Parts of this chapter were originally published in my article, "Proving Sanctity: Selection and Authentication of Saints in the Later Middle Ages," *Viator* 20 (1989): 183–205. © 1989 by The Regents of the University of California.

1. Even with canonized saints there was a gap between papal claims of universality and the actual state of affairs. In his article "canonizzazione" in the *Enciclopedia Cattolica* (1948–54, 3:589) Joseph Löw noted that, "Anche se nelle bolle pontifice generalmente la festa del nuovo santo viene prescritta in termini categorici, in realtà poche di quelle feste sono entrate nell' uso generale della Chiesa: i culti rimasero circonscritti, de facto, a territori più o meno limitati."

tional. The martyrs confirmed by their death not only their personal heroism, but the truth of the Christian message. Moreover, in many cultures those unjustly murdered are ascribed great powers. The injustice done to them creates a moral imbalance which the community corrects by empowering the victim. The Christian prototype of the innocent victim acquiring tremendous powers through his unjust death is, of course, Christ. But this belief transcends the boundaries of any specific religion. A cult often emerged around the burial place of an innocent victim, even if he or she did not die for the faith.[2]

As persecution ceased in the fourth century, martyrdom became a rare event, limited mostly to Christian missionaries. Yet the thirst for new intercessors did not diminish. The closest thing to the martyr was the ascetic, who subjected himself to a sort of spiritual martyrdom. But the ascetic's sainthood was more ambiguous than that of the martyr. For while martyrdom was public and final, the life of the confessor consisted of periods that were spent away from the public eye. One was never sure what the saint did at such times. Furthermore, it seems almost inconceivable that a person would fake martyrdom out of ulterior motives (though the possibility was not ruled out: it was used as a last resort as when the martyrs in question were heretics). For the confessor, however ascetic, such an imputation could not be ruled out completely.

In addition to the psychological uncertainty of the confessor's sainthood, there was also theological uncertainty. Augustine's extreme skepticism regarding moral appearances had a deep impact on Western theology (Kleinberg 1987). His concept of the mysterious and, from a human perspective, arbitrary working of grace made him deny the possibility of determining the real worth of a person from his or her works. A person's behavior does not necessarily reflect his or her true worth. Many who are considered evil are actually saints and many considered saints are in fact damned. Strictly speaking, then, certainty is possible only for God.[3]

2. Examples abound—from the Holy Innocents of the Gospels to the "holy greyhound" (see, Jean-Claude Schmitt 1979b) to Maria Goretti.

3. See, for example, Angela of Foligno, *Le livre de l'expérience des vrais fidèles,* edited by M. J. Ferré, translated by Ferré and L. Baudry (Paris, 1927), p. 516: "Nam multi apud homines videntur dampnati, qui apud Deum sunt salvati. Et multi apud homines videntur salvati, qui apud Deum sunt dampnati."

While many medieval theologians disagreed with Augustine's extreme predestinarianism, his notion that without divine inspiration empirical evidence was no more than a tentative indication of a person's sainthood was generally accepted. Theologians had to concede not only that some saints remain unknown to the church, but also the more annoying possibility—that some nonsaints are venerated as saints.[4]

Until the twelfth century, the Christian community as a body played the role of judge in matters of sanctity. Its inspired verdict was pronounced by the supposedly spontaneous emergence of a cult upon a saint's death. The very existence of a cult, therefore, could be seen as *post factum* evidence of a person's sainthood. If a person was not a saint, it was assumed that a cult would not develop. Although it was recognized that errors did occur occasionally (as when heretics or worldly people were venerated), they were not used to cast doubt on the people's role as detector of sanctity. Before the twelfth century the clergy had neither the incentive nor the means to intervene regularly in the veneration of saints. Local bishops were sometimes called to give their approval, but this did not involve a systematic examination of the saint in question. In most cases they simply gave a formal blessing to a *fait accompli* (see Amore 1977).

For the writers of saints' *Lives* at that time, all saints were specific manifestations of one prototypical life. It was the hagiographer's task to show that the Christian community was in fact venerating saints who, as saints, were identical or nearly identical.[5] Most saints' *Lives* until the late eleventh century sought to convince their readers that the subject of their work was just like all other holy people and must therefore also be holy.[6] Writing about Carolin-

4. On "anonymous" saints see, for example, St. Bernard of Clairvaux, "In festivitate omnium sanctorum," ser. 5.2 in his *Opera,* edited by J. Leclercq and H. Rochais (Rome, 1968), 5:362.

5. See Agnellus of Ravenna, *Liber pontificalis ecclesiae ravennatis* 19.32 *M.G.H.* Scriptores rerum langobardicarum et italicarum saec. VI–IX, p. 297; Hucbald of St. Amand, *Vita S. Jonathi* (prologue) in *Catalogus codicum hagiographicorum bibliothecae regiae Bruxellensis* 2 vols. (Brussels, 1886), 2:273. See also Morse (1991, pp. 147–48).

6. The *Life* written for the canonization of Ulrich of Augsburg by his friend Gerard was found to be too unconventional, and a new *Life* had to be written (see Bredero 1977, p. 77; see also Steinen 1959, pp. 105, 109–10).

gian saints, J.-C. Poulin notes: "What counted in the saint was not the man, but the active presence of God in the man. Since God is one, the more authentic the saint, the less individualized he was."[7] Most saints' *Lives* written between the eighth century and the end of the eleventh century describe saints who died more than a hundred years earlier (see Head 1990, pp. 4–5). The writers' own days were seen as a deterioration from a more worthy past. Previous generations provided examples that could stimulate the morally enfeebled present. This tendency made it easier to present a standardized and unvarying image of sainthood. The biographer related either the life-story of a person whose sainthood had been proved by a long-standing active cult, or chided the people for their negligence in venerating a specific saint. In the latter case, the saint's contemporaries were presented as recognizing the (evident) sainthood of the *Life's* subject. The disappearance of the cult was attributed to the moral degeneration of later times.

From the late eleventh century, however, the number and relative importance of *Lives* of new saints began to rise (see Schmitt 1984; for the prevalence of distant biographies in earlier periods, see Van der Essen 1923, pp. 340–41). There was a widespread feeling that the world was showing signs of rejuvenation rather than decay, and one need not look back to find intercessors and protectors. The new heroes were not looked upon as pale imitations of past glory. The Bernards of the twelfth century and the Francises of the thirteenth century were not seen as dwarfs when compared to their holy predecessors; they were considered as great as the ancient saints.[8] "Ancient generations are renewed in our own time and in the days of new grace the miracles of the Old People [Israel]

---

7. See Poulin 1975, p. 100; see also Zoepf 1973, 33: "Ein Heiliger war ein Heiliger; es konnte ihm keine Tugend eines anderen Heiliger fehlen, sonst hätte er aufgehört ein Heiliger zu sein"; see also pp. 40–46.
8. St. Bernard professed his astonishment at his own unprecedented miracles: "Nil mihi videor in sacris paginis super hoc genere legisse signorum" (*Vita prima S. Bernardi*, 3.7 PL 185:314). Bernard is called "unum ex antiquis sanctis" by the bishop of Constance (ibid., 6 (2).5 PL 185:386). See also Philip of Clairvaux, *Vita Elizabeth sanctimonialis in Erkenrode* in *Catalogus codicum hagiographicorum bibliothecae regiae bruxellensis*, 2 vols. (Brussels, 1886), 1:363. For Francis, see Stanislao da Campagnola (1971), and for Clare, see Z. Lazzeri, ed., "Il processo per la canonizzazione di S. Chiara d'Assisi," *Archivum franciscanum historicum* 13 (1920): 469.

are restored," declared Peter the Venerable.[9] Contemporary saints could focus their society's growing need to experience the holy directly. They could be seen, touched, and imitated.[10] They were a sign that God had not turned away from his world.

The interest in contemporary saints indirectly threatened the notion that saints were identical and sainthood undisputed. The new saint's *Life* had to face greater skepticism than the *Life* of a saint from the distant past. The writer recording the life of a saint dead for many years encountered no challenges from contemporaries, because in most cases they knew nothing about the saint's actual life. Furthermore, the majority of older *Lives* were written for monastic communities by members of the same communities. In the intimacy of a religious community, a consensus about the saint was reached before the hagiographer took it upon himself to provide a written account. Writers and readers alike shared an admiration for the holy founder or for the saint whose relics the community hosted (Gaiffier 1947).

With the growth of literacy and the improvement of communication in the twelfth century, hagiographers faced a reading public that did not necessarily share their feelings about the saint. This readership required a different rhetorical technique. Hagiographers had to adopt a psychologically more sophisticated method of producing a sense of verisimilitude. Instead of portraying the saint as just another epiphany of the ideal saint, they sought to convince the reader of the authenticity of their account by providing enough noniconographic details to demonstrate a familiarity with what was unique to and distinctive of this particular saint. As Norman Bryson has noted in relation to Giotto's *Betrayal*, the realistic effect is achieved because "[the 'neutral' details] are understood as superflux, as detail unrequired by the image's civic or official project the logic of suspicion lowers its guard and accords to the elusive meanings the status of proof" (1985, p. 65). There are icon-

9. Peter the Venerable, *Epistolarum libri,* 4.36, *PL* 189:366. On the general feeling of renewal, see Henrietta Leyser (1984, pp. 3–4).

10. See the process of Joannes Bonus, *AA.SS.,* 22 Oct., p. 851. "De multis partibus infinitae gentes veniebant ad videndum, audiendum et tangendum ipsum tamquam virum justum et sanctum." There is a description in Glaber's histories of how around the year 1000 the relics of many saints are suddenly discovered in various places. (Glaber 1989, pp. 126–29).

ographic and noniconographic elements in any *Life*, but there was a marked increase in the importance of the latter in the new *Lives*. (I will return to this subject in chapter 3.)

The twelfth century also saw the emergence of the first heretical mass movements, a phenomenon related mainly to the emergence of a class of urban consumers of religion. Heretical and orthodox alike, the religious movements of the twelfth century called the laity to participate actively in religious life. Their holy men served as living examples of the truth of their teaching. It was this holy life that threatened orthodoxy much more than the heretics' often confused doctrines. Orthodox saints could be used to prove that the church too had its holy men and women.[11] The problem was that differentiating between "good" and "bad" holy people could be tricky. The papacy felt that the *vox populi* was in need of guidance and approval by the learned.[12]

The papacy began in the twelfth century to show a growing interest in the veneration of saints. A decisive step toward a papal supervisory role was taken by Alexander III (1159–81).[13] In a letter to the king of Sweden, he forbade the veneration of King Eric, who was murdered while drunk. The letter reads: "Even if miracles were performed by him, you are not allowed to venerate him as a saint without the permission of the Church of Rome."[14] The language used in the papal letter may suggest that the pope expected all possible saints to be submitted to papal scrutiny; but this has no bear-

11. See Jacques de Vitry, *Vita Mariae oigniacensis, AA.SS.*, 23 Jun., p. 549; Reginald of Durham, *De vita et miraculis S. Godrici*, edited by J. Stevenson, Surtees Society Publications 20 (1847): p. 17; and *Vita Julianae corneliensis, AA.SS.*, 5 Apr., p. 442: "Scio tamen quod exempla sanctorum nostri temporis, quanto recentiora tanto magis sunt motiva." See also Z. Lazzeri, "Il processo di S. Chiara d'Assisi," p. 469: "Adomandata come sapesse questo [that no female saint, except for the Virgin, was as great as Clare] respuse che de molte altre Sancte haveva udito nelle loro legende la sanctità loro, ma de questa madonna Chiara vidde la sanctità de la sua vita per tucto lo predicto tempo."

12. On the attitude of initial disbelief in the *fama vulgarium*, reinterpretation, and incorporation in the culture of the literati see Brian Stock (1983, pp. 63–73).

13. Stephan Kuttner has questioned the significance of Alexander's move (1980, pp. 172–228). He eventually changed his mind as he notes in the "Retractationes" published in the same volume (pp. 7–11), accepting Eric Kemp's opinion (Kemp 1948).

14. "Cum etiam si per eum miracula fierent non liceret vobis ipsum pro sancto absque auctoritate Romanae Ecclesiae venerari" (X 3.45.1).

ing in reality. The papacy did not expect every small community to await papal permission before it expressed its devotion to a saint. It reserved for itself, however, the right to disqualify a cult it did not approve of.

As papal prestige increased, the more ambitious communities sought to gain papal blessing for their saints as an indication of their importance. Like other prestigious awards, this one too was to be given with caution. A dossier of the candidate had to be submitted to the curia for review. Under Alexander III, formal commissions of inquiry became part of the process of gathering information. The pope rejected the idea that the "people" were divinely inspired. It was not enough to notify Rome that the people considered someone a saint and were expressing their faith in him by attributing miracles to his intercession.

This skeptical attitude toward local intuition was accentuated by Pope Innocent III (1198–1216). The pope declared that the authentication of sanctity consisted of two major elements: the way of life and the power to work miracles. In the bull canonizing Homobonus of Cremona (12 January 1199), Innocent declared: "Although . . . the grace of final perseverance alone is required for sanctity in the Church triumphant . . . in the Church militant two things are necessary: the power of moral behavior [*virtus morum*] and the power of signs [*virtus signorum*], that is, works of piety during life and miracles after death."[15]

To establish a person's sanctity, moral judgment of his or her life was called for. This task was seen as beyond untrained people's abilities. The pope alone should decide on such important matters. The second innovation introduced by Innocent III was the requirement that the committee of investigation transfer to the curia the complete dossier of the inquiry and not just a summary of it (Vauchez 1981, p. 45). The papacy was not going to allow local authorities to decide what was important and what not. It wanted all of the information, both "relevant" and "irrelevant," in its hands.

15. Cf. Innocent III (1964, 1:762). This statement became a standard formula. Cf. Innocent III (1953) on Gilbert of Sempringham, pp. 27–28, and on Empress Cunegunda, *AA.SS.*, 3 Mart., p. 280; Gregory IX on Francis of Assisi, *Bullarium romanum pontificum*, edited by C. Coquelines, vol. 3 (Rome, 1740), pp. 257–58; Innocent IV on Edmund of Abingdon, in E. Marténe and U. Durand (1968), p. 1847.

Procedures regulating the investigation of eyewitnesses and the preparation of a dossier were standardized under Honorius III (1216–27) and Gregory IX (1227–41) (Goodich 1982, pp. 35–36). Under the latter, the investigators began to use *articuli interrogatorii* for the *informatio in partibus* (the interrogation of witnesses on the site of the saint's main activity).[16] After an investigation had been authorized by the papacy, the postulator (the person representing the candidate's cause) prepared a series of statements (*articuli*) about the candidate's life and miracles. Witnesses were then asked to confirm or deny the validity of the statements.

What the *articuli* made possible was a more "objective" examination of a life. Testimony divided into articles allowed the examining chaplains in the curia to organize the material better and to determine whether each item had been proven. By the end of the examination, the total of proved versus unproved articles would help them reach an "unbiased" verdict. How unbiased is, of course, a matter of conjecture. Like other important decisions, these too were probably influenced by a variety of political pressures. It is significant, however, that the papal curia thought it important to regulate and rationalize this process.

In the thirteenth century, canonization came to be conceived of as a judicial-inquisitorial procedure. The role of the hierarchy, until about a hundred years earlier, had been to approve an inspired and rarely disputed popular intuition and to see that the saints were properly honored. The thirteenth-century papacy understood its role mainly in negative terms. It examined claims that were assumed to be highly suspicious, and it tended not to be generous in its approvals. The famous thirteenth-century canonist, Hostiensis, who had a deep influence on the legal concept of canonization, saw the process as a deliberate introduction of obstacles aimed at making sure that only the best cases survived and at preventing inflation: "lest the number of saints be infinitely multiplied, and in

---

16. They were first used in the process of St. Dominic in 1233 (then still referred to as *capitula*), but began to be used more regularly only in the second half of the century. However, *articuli* were not always used even in later processes (see Vauchez 1981 p. 5).

consequence sanctity grow cold and worthless in charity and devotion" (the infelicity is in the original).[17]

If in theory the papacy was the overseer of the cult of the saints, seeing to it that only deserving—and not too many—saints were venerated, in practice things were more complicated. Any attempt to regulate the cult of the saints had to confront not only a confusion of terms and beliefs, but a variety of political and economic interests.[18] In the thirteenth century, when the papal monopoly of canonization was established and the procedure reached maturity, there was already in existence a great number of individuals considered saints. There was no way of curtailing this popular devotion by applying strict standards or bureaucratic barriers. The ecclesiastical authorities could encourage some devotions (by granting indulgences to pilgrims, for example) and frown upon others. But although many of the old saints' *Lives* contained material that would be unbelievable or unacceptable to a thirteenth-century lawyer, they had to be accepted as given. An official reevaluation of the historical validity of existing cults had to wait until the twentieth century.[19]

A cult was not just a body of beliefs; it was a source of local pride and income. Communities could react with great hostility toward any attempt to tamper with their saints. When Abelard tried to suggest to the monks of St. Denis that the Denis in question could not have been Dionysius the Areopagite, their reaction was very unacademic. They dismissed Bede, on whose authority Abelard's claim was made, as a liar, and they planned to deliver Abelard to the

---

17. "Ne contingat in infinitum sanctos multiplicari et per consequens charitate et devotione refrigescere et vilescere sanctitatem." Hostiensis, ad X 3.45.1, *In III librum decretalium commentaria* (Venice, 1581; repr. Turin, 1965), fol. 172A, s.v. Venerantur.

18. For instance, the term *sanctus* was used for charismatic sanctity as well as for sanctity of office, for institutions and for individuals. The terms *beatus* and *sanctus* were, until the fourteenth century, used for canonized and uncanonized individuals indiscriminately.

19. A group of saints was dropped from the *Roman Calendar* in 1969, among them the popular Christopher and Barbara. See *Calendarium Romanum* (Vatican City, 1969), pp. 68–69.

king who would "take his revenge from him as one who would take from him the glory and crown of his kingdom."[20]

Certain cults did deteriorate and fade away, but the appearance of new tastes in sainthood among the elite had only a slow and limited influence on the existing cults. Many of the old miracle-working saints remained more popular for much of the Middle Ages than more "sophisticated" saints whose cults were promoted by the papacy.[21]

The second difficulty facing the canonist was the long established tradition, accepted by the canonists, that the first step toward the identification of a saint was the appearance, theoretically spontaneous, of a popular devotion, a *fama sanctitatis*.[22] Though this intuition was in need of examination and direction, it nevertheless left the initiative in the hands of the saints' communities. The pope was called upon to reach a decision based on an existing, subjective, even rash perhaps, public opinion. He did not (at least in theory) initiate an inquiry; indeed, according to Hostiensis, the pope should not even respond immediately to a community's call for his judgment. He should consent to such pleas only after being besieged "not once but many times and vehemently [*instanter*]."[23]

Candidacies for canonization were presented to the pope in the form of a legal problem: Is a community justified in paying certain honors, attributing certain phenomena (miracles) and a certain metaphysical status (election) to a deceased individual? A negative answer could result in an order to stop all devotions, or keep them

---

20. See J. T. Muckle's edition of Peter Abelard, *Historia calamitatum* (1950, pp. 197–198). See also, Thomas Antonii de Sensis "Caffarini," *Libellus de supplemento*, 2.7.3, edited by I. Cavallini and I. Foralosso, in Testi Cateriniani 3 (Rome, 1974), p. 175.

21. Hostiensis, facing this confusion of old but ineradicable cults, suggests that as saints were rare in old times, the processes had been rather unorganized. Of course, in his own day, he maintains, things should be different. Thus he got rid of the old notion but was still left with the old cults (for example, the cult of Charlemagne at Aix). See Hostiensis, ad X 3.45.1 *In III librum decretalium commentaria*, fol. 172A.

22. The first three stages, out of twelve Hostiensis suggested in his *Lectura*, deal with establishing that a *fama* really exists (Hostiensis, ad X 3.45.1 *In III librum decretalium commentaria*, fol. 172A, s.v. Venerantur).

23. Hostiensis, ad X 3.45.1 *In III librum decretalium commentaria*, fol. 172, s.v. Venerantur.

limited. A positive answer meant permission to pay greater honors and spread the devotion.

From the beginning, the papacy was not expected to look for saints according to some given standard of identification, but to accept or deny a claim that a saint had already been identified (see Hart 1948 for an important analysis of legal processes). This does not mean that popes or lesser prelates could not influence or even manipulate the process. A pope could suggest that a certain person deserved devotion, with all the influence that such a suggestion would have. But a reputation of sanctity had to exist, whether through papal influence or independent of it. In certain cases, processes of canonization had to be stopped, sometimes to the pope's dismay, because of the stubborn indifference of the populace.

Innocent III complained that the incredulity of the people of Languedoc was to blame for the poor miraculous performance of Pierre of Castelnau (Petrus of Castro Novo) "who, having shed his blood in martyrdom for the faith and for peace, than which no nobler reason exists, would have shone, we believe, in bright miracles, had not their incredulity prevented it. . . . Concerning their like," notes the pope, "it is read in the Gospel, that Christ did not perform many miracles there because of their incredulity" [Matt. 13:58].[24] Innocent confirms, then, that even for true saints (and he considered Pierre a true saint) the reputation of sanctity is not automatic. He also admits his own dependence on the same incredulous and irresponsible people which he has just criticized. The formula is quite simple: there was no canonization without popular devotion.

The account of the debate over the sainthood of Marcolinus of Forli, very vividly told by John Dominici, exemplifies the complex and uneasy relationship between popular devotion and formal acceptance. It demonstrates that "the people" were not passive receivers of learned ideals, nor did they lack the means to make their wishes known. When Marcolinus of Forli died in 1397, his Do-

24. "Qui profecto cum ob fidem et pacem quibus nulla est prorsus causa laudabilior ad martirium sanguinem suum fuderit, claris iam ut credimus, miraculis coruscasset nisi hoc horum incredulitas impediret. De quorum similibus in Evangelio legitur, quia ibi virtutes Jesus non faciebat multas propter incredulitatem eorum" (*AA.SS.*, 5 Mart., p. 413—Petrus was murdered in 1208). For other processes failing for the same reason, see Vauchez (1981, p. 49).

minican confreres, wishing to give him a simple burial, found the church packed with people who complained: "You want to bury a saint in secret!"[25] The only friar willing to accept the popular opinion was the convent's cook, himself a man of the people. When he washed Marcolinus's body, he noticed hard skin on the dead friar's knees, a sign, he maintained, of long hours of prayer. (It should be noted, however, that the popular identification preceded the cook's revelation.)

The cook, being a Dominican and a man of the people at the same time, attempted to reconcile the as yet formless *vox populi* with the friars' concept of sanctity. The rest of the friars, however, did not share the popular sentiment and, hoping to put a quick end to the affair, buried Marcolinus during the night.

But the next morning the crowd returned to the church and renewed the debate. "Those [the friars] say: it is not right to venerate a simple man as saint. The others [the people] object: it is much worse to hide his sanctity, which God has revealed."[26] There was a great commotion in church with cries of "he is not a saint!" and "yes, he is!" exchanged. The people supported their case with a number of stories told by persons present in the church. A carpenter told how his hand had been healed by the friar. Another man had been moved by a vision of Marcolinus to confess his sins. A boy that had served the friar in his old age told a story of continuous prayer, self-flagellation, and celestial visions. Many said that Marcolinus was a great prophet (*magnus propheta*), "since he frequently revealed to them hidden, unknown and future things as well as se-

25. "Sanctum occulte vultis tradere sepulturae." The story of the birth of Marcolinus's devotion is told in a letter of John Dominici. See Flaminio Corner (or Cornaro), ed., *Ecclesiae Venetae, antiquis monumentis nunc etiam primum editis illustratae ac in decades distributae,* 13 vols. (Venice, 1749), 7:189 (hereafter cited as Corner). A similar story is told by the anonymous author of the *Vita Margaritae de Città de Castello:* "Post mortem vero Margaritae, cum corpus illius ad ecclesiam fratrum Predictorum portabatur, hominum et mulierum magna multitudo congregatur cumque fratres vellent corpus illius in claustro sepelire, quasi divinitus in populo clamor stupendus attolitur: 'non in claustro, sed in ecclesia sepeliatur; sancta enim est et ab omnibus hec sancta reputetur.'" M. H. Laurent, "La plus ancienne légend de la B. Marguerite de Citta di Castello," *Archivum fratrum praedicatorum* 10 (1940): 126.

26. "Illi dicunt, injustum esse, simplicem hominem revereri ut Sanctum: obiiciunt isti, nimis fore iniquum eius abscondere sanctitatem, quam Deus revelat" (Corner, p. 189).

crets of the heart, although in his life," the writer notes, "he was said to make these predictions through divination, a reputation from which the humble and holy father did not purge himself."[27]

The first three stories of the witnesses demonstrate the difficulty of translating the saint from one type of discourse to another. The carpenter's story is an account of a healing, but it is an ambiguous healing. Marcolinus used an unknown herb to heal the wounded hand. We are assured by the carpenter that the herb was of no significance. "He picked the first herb that occurred to him in the field; . . . the herb was used to conceal the power of God, invoked in humility."[28] Were these details added by the writer to rebuff a suspicion of popular medicine or even magic? Marcolinus's reputation as a fortune-teller would make this reasonable. Whether they were the writer's addition or the carpenter's, from the establishment's point of view this miracle was dubious.[29]

The second story, of the man moved by a vision of Marcolinus to repent of his sins, is a private piece of information. It depended on the status in the community of the person who recounted it—as far as the friars were concerned it was apparently not good enough. What is more, the vision seems to have taken place after Marcolinus's death. It is the result rather than the cause of the *fama*. It could certainly add to the pressure, but it was not as effective as a public miracle would have been. The boy's story was of the right kind, even from the friars' point of view, but it seems strange that it was revealed only after circumstantial evidence (the cook's revelation) had been used and, again, it depended on the boy's credibility, for like the previous person, he was the only witness to the related events.

<hr />

27. Corner, pp. 189–90. "Protestabantur etiam multi, et multi ipsum fuisse magnum prophetam, cum praedixisset eisdem occulta, et ignota, et futura, et cordium secreta frequenter, licet in vita dixissent eum arte divinatoria talia praedicere; a qua fama se non purgat pater humilis et sanctus (p. 190).

28. Corner, p. 189. "Herbam primam sibi occurrentem electam de prato apponit vulneri; [. . .] et nesciebat [carpentarius] quod herba apposita erat ad occultandam dei virtutem in humilitate praefata."

29. See the process of canonization of Thomas Cantelupe in *AA.SS.*, 2 Oct. pp. 589–590. The commission inquired "si in operatione dictorum miraculorum fuerunt appositae herbae vel lapides, vel aliquae aliae res naturales et medicinales." A positive answer would, most likely, disqualify the miracle.

Finally, there were two arguments coming from "many." The deceased was a prophet, although he had a reputation of using the *ars divinatoria,* and was a charitable man, as the poor of Forlì testified. The first three stories are private and posterior to the initial public recognition of Marcolinus as a saint. The initial response must have sprung from those stories told by "many": the friar's reputation as a successful fortune-teller and perhaps a popular healer. Also important was the fact that he refused to gain any material advantage from his powers and preferred to remain poor and share what he had with others. Marcolinus was different from other Dominicans, and it is always difference that attracts attention.

The purpose of the stories was to strengthen the faith of those who were hesitant about the friar's holiness and to make Marcolinus closer to the friars' ideal of sainthood, but in a significant way they failed to achieve this objective. The healing and the vision, besides their private and unattested character, should have come after a spectacularly virtuous life. This, as far as the other friars were concerned, was lacking. The prayers and mortification were not properly proven, the prophesies and healing suspicious, and the charity insufficient. For the friars, Marcolinus could not be a saint (*non licere fieri novum sanctum*), because he was "a simple man, without much learning; neither keen nor graceful in words, sleeping during mass and at the table and even while walking."[30] In other words, Marcolinus left no great impression on his community, and their refusal to be convinced by the popular stories does not so much show a skepticism vis-à-vis miracles as a disbelief that they could be justifiably ascribed to *him.*

The dynamics of the debate added a new factor to the scene. The friars had consistently put themselves in opposition to the people, and at some point Marcolinus became a prize to be won in the conflict. The public might have responded to curiosity more than anything when it first heard about the death of Marcolinus, who was "very well known, though everyone considered him a simple man."[31] By the second day, however, the stories told to promote Marcolinus's cause and the friars' obdurate and contemptuous re-

30. "[Dicentes eum esse] hominem simplicem, nec magnae litteraturae, in verbo non acutum, vel gratiosum, dormientem in missa et mensa et in via ambulantem" (Corner, p. 191).

31. "Notissimus licet simplex homo ab omnibus reputatus" (Corner, p. 189).

sistance had made a unified and excited mass out of the people gathered in the church (cf. Gellner 1969, p. 74). After the final refusal by the friars, an impasse was reached. It became clear that the people's attempts to make Marcolinus closer to the Dominicans' ideal failed, and so did the Dominicans' attempts to convince the people of the nonsainthood of the dead friar.

An act of violence terminated the deadlock. The people forcibly opened Marcolinus's tomb, wishing, probably, to transfer the body to a more worthy place. As the body was being removed from the grave it was found to be in perfect condition, showing no signs of decay. Furthermore, it gave off a fragrant odor. In the heated atmosphere in the church, it is hard to believe that these signs were examined carefully and calmly. How many people actually smelled anything? It is hard to know. It is likely that the physical phenomena were announced by those nearest to the body and created a chain reaction. There was total chaos in the church.

Although all canonical authorities dismiss both bodily preservation and fragrance as proof of sainthood, the people carried the day.[32] Their now vindicated faith in Marcolinus was expressed by such a deluge of miracles that the friars could no longer resist and had to allow very intense devotional activity in the church. (Marcolinus was eventually beatified and his cult in Forli is still active.) But the people's victory was not complete, for they were not allowed to venerate Marcolinus as a simple and unpretentious faith healer. His sanctity was accepted by the friars, but his simplicity was reinterpreted as a sign of humility, and the very lack of the extraordinary in him now came to be seen as premeditated and deceptive.

The popular "canonization," then, started with an identification: "Marcolinus is a saint!" This proposition resisted attempts, either official or unofficial, to defeat it. The candidate's opponents argued that the candidate did not conform to their notion of existing canons of sanctity. His supporters either denied this by arguing that the incompatibility was only apparent or by arguing that the

---

32. See, Hostiensis, ad X 3.45.2 *In III librum decretalium commentaria*, fol, 173, s.v. extra capsam: "Nam ex hoc sumunt [laici] materiam detrahendi et blasphemandi, videntes enim ossa nuda dicunt: truphae sunt, si enim sanctus esset, non esset sic consumptus." Hostiensis rejects out of hand any such sign as proof of sanctity.

old definitions were too narrow and needed reinterpretation. If the saint successfully passed public trial, his holy essence spread over his person and his actions acquired a new meaning. Marcolinus's simplicity became a sign of humility, but also the concept of sanctity was broadened to include "that which Marcolinus was," or more specifically, "that which Marcolinus did."

Not all of the saint's actions were deemed suitable for remembrance. Some of his or her more problematic or insignificant deeds (from the point of view of the then current concept of sanctity) could be passed over in silence by the writers of *Lives*, who, being learned, were more faithful to contemporary canons. Given the pluralistic character of medieval sainthood, however, it was possible not only for old concepts to "adjust" a specific saint's life, but also for an individual saint's life to modify the existing paradigms (Dinzelbacher 1985). For once an individual had been acclaimed, he or she became a new entity—a saint. Such a person was given the status of an authoritative precedent and a certain surplus of sanctity was created around him or her.[33] These men and women possessed the common saintly core, but since their behavior was seen as an authoritative interpretation of the essence of sanctity, some of their accidental traits were added to the range of the saintly possible.[34]

The saints' advocates used isolated elements from the accounts of other saints out of context and gave them a meaning that would suit their own saint. Raymond of Capua, having to defend St. Catherine's total abstinence from food, invoked in her defense the desert fathers and St. Mary Magdalene who lived with no food for thirty-three years "as the story of her life clearly indicates."[35]

The past was rarely invoked to impede saints from taking their own path. That other saints in the past behaved in a certain way did

33. On the saint as one not bound by the norms that bind ordinary human beings, see Bernard of Clairvaux, *Vita S. Malachiae* 3.6, in *Opera* (Rome, 1963), 3:315.

34. For an interesting parallel in medieval Judaism, see Haym Soloveitchik (1987: 205–21, especially p. 211).

35. See Raymond of Capua, *Vita S. Catharinae Senensis*, 2.5, *AA.SS.*, 30 Apr., p. 905; also *Vita Gertrudis ab Oosten, AA.SS.*, 6 Jan., p. 350; Thomas of Cantimpré, *Vita Lutgardis, AA.SS.*, 16 Jun., p. 209; *Vita fratris Abundi*, Brussels, Bibliothèque Royale de Belgique. MS. 3255 (19525) fol.10 vᵒ. See also Chiara Frugoni (1982).

not compel saints to do likewise. The tendency was to expand the repertoire of saintly behavior and not to contract it. Though not everything that was possible would be in constant use, it was at least available for the advocate who knew where to look.

We see, then, that in the process of accepting a person's sainthood, both the saint and the concept of sainthood changed. What remains to be considered is how this local consensus was affected by the confrontation with the highest religious authority of all—the papacy. All evidence suggests that the curia saw the process as a trial resulting in a sentence, not as a philosophical investigation ending with the discovery of truth. The papacy was satisfied with reviewing those few cases that were presented to it; in all other cases it maintained the right to veto a veneration, a right that was rarely exercised until the seventeenth century. It is also clear that the papacy did not try to form a coherent picture out of all the cases reviewed.

Papal canonizations were a luxury open to very few candidates whose followers could afford the expenses it demanded. Though canonization meant that the person was a saint, or at least must be regarded as such, its absence did not mean that he was not a saint. Most communities were satisfied with a local and, in the technical sense, "private" devotion for their saints. In practice, the "private" devotion was often hardly distinguishable from a public cult.[36] It would be very misleading to generalize from the small number of canonized saints about the nature of the veneration of saints in the Middle Ages. When papal authority was not challenged, the papacy was willing to tolerate the many hundreds of unauthorized new cults that were constantly emerging and disappearing in a rhythm of their own.

The case of Armanno Pungilupo can demonstrate the papacy's reluctance to interfere in local cults. Shortly after the death of Armanno in 1269, the Dominican inquisitor in Ferrara, Aldobrandinus, discovered that the man, venerated as a saint in the city, was a

---

36. According to Innocent IV, the difference between a public and a private cult, besides the universality of the former, is the singing of an office for the saint and the solemnity of the prayers. "Item non negamus quin cuilibet liceat alicui defuncto quem credebat bonum virum porrigere preces ut pro eo intercedebat ad Deum: quia Deus fides eorum attendit. Non tamen pro eis licet facere officium solenne vel preces solennes" (Innocent IV, ad X 3.45 *Commentaria in III,* fol. 457 vº).

Cathar heretic. Aldobrandinus tried to exhume Armanno's body and burn it, but was resisted by the canons of the local chapter. He excommunicated the canons and put the cathedral under interdict. The canons appealed to the pope (Gregory X), who after an investigation ordered the inquisitor to lift the excommunication and the interdict (Zanella 1986, pp. 23–27).

In their appeal to the pope, the canons sought to prove Armanno's orthodoxy with signed statements from priests who had heard his confessions. They also produced a long list of his miracles. The canons' letter included a two-line list of vague clichés describing Armanno's virtues (he was humble and patient, simple like a dove, pure and faithful). Unlike the miracles and the orthodoxy, the virtues were not supported by testimonies (Zanella 1986, pp. 72–89).

The canons did not even try to refute one by one the specific allegations against Armanno. The confessors' testimony, after all, did not prove much. Armanno could, and probably did, lie to his confessors. What the canons affirmed was the orthodox nature of the cult. Whatever Armanno might have been, the cult, they maintained, was not heretical. They denied all knowledge of Armanno's heresy and demonstrated by the list of miracles the people's faith in him. Had they asked for a canonization they would need much more than that, but the canons simply asked to be allowed to continue the cult with neither approval nor denunciation by the pope.

In spite of the overwhelming evidence he managed to collect, Aldobrandinus failed to convince either Gregory X or Nicholas III to intervene. In 1284, Aldobrandinus's successor, Florius, renewed the effort to crush Armanno's cult. In 1301, he finally succeeded and, with Pope Boniface VIII's permission, the body was exhumed, burned, and the ashes dispersed (Zanella 1986, pp. 28–29). In all, it took the papacy (or the ten popes who reigned during that period) more than twenty years to stop the cult of an active heretic. The cult of an orthodox person, whatever his merits, would not have been interrupted.

Even in canonization proceedings, where a careful examination of the candidate's life was called for, the papacy did not judge the behavior of local communities toward the living saint. Candidacies could be rejected because the postulants failed to produce sufficient miracles or because they were technically faulty, but not because the community's ascription of virtue to a specific saint was unacceptable (see Vauchez 1981, pp. 60–63). The papacy rarely, if ever, questioned a community's taste in sainthood. It did not point out to a community that it paid too much attention to miracles and not enough to almsgiving, for example, or that one set of attributes was more important than another.

The papacy made no attempt to make the content of sainthood consistent.[37] Each case was examined in isolation from others. A saint was not expected not to contradict other saints. This included even the information the saint related in his or her visions. It could have been possible to collate such information to discover inconsistencies. For if two saints had different visions of the same thing (say the number of people present at the Crucifixion), only one vision, strictly speaking, could be true.[38] In practice, however, no such formal examination was ever attempted. Sainthood was an inconsistent notion. The popes had their own individual tastes, which influenced their behavior in particular cases, but the papacy developed no canonical model sainthood that all communities were to follow. It was left for the saints and their communities to develop their own interpretations of holiness.

37. As Pierre Bourdieu observed (1986, pp. 141–42), "Practical logic . . . functions practically only by taking all sorts of liberties with the most elementary principles of logical logic: thus the same symbol can relate to realities that are opposed even from the axiomatics of the system—or rather, we must include in that axiomatics that fact that the system does not exclude contradiction."

38. The eighteenth-century editor of the *Life* of St. Benvenuta Bojani, exasperated by such inconsistencies finally commented: "Sunt nempe piarum meditationum, ac mentis fervore affectae, inoxiae phantasmata." See *Vita Beatae Benevenutae Bojanae,* edited by Johannes F. de Rubeis (Venice, 1757), p. 62.

III

WIDE-EYED WITNESSES AND PARTIAL OBSERVERS

THE *Lives* of the saints ranged from the ordinary to the eccentric, from very crude compositions to works of great sophistication. How were they written and by whom? Why do they contain so much that we—and some medieval readers—find hard to believe? What may we believe? What can we choose to believe? Should questions concerning the veracity of the *Lives* be asked at all or do such questions reflect a misunderstanding of the genre? How different is the way we read the saints' *Lives* from the way they were read in the Middle Ages? That is the scope of this chapter's discussion.

The process of recording the saints started already in their lifetime. Those considered holy were observed with special attention by their followers; their words and gestures were carefully noted and committed to memory. In the general sound and fury of everyday life, the saints signified something. It was not always clear what their actions and words meant, but they could not have been meaningless. The saints of God were there for a reason. They demanded attention and consideration. Their spectators had a sacred duty to save the saints from oblivion.

The saints, even those whose lives passed with little external activity, were "worthy of memory," and what is worthy of memory, in the words of Isidor of Seville, should not be forgotten.[1] Their words and deeds must not vanish with those of ordinary people. "You, who have a good memory," says one of St. Clare of Assisi's Sisters to another, "keep well in your mind that which the lady [Clare] says."[2] Remembering the saints was an act of piety, part of the praise that was due to the friends of God, and the fulfillment of

1. See Isidor of Seville, *Etimologiae* 1.41, "Quia quidquid dignum memoria est litteris mandatur."

2. Z. Lazzeri, ed., "Il processo per la canonizzazione di S. Chiara d'Assisi," *Archivum Franciscanum Historicum* 13 (1920): 456–57.

a duty to posterity. The saints of the past reassured each passing generation that doing good was possible, that holiness should be aspired to.

But human memory is frail. In the prologue to the *Life* of Lukardis of Oberweimar, the writer states that what moved him to write, in spite of his unworthiness, was the fear that "just as forgetfulness had destroyed, alas, so many lovely stories [of Lukardis], so would negligent sloth, idle procrastination, and useless oblivion destroy these too.[3] Those lovely stories were lost because by some negligence they were not all written down. The writer knows that Lukardis told the stories to certain people, but these people, unfortunately, died.[4]

The *Life* of Juliana of Cornillon relates a similar loss, perhaps even more tragic. None of the saint's friends was at hand at the hour of her death. She did not know who she could trust to bear witness to her final message. Juliana called for a notary, but none was to be found. Having suffered rejection and hostility in her last years, she did not feel she could trust the boy who was sent in place of a notary; so her last words are lost. Juliana's resort to the notary reflects her belief that a professional would record her words faithfully. Even more important, it reflects her faith in the written word. Events recorded in ink could be saved from the frail memories of humans. Raw material was often written down in the vernacular shortly after the event, collected in notebooks, awaiting a more learned writer to translate it, both literally and metaphorically, into a higher language.[5]

There was a moral dilemma involved in the process of recording the saints. The object was not unaffected by the process of recording itself. The devotee taking notes, or writing a full biography in the hagiographical mode, could not help but convey to his subject

3. *Vita venerabilis Lukardis,* in *Analecta Bollandiana* 18 (1899), 310: "Timeo etiam quod, sicut heu plura huius materiae delectabilia delevit [oblivio], sic et ista negle[g]ens acedia, tarda dilatio ac inutilis deleat oblivio." The Latin is somewhat confused, but the meaning is clear.

4. Ibid., p. 314. Cf. Peter of Florence, *Vita B. Margaritae Faventinae, AA.SS.,* 26 Aug., p. 851.

5. Thomas Caffarini, *Libellus de supplemento* 3.6.1, p. 377. Catherine of Siena's first confessor, Thomas de Fonte, who is described as "illiteratus" (that is, not proficient in Latin) transferred his notebooks, written in the vernacular, to Raymond of Capua. Raymond used these notebooks for his *Legenda.*

the fact that he was considered worthy of veneration.[6] The lives of ordinary people were not worth remembering. This awareness could endanger the supposed unself-conscious nature of the saint. The saint was supposed to be holy for holiness's sake. The mirror put in front of him could focus his attention on himself, instead of on God.[7] The saint, in other words, could become proud and self-conscious.

But the dread of forgetfulness was so great that all these risks were deemed worth taking.

I [William of St. Thierry] thought that after his [Bernard of Clairvaux's] death, if I would outlive him, the task [of writing his *Life*] would be better and more effectively done, when a man is no longer harmed by his praise, and it would be safer from the turmoil of men and the objection of tongues. But he, thriving and vigorous, the feebler his body, the stronger he became. And, being strong, he had not ceased accomplishing things worthy of memory; constantly adding greater to great things which—he himself being silent—required a writer. Already consumed by pressing infirmities of this body of death, and all my members beginning to sense death close by, I feel the time of my demise approaching, and I fear greatly that I would regret, late in the day, having put off for so long that which I would have wanted to carry out at all costs before I pass away.[8]

The saints themselves were often torn between a desire to preserve their deeds (or at least the manifestations of God's work in them), and an uneasiness with the praise implied in the process of recording, and the damage it could do to their souls and to their reputations. For all their self-deprecation, the saints were quite sensitive about their reputation.[9] Johannes Bonus, for example, did not hesitate to relate his own miracles "ad corroborationem fratrum suorum," but he was less comfortable with a written record.[10]

6. In one of her letters, Heloïse writes to Abelard: "Whence it is also written: 'Do not praise a man in his lifetime.' Do not praise a man, that is, when by praising him you could make him unworthy of praise" (*PL* 178:198).

7. For the dilemma of writing the *Life* of a living person, see *Vita fratris Abundi*, fol. 10v; Jacques de Vitry, *Vita Mariae Oigniacensis, AA.SS.,* 23 Jun., p. 549; Thomas of Cantimpré, *Vita Lutgardis, AA.SS.,* 16 Jun., p. 203.

8. William of St. Thierry, prologue to *Vita prima S. Bernardi, PL* 185:225.

9. See, for example, Henry Suso, *The Life of the Servant* (London, 1952), p. 68. Suso was ready to suffer any tribulation, but pleaded God not to allow his reputation to be affected.

10. *AA.SS.,* 22 Oct., pp. 774, 775.

Johannes's miracle stories were being collected in booklets (*quinterni [sic]*) and circulated by some friars. There was criticism about this practice in the order, and it came to Johannes's attention. He found the booklets and secretly cut them up with a knife. The deposition in the process of canonization suggests that it was the objections of others that drove Johannes to destroy the booklets. The possible damage to the saint's image was greater than the value of the recording. But the disciples were distressed by the saint's action and reproached him bitterly for it. Johannes had to console them by promising that he would work even greater miracles after his death.[11]

Very often the saint was willing to collaborate with interviewers only on the condition that the information divulged would not be published until after her death. In this way, the saint could guarantee that her story would be told without arousing doubts about her humility.[12] Another common device was the saints' modest use of the third person in talking about themselves.[13] Benvenuta's Bojani's *Life* provides us with examples of both methods. Benvenuta's confidante (*secretaria*), Jacobina, played the role of living recorder. Her job was to accompany Benvenuta, be privy to her secrets, and to remember everything until her recollections would be needed for the saint's biography. Benvenuta's confessor ordered her to repeat the things she told him in confession to Jacobina, so that he would not be the only one to have that information.[14]

Benvenuta recounted her own marvels in the third person. However, she was sometimes carried away by the narrative and switched inadvertently to the first person. When she realized this, she was shaken and very embarrassed. "Why do you bother to hide these things from me?" asked Jacobina. "I know that it is you yourself you are talking about." Benvenuta did not deny that this was so, but she warned Jacobina not to tell anyone as long as she lived. In her eagerness to please Benvenuta, Jacobina promised not only not to tell a soul as long as the saint lived, but also not to tell anyone

11. Ibid., p. 783.
12. *Il processo per la canonizzazione di S. Nicola da Tolentino,* edited by N. Occhini (Rome, 1984), p. 84; Reginald of Durham, *Vita Godrici* (1847), p. 316.
13. For example, Johannes Suso and Margery Kempe; see also, Reginald of Durham, *Vita Godrici,* p. 18.
14. *Vita Benevenutae* 5, *AA.SS.,* 29 Oct., pp. 161–62.

after she had died. "This I did not say," Benvenuta hurried to make clear, "rather if you would see a chance to edify I want you to reveal [these things]."[15]

But those who recorded the lives of the saints contributed more than requests for information to the saints' stories. They were engaged in a dialogue, though the biographer's part is not always recorded. When the saint said things that sounded strange or problematic to the biographer, the latter would ask the former for an explanation. If the saint herself could be made to modify her message or add her own authoritative gloss, then much embarrassment and exegetical acrobatics could be avoided later on. However, the saint sometimes refused to accommodate her pious examiners, and the problematic original text was nevertheless allowed to stay (see Roisin 1947, p. 220).

Consider the following episode from Raymond's *Life of St. Catherine of Siena*. On one occasion, Catherine informed her confessor, Thomas de Fonte, that Christ opened her left side and removed her heart. She told the surprised friar that she no longer had a heart in her breast.

He laughed at this, and in a joking way reproved her; but she repeated it and insisted that she meant what she said. "Truly, Father," she said, "insofar as I feel anything at all, it seems to me that my heart has been taken away altogether. The Lord indeed appeared to me, opened my left side, took my heart and went away." Her confessor then pointed out that it is impossible to live without a heart, but the virgin replied that nothing is impossible to God, and that she was convinced that she no longer had a heart. And for some time she went on repeating this, that she was living without a heart.[16]

Thomas, like his namesake, had doubts. When confronted with Catherine's account, he found it unbelievable; for what Catherine was saying sounded impossible, and she offered no proof to make it more credible. Thomas tried to solve the difficulty by suggesting that she should not insist on a literal interpretation of her words. But, when Catherine refused to accept his advice, he remained undecided. Clearly he was not fully convinced or we would have been

15. Ibid., epilogue, p. 185.
16. Raymond of Capua, *Vita Catharinae* 2.6, *AA.SS.*, p. 907. Cf. Thomas Caffarini, *Libellus de supplemento* 2.7.1, p. 127.

told that he was. But Thomas was not certain that the claim was false either. He recorded Catherine's claim, because she was so resolute, and because, in spite of his doubts in this particular case, he did think she was a saint.

Besides, Thomas was not composing a full biography. He was simply recording memorable words and actions of the saint. It was always possible that others would not share his doubts. If he decided not to record the story it would simply be lost, but if he did record it, others might find it acceptable or discover new significance in it. And indeed Raymond, who incorporated this episode in his biography of Catherine, docs not leave us in suspense for too long. He learned from "those who saw it" that Catherine had a scar on her side whence the heart was removed and Christ's heart put in instead. "He questioned Catherine most strictly about it [the removal of her heart by Christ]," and she "could not deny it," but had to admit that everything happened as she had told Thomas.[17]

Note how Raymond uses language that suggests implicitly that he obtained new information through his persistence: he "questioned Catherine most strictly"; "she could not deny"; "she had to admit." Why should she deny any of this? After all, she provided this information in the first place.[18] Catherine did not say anything she had not said already. Raymond's mention of a scar is both insufficient (when and how did it appear?) and vague. In contrast to his habit of identifying his sources, Raymond speaks here about unnamed companions who told him about the scar. It was not new evidence, but Catherine's insistence on its occurrence that convinced Raymond to include the incident in his work in spite of its problematic nature.

The attitude of the follower vis-à-vis his saint is one of submission to a higher authority. Commenting on the statement in the Gospel of St. John, "we know that his testimony is true" (John 21:24), Paul Veyne observes: "If that was a testimony in the Greek sense (the witness was there and saw the thing with his eyes), the

17. Raymond of Capua, *Vita Catharinae* 2.6, *AA.SS.*, p. 907.

18. Raymond is often suggesting bashfulness and reluctance to talk on Catherine's part to avoid accusations of self-advertisement. See *Vita Catharinae* 1.7, p. 890 ("sicut ipsa mihi secrete et verecunde confessa est"); ibid., p. 891 (confessa etenim, licet verecunde, mihi saepius est, quod semper annulum illum [the invisible wedding ring she received from Christ] videbat in digito").

phrase would be absurd, for how could they testify to the truth of the account that St. John made of the death of Christ when they were not there? But the disciples mean that they knew John well and recognized a sincere heart incapable of lying" (Veyne 1988, p. 138 n.44; cf. *Vita Benevenutae,* epilogue, *AA.SS.,* p. 185).

Hagiographers were expected to edit the raw material they gathered from eyewitness accounts and the rough notes that were taken on the spot by the saint's followers. But the hagiographer who knew the saint personally could not easily edit what the saint himself recounted. He found himself undecided between the role of editor and eyewitness. We often find the hagiographers trying to explain what a less scrupulous narrator would have omitted altogether. In their desire to record the saint, the writers tell us too much. Their narratives are hesitant, indecisive, full of details that distract and trouble the reader instead of reassuring him or her. The personal encounter with a holy individual was often too powerful and too bewildering to allow a truly iconic portrayal of the saint.

The urge to produce a faithful account of the person admired was particularly powerful in the recording of mystical experiences. But the life of the saint, her every act, was often seen as having a sacred quality that called for recording. "Whatever daily and minute act," writes the prior of the Camaldolese house in Florence, "every movement of her [St. Catherine's] feet, so to speak, every gesture, every place where she stopped, her words—all should be described, because such words and actions are the instruction of churches and a stimulus to virtue for the good."[19]

Fra Arnaldo's account of how he recorded the revelations of Angela of Foligno demonstrates the recorder's awe toward his material. Arnaldo was Angela's relative and her confessor. He began writing down Angela's revelations quite by coincidence. The friar saw Angela screaming and yelling incomprehensibly in the basilica of San Francesco in Assisi. He was embarrassed by his relative's behavior and ordered her to leave the place and never to return. Later he went to see her in Foligno to find out what caused her outburst.

---

19. "Sed quique cotidiani et minuti actus et, ut ita dixerim, omnes motus pedum, omnes gestus, omnes mansiones et dicta describenda essent, quia talium verba et opera ecclesiarum sunt instituta et bonis quidem virtutis stimulus" (Matteo Guidoni in a letter to Thomas Caffarini, *Libellus de supplemento,* prologue, p. 3).

Angela agreed to reveal her experiences to Arnaldo and he was immediately struck by their power. He began to write down what she was saying to him, translating her words into Latin, transposing her speech because of his haste from the first to the third person (it is easier to remember the Latin conjugations of the third person).[20] But he states again and again that these were the only changes he made willfully. As much as he could, he tried not to add anything of his own to her words (Angela, 34, p. 42).

Faithful to his conception of himself as a passive recorder, Arnaldo went to almost absurd extremes. For a few months in 1294, Arnaldo was forbidden by his superiors to talk to Angela. He arranged for her to relate a vision to a boy, who recorded it in Italian. The text was so badly written that Arnaldo could not understand it at all. Nevertheless, he translated the words into Latin, not adding anything "as a painter paints, for I did not understand it" (Angela, 68, p. 148; see also 96, p. 192).

In one place in his account, Arnaldo launches into an apologia for his work as a whole. It is worth quoting in full.

I, brother scribe, wrote as much as I could grasp, with great fear and reverence, and with much haste, just as I have heard it from the mouth of the said Faithful of Christ, while she talked in my presence. I did not add anything of my own from beginning to end, but I have omitted much of the good things which she said, because I could neither understand them nor write them down. And she spoke about herself in the first person, but it happened sometimes that I wrote in the third person, because of my haste, which I did not correct. And from beginning to end I have hardly written anything except in her presence. And then I wrote with great haste, as she spoke, because I was forced to hurry by the many obstacles put before me by the Brothers and their prohibitions. I tried to write as much of her words as I could get, not wishing to write after I had withdrawn from her presence, and not knowing what to write later for fear that I should include, be it even one word, which she did not say herself. Whence I have

20. Angela of Foligno *Le livre de l'expérience des vrais fidèles,* edited by M. J. Ferré, translated by M. J. Ferré and L. Baudry (Paris, 1927), chap. 34, p. 42 (hereafter cited as Angela). There is a summary of the circumstances of Arnaldo and Angela's collaboration in Rudolph M. Bell (1985, pp. 103–5). Bell misunderstood Arnaldo's explanation of his use of the third person. He seems to think that Arnaldo initially transposed Angela's first person to the third and that he stopped this practice because of his haste (p. 104). In fact, Arnaldo says that he gave up trying to keep things in the *first* person (see Angela, pp. 126, 247).

always read aloud to her many times what I have written so that I would only include her own words.[21]

Arnaldo's excitement is obvious from his repeated and confused exclamations. In this passage alone he repeats three times his claim of utter passivity. He is merely a sieve, to use his own word.[22] The material passes through him but takes nothing from him. This claim is made repeatedly, in one form or another, throughout the text.[23]

This is very different from the common perception of the hagiographer as one quite free with his material. But the skeptic might still object that Arnaldo could have edited Angela's communications or even invented part of the narrative while claiming with great vehemence that he had not. Does not Benôit de St. Maur state in his *Roman de Troie* that he "shall follow the Latin to the letter. I shall put in nothing," he writes, "but as I find it written" (Nelson 1973, p. 24). Since we are familiar with Benôit's sources, we know his claim to be false. Unfortunately, we have no knowledge of Angela's words other than Arnaldo's account. But is it really necessary to be so skeptical? It is unlikely that anyone wishing to fabricate would produce such a problematic text. The con-

21. Angela, chap. 126, p. 248: "Ego, frater scriptor, cum magno timore et reverentia et cum multa festinatione scripxi [*sic*], sicut ab ore predicte fidelis Christi, dum ipsa presence mecum loquebatur, capere poteram, non addens aliquid de meo a principio usque ad finem, sed multa dimittens de illis bonis que dicebat, quia ego non poteram ea capere intellectu meo nec scribere. Et ipsa loquebatur de se in prima persona; set accidebat aliquando quod ego scribebam in tertia persona propter festinationem, quod et non correxi. Et a principio usque ad finem, vix aliquid scripsi nisi quando ipsa presence loquebatur. Et tunc cum magna festinatione, ego scribebam, sicut ipsa proferebat verba, quia valde cogebar multis impedimentis illatis a fratribus et prohibitionibus festinare. Set et ego conabar, et propria verba sua ponebam que ego poteram capere, nolens ea scribere postquam recedebam ab ea et nesciens ea postea scribere pro timore et zelo, ne forte accideret quod ego aliquid vel unum tantum verbum ponerem quod ipsa proprie non dixisset. Unde et que scripxeram semper sibi relegi et iteravi pluries, ut tantummodo ponerem propria verba sua."

22. Angela, 34, p. 40: "eram sicut cribrum vel stacia."

23. See, for example, Angela, chap. 52, p. 100; chap. 56, p. 112; chap. 68, p. 148; chap. 96, p. 192. Cf. *Vita Godrici*, pp. 315–16: "Adhuc siquidem eo vivente, quicquid digna ex eius ore sacrato dideceram veridica piae fidei ipsius exemplaria secutus, calamo quotidie currente, membranulis commendaveram, et haec ea pro occasione feceram quod eadem verba quae dixerat eodem tenore quo illa explicaverat scriptis inserere contendebam."

fused and repetitive nature of Arnaldo's text (like many eyewitness accounts) strongly supports his claim that he was writing from dictation, often without completely understanding what he wrote. There is no reason to doubt that Arnaldo was so totally convinced of Angela's divine inspiration that he was not aware of making any (significant) willful alterations of her account.

However, no human being is merely a tape recorder, and Arnaldo certainly was not. To begin with, we have here a process of double translation going on. Angela speaks in Italian and Arnaldo translates into Latin. Arnaldo then translates his own text back into Italian for Angela and translates her corrections into Latin again.[24] As Arnaldo was translating both ways, his reading of what he wrote to Angela did not solve the problem of changes in content through translation. It is obvious that the process of translation is an interpretative process, involving numerous ambiguities that need to be solved one way or another. Arnaldo translates Angela's words into a higher, more canonical language, and in the process he is bound to change the original. But Arnaldo's role went beyond merely translating.

While he was recording Angela's words, Arnaldo did not remain as totally passive as he claims. He may not have changed Angela's words, but he did have an influence on what she said. Whenever Angela's statements seemed particularly troubling to Arnaldo, he stopped her to ask for clarifications. He asked how she could say that the Holy Spirit was crucified for her (Angela, 39, pp. 58–60). He objected (*cepi contradicere*) when she said that sharing in Christ's suffering was pleasant for the elect (Angela, 53, p. 104). Sometimes he asked questions or commented on Angela's words (Angela, 67, 93, pp. 142–46, 184). And there was always a reaction from Angela. Angela considered what Arnaldo had said to her and provided clarifications, new revelations, excuses.

Arnaldo might not have been aware that by these questions, and even by his requests for clarification when he could not understand Angela's words, he was guiding her in certain directions. He wanted no more than the saint's authoritative gloss on her own pronouncements. But his questions forced the saint to restate her words, sometimes to retract statements that his reaction showed to

---

24. Cf. Philip of Clairvaux, *Vita Elizabeth sanctimonialis in Erkenrode*, 1:373.

be dangerous. The final product was shaped in the back-and-forth dialogue between Arnaldo and Angela, between the saints and the persons with whom they interacted.

Arnaldo was different only in degree from other recorders. His account, like more eyewitness accounts, is a compromise between the conflicting urges to record faithfully and to produce a "well-written" (canonical) *Life*. Every *Life* that is not completely fabricated sends a blurred message. The medieval storytellers/witnesses wanted their saint's holiness to be accepted. But their testimonies were influenced by the fact that the saint was seen by other people and by their desire to provide a full account.

Reading the *Lives* of the Saints

Having examined how this particular type of *Life*—the eyewitness account—was written, let me now turn to the modern historian's treatment of such *Lives*. Saints' *Lives* are only reluctantly accepted as historical evidence by the modern historian. Some historiographers do not even consider them part of historical writing in the Middle Ages. Hagiography is presented more as an aberration of history than as a special branch of it (Certeau 1975, pp. 274–88; Guenée 1980, pp. 53–55). It is not hard to see why. Consider the following passage from Peter of Dacia's (on Peter, see Gallén 1946, 225–44; Nieveler 1975, pp. 58–75) *Life* of Christina of Stommeln:

Having entered [the room], I sat on the ground in front of Christina's bed. The lord prior Gottfried sat at the head of her bed, that is, to my east, and the lord cellarer at the foot of the bed, that is, to my west. The lord priest sat at the north, together with me, and the room's wall was at the south. With all these people guarding the said bed, . . . each of whom could touch with his hand, not only the bed, but also the person in the bed (for they all sat close by), the demon defiled Christina, as far as I could see, more than twenty times in different ways. Those present called this hardship "defilement," because she was stricken with the most fetid matter, that is, with human excrement. At times the demon covered her completely under her gown with this matter; at times only her face; at times he covered her under the veil with a sort of paste, and—which seemed even more marvelous—he put together thick filth between the eyelids and the pupils. Sometimes he even filled her mouth with the said filth. Sometimes he stuck it so forcefully and firmly between her teeth that it could hardly be removed and cleaned with a piece of cloth. Call me a liar [*falsum dico*], if I did not remove the filth administered in this way from the said places with my own hands.[25]

There is something disconcerting about this passage for the modern reader. First, one finds it hard to overcome the repulsion that the author's detailed description arouses. It is one thing to say that the saint was covered with filth, but Peter's description shows the eyewitness's fascination with detail—filth in the form of paste, thick filth under the eyelids; filth that sticks firmly and filth that is more easily removed—not descriptions a modern reader expects to find outside, perhaps, medical journals. But worse still, Christina comes out of the episode looking ridiculous. There seems to be little or no danger in the demonic attack. Christina is simply made the victim of scatological slapstick. I cannot help feeling that there is something slightly comic about this episode.[26]

But leaving our repulsion aside, what about the account's veracity? The medieval writer who produced it supposedly assumed that his readers would be moved by descriptions such as this to regard the heroine with compassion and admire her patience. Why does the description strike us as possibly comic? Is it not because,

25. Peter of Dacia, *Acta B. Christinae Stumbelensi, AA.SS.*, 22 Jun., p. 250 (hereafter cited as *Christina*). The Bollandists' edition is very unreliable. The student should consult J. Paulson's transcription of the second book of the *Codex Iuliacensis*, (*Vita Christinae Stumbelensis*, Scriptores Latini Medii Aevi Suecani 1 fasc.2 [Götenborg, 1896], hereafter cited as *Paulson*). However, Paulson's edition is very hard to find (I used a photocopy I got from a Swedish friend). I also preferred to make all my references to the same text. Since the third book of Christina's tribulations and the *Vita anonymi* are printed in the *AA.SS.*, but not in Paulson, all references are to the Bollandists' text. I provide Paulson's reading whenever there is a significant difference between the two editions.

26. It seems that for many modern readers excrement is somehow worse than other excretions. The Visitandines' English translation of their foundress's *Autobiography* reproduces without comment episodes of licking wounds and eating vomit. They omit, however, an episode where the saint filled her mouth with a patient's excrement (Marguerite-Marie Alacoque, *Vie et oeuvres* 3 vols., edited by Mgr. Gauthey [Paris, 1915], 2:83), commenting that, "the saint then performed an act so repulsive to nature that not only would no one have advised it, but no one would even have permitted it" (Margaret Mary Alacoque, *Autobiography*, translated by The Sisters of the Visitation, 2d ed. [Roselands, Walmer, Kent, 1952], p. 83). See also Ernest Renan's "Une idylle monacale au XIIIe siècle: Christine de Stommeln" (1884, p. 365).

in spite of its rich detail, its freedom from hagiographical stereotypes (this is *not* a hagiographical topos), and the writer's solemn avowals to the contrary, we do not believe that this incident really happened? After all, had Christina's tormentor not been a demon but a human being, the description would have roused nothing but outrage and sympathy.

Can we assume that in contrast with their modern descendants, medieval readers would have accepted the veracity of such an account without further question and therefore immediately conceived it as tragic rather than comic? Although we are dealing with speculations, it is more probable that without supplementary data, a medieval reader would not be able to assign truth value to the episode. He would have to suspend judgment until he knew more about Christina and Peter: Were they reliable sources? Would other individuals mentioned in the description corroborate Peter's version? Is it not possible that the episode was a demonic delusion and not a real event? For me and for a great number of modern readers like me, all these considerations are redundant. We would unequivocally affirm that the incident did not happen.

How did an episode written to convince readers end up arousing their suspicion? Why does the careful realism of Peter's account cast more doubt on his narrative than would a more casual description? The answer is that Peter's text was designed for readers with one set of expectations and is now read by readers with a different set.

The first question we need to ask is whether the reader expected the text to be taken as history or as fiction. For medieval readers, defecating demons were, at least theoretically, possible. But like all manifestations of the supernatural, they were suspect. If medieval readers expected the account to be factual, they would want to be convinced that this extraordinary (though not impossible) occurrence really took place.

All hagiographers expect to be believed on some level. At least formally they all write history. The hagiographer's obvious interest in edification should not make us forget his claims to historical truth. The saints' biographies were to be read as the written record of virtue practiced in the actual world. The saints were real people whose relics could be seen and touched. The miraculous powers of their remains, of their images, and of the very invocation of their names attested to the saints' historical existence in real space and time. If the saint were to serve as evidence that perfection was humanly possible, he had to be more than a literary construct; he had to be real.

But not all the specific stories told about the saints were of equal significance, nor were all saints equally open to critical enquiry. *The Golden Legend* and the stories of saints like Barbara and Alexis, for example, take the reader's sympathy for granted. Did everything in these tales happen exactly as the writers claimed? Maybe it did and maybe it did not. The saints about whom the most incredible stories were told usually existed in that unwitnessed past where people dressed, talked, and behaved in a different way. But more important, the writers were just reaffirming tradition. They were not thought to be seeking any gains through telling their stories. Why should the writer not be allowed to embellish his narrative the better to praise the saint?

The saint whose sainthood was affirmed by tradition could be made into an ideal stereotype. His personality, with the exception of his iconographical attributes, could merge into the quality of sainthood that is nonspecific and unquestioned. But the *legenda* that tried to change the status of a nonsaint into that of a saint attempted to reach a new consensus, not just reaffirm an existing one. The papacy, likewise, was willing to accept fantastic stories about saints of the sacred past, but subjected new saints to a most rigorous examination. The readers of a new saint's *Life* would not be edified unless they were convinced that the events described by the author were true in a concrete and verifiable way and that the events described a person who was worthy of the title of saint.

As Walter Daniel learned to his dismay, his readers expected his account of the life of Ailred to be proved by formal and public proof "as though crime and virtue are established by the same canons of faith."[27] It is unlikely that a *Life* narrating the wonders of a Roman martyr would arouse similar demands. Not only was it impossible to provide such proofs, it was unnecessary. The only exception made was when the writer tried to go beyond the limits of the existing consensus by claiming, for example, that the said Ro-

---

27. Walter Daniel, *Vita Ailredi abbatis Rievall'* (*The Life of Ailred of Rievaulx*), edited and translated by F. M. Powicke (London, 1950), p. 69.

man martyr ordered his admirers to make their donations to one particular location over all others. This claim would be treated with much greater suspicion. Skepticism regarding the saints of the past was usually limited to their relics. The claim of possession of a saint's relic had practical implications that made it potentially suspicious (Schreiner 1966).

The biographer of a new saint had to produce just enough hagiographical commonplaces to convince the reader of his subject's sanctity and enough neutral and unconventional material to convince the reader of the writer's sincerity. As for miracles, the most convincing demonstration of sanctity—and for medieval as well as for modern readers the most suspicious material in a *Life*— the writer provided as accurate a description of the miracle's setting and as many eyewitnesses as he could muster. The details identified the writer as an eyewitness or as being in immediate contact with eyewitnesses whose names gave additional weight to his version.[28]

In the *Lives* of accepted holy men and women of the distant past, only the barest description of the setting is usually given since the real point of the narrative was to get to the description of the miracle itself. Witnesses are rarely named and are vaguely described as, for example, "a monk," "a peasant." Events in the *Lives* of old saints are often written in a "generic" form, even when they are based on real occurrences. In contrast, events in the *Lives* of new saints had to be related in such a way as would convince the reader that they were real, even when they were fabricated by the writer.

The modern reader approaches sources that are allegedly true in a concrete sense, with the disadvantage that his extratextual information is often extremely limited. Walter Daniel's readers could cast doubts on his *Life of Ailred* because they had access to people who knew the saint. Other contemporary readers, however, might be convinced through personal experience or eyewitness accounts that, the writer's literary deficiencies notwithstanding, an event really took place. But the modern historian cannot; she is very often totally dependent for authentication of her texts on internal evidence. In addition, modern historians, even religious ones, have little sympathy for medieval hagiographical models. They are quite

---

28. See Roland Barthes (1982, pp. 11–17); for details as a means to create the "reality effect" in art, see Patricia Fortini Brown (1988, pp. 125–64).

capable of separating sainthood from miracles, a feat that, though theoretically possible, was emotionally unacceptable for most medieval people. Modern historians therefore can feel that the hagiographical core of the *Life* is unnecessary even for the purpose of proving sainthood. Hagiographical topoi rouse, ipso facto, the modern scholar's suspicion.

But the a priori suspicion of the hagiographical schema makes the modern reader particularly susceptible to the *Life* that breaks its conventions. The very existence of the iconographical convention determines the credibility of statements that would otherwise be of little significance. Consider the following statement: "He tried to preach to a flock of birds, but they flew away."[29] In itself the statement does not have a great impact on us. True, there is no reason to suspect its veracity, but the information it conveys seems trivial and mundane. Now, consider the statement in the context of a saint's *Life* and immediately it becomes very powerful. For the purpose of hagiographical works is, in the absence of more worldly gains, the glorification of the saint and the edification of the reader. Because we expect the hagiographer to tell us that the saint was able to preach to spellbound fowls, his admission of failure strikes us as detrimental to his own cause, thus lending it a credibility it would not have had otherwise. It is not simply the fact that the birds' reaction in this statement is more natural. A hagiographer who describes a saint as telling tasteless jokes, for example, sounds more believable than a hagiographer who describes him as serious and devout. Descriptions, in other words, acquire their status against the background of other descriptions within the genre.[30]

Peter of Dacia's *Life* of Christina, which I cited at the beginning of this chapter, can demonstrate how confusing a medieval writer's breaking of the hagiographical conventions can be for the modern reader. Peter was a Swedish student of theology in the Dominican *studium generale* of Cologne. He became a devoted admirer of Christina, a Beguine who lived in nearby Stommeln. His recollections of their meetings between 1267 and 1269 and then again in

29. Such an account was in fact attributed to Brother Masseo of Assisi in a fairly early tradition. As can be imagined, it did not become as widespread as the saint's more successful sermons to the birds (see B. Bughetti 1927: 546–47).

30. On the immediate credibility of statements that seem to be in the speaker's worst interest, see Erving Goffman, (1971, pp. 110–13).

1270 and 1279 are narrated in a memoir he wrote after his return to Sweden. Our source in this case, then, is an educated cleric who also claims to be an eyewitness to some of the events he describes.

The first peculiarity in the *Life of Christina* that we notice is the authorial role assumed by Peter. Unlike most hagiographical narratives, Peter's composition does not start with an account of Christina's birth and early life, nor even with Christina. The narrative opens with Peter. He tells the reader how he always hoped God would one day show him a saint that would remove his doubts about "what pertains to the lives of the saints" (Christina, p. 239). He saw many saintly men and women, but his doubts were not removed. Then, one day, he met Christina. Without pausing to tell us about her life until that moment, Peter describes, with detail and emotion, their first, then subsequent, encounters.

The missing biographical background of the saint appears much later in the text. It is clear from the outset that this is as much Peter's story as it is Christina's. This approach stands in stark contrast to other accounts of Christina's life which Peter incorporated in his text—the local priest's account of her early life and the schoolmaster's account of her later life. The other narratives follow a traditional chronological pattern with the author either completely absent or appearing in the appropriate places as an eyewitness. That Peter's choice was unusual is shown by the Bollandists' decision to reverse the order of the chapters in the manuscript and begin with what in Paulson's more faithful edition starts only on page 109–Christina's early life.[31]

This breach of traditional models was hard to swallow for contemporaries. It put too much emphasis on the person who was, after all, a mere instrument for recording the saint's life. The second *Life* of Christina, composed by an anonymous writer after Christina's death, reflects this dissatisfaction. Although the writer of this *Life* depends on Peter's narrative for his information, he does not simply abbreviate Peter's account and relate the story of Christina's last years. He reverses the order of the chapters to return the emphasis to Christina and relegates Peter to the role he

---

31. This was a conscious decision on Peter's part. The *Life* as we have it is not a journal Peter kept while events were taking place, but a work he started in Sweden eleven years later (see Jarl Gallén 1946, p. 228).

should have played in the first place—a minor player and an eyewitness. Peter's various personal reflections and many of the episodes in which he was involved were removed from the text. It is not often that the account of a learned Dominican was seen to be in need of such radical revisions.

Peter's arrangement of his material and his active authorial role serve to strengthen his narrative's effect on the reader. Instead of burdening our belief from the outset with tales of a miraculous birth or early miracles, about which he has only secondhand knowledge, Peter begins from a shared rhetorical doubt in "what pertains to the lives of the saints," then moves to a firsthand conversion that the reader is expected to share.

Peter's credibility as an eyewitness/author is enhanced by his demonstrating his incredulity in more concrete ways. He verifies with Christina various details of other people's accounts of events, thus implicitly suggesting that he shares our suspicions of the secondhand report.[32] The eyewitness/author can also use his own reactions, physical and emotional, as a simultaneous gloss on the events that he describes. The psychological authenticity of these descriptions is seen as proof in itself of the writer's personal experience of the events. We empathize, in a sense, with the writer's "normal" reactions to anomalous events. If the author's reactions strike us as psychologically convincing, our readiness to accept the veracity of the events increases considerably.[33]

Peter's unorthodox choice of narrative technique combines with another fact to increase his credibility. Peter included fourteen of Christina's letters in his text.[34] They contain personal messages of all sorts, and in the first years express great longing for Peter (see,

32. For example, Christina, pp. 237; 259; 278. Peter also examined four of Christina's close friends "seorsum et divisim" (p. 245).

33. An equally powerful authorial involvement, though of a somewhat different type, is practiced by Raymond of Capua in his *Life of St. Catherine of Siena.* However, Raymond is less willing to put himself at the center of attention. He is careful always to play second fiddle to Catherine.

34. Letters 2, 4, 7, 13, 16 (there are two letters marked 15 in the *AA.SS.*— this is the second one), 17, 18, 19, 21, 25 (not given a number in *AA.SS.*), 26 (marked 25 in *AA.SS.*), 28 (27 in *AA.SS.*), 29 (28 in *AA.SS.*), 30 (also 28 in *AA.SS.*). They can be found in pp. 257, 258, 261, 266, 272, 272, 273, 274, 276, 281, 286, 289, 293. The rest of the letters are added without chronological order at the end of the manuscript and might not have been intended for publication.

for example, Christina, p. 272). The letters also contain numerous descriptions of demonic assaults on Christina. What the letters lack are accounts of mystical experiences, or even a developed spirituality. This, for an ecstatic visionary, is very unusual.

It is enough to glance through the writings of any one of Christina's contemporaries—Margaret of Cortona (d. 1297), Gertrude of Helfta (d. 1302), or Angela of Foligno (d. 1309), to name but a few—to realize the difference. In the sixty-seven pages her letters occupy in Paulson's edition, Christ is almost completely absent. The scribes allude to him indirectly as Christina's bridegroom, but there is not even one dialogue with Christ to be found, no meditations on the Passion, no visions of Christ's life or his glory in heaven. The closest thing to a traditional mystical experience is a single description, about five lines long, followed by a short account of a vision of the Blessed Virgin that Christina had as a child (Christina, p. 291).

Peter's letters to Christina, in contrast, are filled with discussions of Christ's love, Christina's spiritual marriage with Christ, and the mystical significance of her stigmata.[35] Christina's letters, then, did not conform with Peter's notions of spirituality. Yet Peter resisted the temptation to make Christina the mystic she was not. Her letters are incorporated in the text seemingly unedited. Peter adds short comments, but does not change the tone, or the crude style of the letters.[36] This faithfulness to the letter, so to speak, is usually taken as a sign of a trustworthy witness.

Much of the *commune sanctorum* is also absent from Peter's account. There are only two (rather ambiguous) miraculous cures in the narrative.[37] The text makes no mention of prophecies, clairvoyance, exorcism, or other such activities. Some ascetic practices are related in the priest's account of Christina's early life, but almost

35. See, for example, letter 5 (Christina, pp. 259–61) and letter 24—no number in *AA.SS.*—p. 280).
36. See, for example, Christina pp. 258, 262. This is especially significant since Peter did edit (at least stylistically) his own letters (see Monika Asztalos 1986).
37. For the miraculous cures, see Christina, pp. 254, 278. In the first, a tumor disappeared from a friar's arm. In the second, Christina herself was healed of a wounded shin without medical treatment. There is no indication that either the wound or the cured member were seen by others.

none in Peter's narrative.[38] Peter mentions no significant charitable activity in relation to Christina. She did not feed the poor or attend the sick. This cannot be attributed to Peter's negligence. One of his spiritual daughters in Sweden was also a stigmatic and an ecstatic visionary. In a letter to Christina, Peter does not fail to mention both the former's ascetic practices and her almsgiving and service to the poor (Christina, p. 352).

All this cannot be explained solely by Peter's faithfulness to the truth at all costs. Peter apparently saw Christina as first and foremost a patient victim, a genuine martyr. For the martyr the most important quality was patience. The more horrible the torments the more striking the martyr's equanimity. And yet, even in the *Lives* of martyrs, written during that period, there is usually an attempt to provide enough of the *commune sanctorum* for the saint to make the martyrdom just the crowning effort of a virtuous life. That Peter chose not to do so might have surprised (and perhaps disappointed) his contemporaries, but for the modern reader the absence of the conventional serves to increase the credibility of his account.

What is most confusing about Peter's account is that his "realism" seems to defeat his principal goal. It was not enough, after all, for a hagiographer to convince the reader that he was telling the truth; he had to convince him also that his subject was a saint. The absence of conventional hagiographical elements might convince readers that Peter was telling the truth, but at the same time it raises serious doubts regarding Christina's sainthood. It is probable that this is exactly what happened. The *Life* contributed very little to Christina's cult. What little veneration developed after her death cannot be traced back to the *Life,* which survived in only one medieval manuscript.

For the modern reader, the combination of literary independence, realistic descriptions of behavior, and such disregard for audience expectations that lead to the failure of the work's practical objective should have made Peter the ideal source. Instead, all this

38. For asceticism in the priest's story, see Christina, p. 237. We are also told in the second *Life* that for a year and a half she ate nothing but ginger (Christina, p. 386).

convincing form is wasted on modern readers who cannot accept the content. At the very heart of the vita, Peter reports a number of incidents, which he claims to have witnessed himself, of demons covering Christina's and other people's bodies with large quantities of excrement. We just do not believe in such things. This is not for lack of convincing evidence. Our disbelief, just like Peter's belief, in their possibility is unconditional and nonempirical.

David Hume states this position in typical directness. Suppose, he says, we had overwhelming, and in every respect trustworthy, evidence that Queen Elizabeth I had died and then returned to life.

You would in vain object to me the difficulty and almost impossibility of deceiving the world in an affair of such consequence; the wisdom and solid judgment of that renowned queen, with the little or no advantage which she could reap from so poor an artifice. All this might astonish me, but I would still reply, that the knavery and folly of men are such common phenomena, that I should rather believe the most extraordinary events to arise from their concurrence, than admit so signal a violation of the laws of nature. (Hume 1921, 10.2, p. 133)

If the historian, like Hume, is unwilling to believe in miracles, she faces a serious dilemma. Does she declare this *Life* worthless as a historical source? Does she retain some parts and discard others, and which ones should she keep?

The problem is not related to this *Life* only. To a greater or lesser degree, many medieval *Lives* present the reader with a mixture of believable and unbelievable elements. Even if the reader is willing to accept my claim that the firsthand accounts of the lives of new saints contain at least some real elements, it is not always easy to tell those elements apart from the unreal ones. The only thing we do know is that certain stories cannot be accepted literally. To be useful, these elements must somehow be explained or else they cast doubt on the reliability of the source as a whole.

In theory, one could dismiss all these *Lives* as unreliable, but that would make further research in the field practically impossible. There is a tacit agreement among historians that if the object of study is important enough, existing material should be considered sufficient for conducting research. This is a strong and arbitrary claim. Our interest in a subject does not, unfortunately, have much effect on the quality of the data. Nevertheless, this belief is held as an article of faith by people active in fields where data are problematic. The outsider trying to challenge the very legitimacy of the field—the economic history of premodern societies or the religious and social history of the Middle Ages, for example—is seen as a mere nuisance to be ignored.[39] Research must be possible, because it is done.

There are some historians, however, who argue that it is possible to avoid the Humian dilemma altogether. They maintain that saints' *Lives* tell us about perceptions, not about reality. *Lives* are an expression of what the hagiographer and the saints considered ideal or canonical sainthood, not a factual report of real events. If some events recounted in the *Lives* happen to be true, it is nevertheless their symbolic value that matters, their reflection of "perceptions" not historical "facts."[40] To try to distinguish between what did and what did not actually happen is to misunderstand the nature of medieval *Lives*.[41]

But to assume that everything in the *Life* is, in one way or another, what the writer considered ideal sainthood is simply false. When Raymond of Capua struggles to explain the failure of Catherine's prediction of a crusade that did not materialize, he is not dealing with ideal sainthood. Ideally, such unfortunate accidents should not have occurred. He had to deal with the mishap because it did occur, and because other people knew about it. As I have argued earlier, not only the saint's public failures entered the text (in the form of apologetic explanation). Some information was included because it left a strong impression on the biographer, or because the participants had put pressure on him to include it. Thus, not only does the fabricated material cast doubt upon the nonfabricated, but the reverse is also true. If some elements entered the text because the writer felt constrained to include them, they cannot be treated as if they were a reflection of the writer's or even the saint's perceptions.

39. On the tacit hermeneutics of professional groups, see Gyorgy Markus (1987).

40. See Weinstein and Bell (1982, p. 13): "Our 'facts,' then, are perceptions"; Rudolph Bell (1985, p. xi); see also Caroline Walker Bynum (1987, p. 8).

41. This position often leads to the naive idea that for medievals fact and fantasy were not clearly distinguished (see, for example, Thomas J. Heffernan 1988, pp. 66–71).

An invented carpenter father is one thing; a real carpenter father quite another. In the former case, an explanation is required in terms of the logic of the author's choice, in the latter it is not. It would be a mistake to explain a flesh and blood carpenter as a christological allusion, unless the author himself gives us a cause to do so. In the case of miraculous events too, the historian's analysis would surely be very different, depending on whether something interpreted as a miracle actually took place: the cure of a psychosomatic problem, for example, or whether the event was invented lock, stock, and barrel. In the former case, the historian would be justified in trying to reconstruct social reality—how real people reacted to an extraordinary occurrence—in the latter case, she may only reconstruct the mental world of the author: this is how author *x* imagined the reaction of an ideal audience.

We do not know whether an event occurred in the real world or in the imagined world of the author. We do not even know whether an author describes an event more or less faithfully, or modifies it to make it consonant with his ideal. What we do know is that the two positions are not interchangeable: literary inventions are not real people, nor are descriptions of real people mere reflections of authorial perceptions. I would like to argue that the categories "real/fabricated," or "authentic/inauthentic" are indispensable for historical analysis.

What troubles me about the "perceptions" strategy is that it seeks to relieve the historian of the need to make decisions—to take sides. It introduces a semblance of consistency where consistency does not exist. The texts we are dealing with cannot be interpreted either as pure literary invention or as reliable real-life testimony; they are both. The historian must tell the reader how *she* interprets specific elements in the text. By so doing, the historian acknowledges that she is not simply an observer of her text, but an interlocutor, a distorting lens, that she is constantly taking sides.

In what follows I will tell the reader how I make sense of the text. This is not an investigation of truth (other readers may take sides differently, with equal justification); it is, rather, a methodological confession. I chose to focus on the supernatural elements in the *Lives,* because they tend to present the most difficult problem in this type of text. I will tell the reader how and at what cost I justify my claim to study "lived sainthood."

Saving the Text

Historians use a number of unstated mechanisms to reduce the incredible in hagiographical sources or remove it altogether. As much as possible, the historian prefers to think that his witnesses are telling the truth, at least as they saw it. The historian might have to reinterpret the data made available by the eyewitness, because the latter was biased, naive, or ignorant. Medieval credulity can be used to save the credibility of the medieval writer. If our source was quick to believe, the more disturbing option—that he was lying—need not be entertained. This solution, however, does not work for the eyewitness. It would not do to say that he was credulous in the same way, for he claims to have experienced the things directly. The most common saving techniques for the eyewitness account are the hallucinating witness and the deceived witness. Both can have stronger and weaker forms.

The hallucinating witness can be said to be mad or, more often, unable to distinguish dreams and other subjective experiences from reality. Deception, on the other hand, can be the result of a premeditated effort or of an unconscious one. For example, if the saint claims that she survives on nothing but the host for many years, she can knowingly be eating and lying about it, or eating in some state of unconsciousness and believing in all sincerity that she does not. In the latter form, this explanation is a variant of the hallucination strategy. The main difference is that hallucination is used when the person in question does not gain anything material by his or her words and acts, or when such gains are conceived as minor and indirect. The term deception always carries a pejorative sense and tends to be used when a person conceals certain facts which would allow others to realize his or her "true," supposedly less appealing self.

The difference between a conscious deceiver and a dissociated visionary depends more on the observer's attitude toward the performer than on the nature of the acts themselves. It is hard nowadays to consider the possibility of "conscious" deception without being regarded judgmental or, worse, a positivist. The question may in fact be, as Thomas Szasz has suggested, a pseudo-problem: "for consciousness—or, self-reflective awareness—depends partly on the situation in which a person finds himself. In other words, it is partly a social characteristic rather than simply a personal one (Szasz 1974, p. 219).

Peter can be seen as the victim of either conscious or unconscious (depending on how we want to see Christina) deception. He tells us that on his first visit to Stommeln, Christina drew two iron nails covered with blood from her sleeves. For Peter, these were instruments of demonic torture, which he kept as relics. Had Peter been less ready to believe Christina, the nails would have raised the possibility in his mind that her stigmata were self-inflicted. Had he wished to deceive us, he would have withheld this piece of information. As it was, he did neither. The facts he describes, though not perhaps his interpretation of them, can be believed.[42]

If we choose to believe that Christina was totally sincere in all her actions, we can view her visions and demonic attacks as examples of a blurred sense of reality. Although she said that these incredible things actually happened to her, we may, and regularly do, assume that they were internal experiences that the saint confused with real events. The third part of Christina's *Life* is an account of her tribulations dictated to the schoolmaster, John. Every page of his account is more marvelous than any of Peter's descriptions. Christina saves numerous souls from purgatory; she is assaulted by thousands of demons (on one occasion 200,000),[43] torn to pieces, burned alive, hanged, drowned, reduced to dust by hammers, and is again and again miraculously cured.

All these marvelous occurrences are presented as reports made by Christina. She reported these stories to her secretaries and they wrote them down. The events themselves were experienced only by the saint. Her friends believed them to be events in the real world; we do not. We might wonder, like Catherine of Siena's critics, whether the saint experienced them in her mind or made them up, but the credibility of the writers is not reduced because they believed in the reality of the saint's stories.[44]

---

42. In spite of the nails, it is not impossible that the stigmatic wounds were spontaneous and that the nails were only meant to increase the impression. The description of the physical stigmata is not unlike that of authentic cases. See (for descriptions of the stigmata), for example, Christina, p. 245 and pp. 255–56. For a medical discussion of stigmatization, see F. A. Whitlock and J. V. Hynes (1978).

43. Christina, p. 322.

44. Cf. Raymond of Capua, *Vitas Catharinae senesis* 1.5, *AA.SS.*, 30 Apr.,

Another device to save the author's credibility is the ambiguity of language. Statements concerning measurements (either temporal or spatial) can be saved by assuming a semiskeptical attitude. Medievals are notoriously bad with numbers, and their description can be viewed as exaggerated but basically true. Linguistic ambiguity can sometimes be more intentional. As Walter Daniel says in the defense for his *Life of Ailred,* he had indeed said that Ailred's body "shone like a carbuncle and smelled like incense," but he was merely availing himself of a rhetorical device and was not to be taken literally.[45]

In another type of supernatural event, the miraculous cure, it is possible to hold that the witnesses faithfully recounted what they saw. The majority of miraculous cures involved what might have been psychosomatic disturbances: temporary paralysis, blindness, loss of speech, possession, etc. Even the most spectacular miracle, the resurrection of the dead, could be interpreted as based on what we would consider inappropriate diagnosis of death. As Pierre-André Sigal has noted, the overwhelming majority of medieval miraculous cures he had examined would nowadays be considered quite natural.[46] It is important to bear in mind, then, that many medieval people actually witnessed events that they considered miraculous and that their willingness to believe accounts of others—categorically different from our point of view, but similar from theirs—was much greater than ours even among medieval skeptics. However, even this relatively effective technique is not always easy. Providing natural explanations for incredible stories can often be done only with great difficulty. For though deception by the participants can be summoned as a last resort to explain certain occurrences that defy any other solution, it is often hard to see how exactly it was arranged.

---

p. 883. In his essay "Apparently Irrational Beliefs" (1985, pp. 35–63), Dan Sperber argues convincingly that there is nothing irrational in the belief in dragons, for example, in a culture where such beliefs are sanctioned by tradition. However, he conveniently ignores the trickier question—not why some people believe supposed eye-witness accounts of this sort, but why others tell them.

45. Walter Daniel, *Vita Ailredi abbatis Rievall',* pp. 76–77.

46. See Pierre-André Sigal (1985, p. 255); for medieval definitions of death see "Rapport d'un curialiste sur la vie et les miracles de S. Thomas de Cantiloupe évêque de Hereford (d. 1282)" in André Vauchez (1981, p. 642).

Some texts, however, cannot be saved by any of these techniques. Peter's *Life* cannot be saved, mainly because Peter would not let us save it. Consider the passage with which I opened this chapter. It was a straightforward, unambiguous report of a personal experience. The setting of the bedroom scene as Peter described it blocks any attempt to suggest error, deception, or naiveté. Peter, addressing an audience that believed in the possibility, and frequent occurrence, of miracles did everything to provide his readers with as many reassuring details as he could.

First, Peter tells us that he was not alone (this excludes the possibility of a private experience). Second, he and his friends surrounded the bed from all sides, sitting within reach of Christina. The appearance of excrement in Christina's mouth and on her eyes could not have been achieved by artifice, without the knowledge of those present. So it is precisely Peter's "thick" description, aimed at convincing his contemporaries that fraud or delusion were impossible, that makes his account unsalvageable from our point of view.

The modern historian has to decide whether Peter was mad or hallucinating, in which case his account would fall into the category of the purely subjective, or whether he was lying. (These are, naturally, only the two extreme positions on a very wide spectrum, but one always opts between these two poles.) The *Life* itself and Peter's career in the Dominican Order do not lend support to the first possibility. Peter must be lying. But why this particular lie, why not other, more impressing, more beautiful lies? For if we must assume that our witness is lying, we would like at least to understand why.

The most obvious reason is interest. Peter might have been driven to lie by his desire to see Christina venerated by others. Yet, this does not provide a much better explanation in this case, for if some of Peter's problematic descriptions, such as the one quoted at the beginning of this chapter, can be seen as portraying Christina as a patient victim, others are less easy to explain. How do we account for a passage like this:

After Brother Gerardus greeted Johannes of Mussindorp, his friend, the lord priest, Christina, and those who stayed with her, he added jokingly: "do not shit on me, Mr. demon, for I am your friend." I [Peter] reacted: "If you are a friend of the demon then I am an enemy of both you and him." Those present laughed at these words, and with one voice expressed their wishes that the devil would greet his friend with his usual ornaments. . . . After supper Brother Gerardus rose and wanted to go to the fire . . . dressed in a white new scapular, which he wore that day for the first time. When he reached the center of the room, the devil steeped his face, his scapular's cowl as well as his whole chest with the vilest liquid, stinking human shit in such abundance, that standing in the center of the room, in sight of us all, he made the said filth drip from his face and nose; which did not displease some of us, for he [the devil] disfigured thus the one who called himself his friend. (Christina, p. 252)

Christina is not even the heroine of this episode, nor does it stress patience. Brother Gerardus is not a detractor receiving his just deserts,[47] but one of Christina's most loyal devotees. In fact, it functions, if anything, like a comic relief. The devil is more a prankster than a threatening agressor. If Peter wanted to lie in order to increase his heroine's fame, why did he not attribute a greater number of miracles to her? This would have been much more effective for a canonization process or a nascent cult than Christina's bizarre demonic assaults. Hume's belief in the "knavery and folly of men" may make further explanation for Peter's behavior unnecessary for *him*, but it is an admission of failure to provide more specific answers.[48]

All this leaves us in a very uncomfortable position. Because we do not understand why Peter was lying in this particular way, we cannot be sure that we may trust seemingly nonproblematic parts of his text or exercise our exegetical tactics with much certainty. If we knew that the whole document was a mental construct, we could at least learn something from it about a "medieval mind." It seems quite likely, however, that parts of the narrative are true records of actual events. But which ones? We find ourselves under the spell of a demon who—like Descartes's metaphysical demon— sometimes lies, but sometimes tells the truth.

It would have been wonderful to have other sources or more sources, but in the absence of the ideal source, the question is often how badly we want a specific text or category of texts. This is an

47. On one occasion, the demon covered Christina's detractors with excrement as they were sitting in the local church (Christina p. 255).

48. "The vulgar, that is indeed, all mankind, a few expected, being ignorant and uninstructed, never elevate their contemplation to heaven" (David Hume 1976, p. 57).

admission, in other words, that I, too, as part of the community of historians, regard existing data as sufficient for meaningful study.

Witnesses, as Aquinas had noted, are a fallible medium, and therefore no certainty is possible in canonization. Unable to live with such an uncertainty, Thomas had to summon divine providence to safeguard the church against error. His contemporary, Hostiensis, refused to have recourse to the Almighty to resolve his uncertainties. Error, he boldly asserted, is possible. One must do what is humanly possible to avoid it and trust God to consider our good intentions rather than our limited abilities.[49]

Historians are closer in their approach to medieval canonists than to medieval theologians. They pass judgments that are as fallible as the evidence they are based on, but they are very serious about them nonetheless. Like the canonist, the historian should strive to reduce, as much as possible, the likelihood of error and distinguish between the more credible and the less credible.

Unlike medieval canonists, however, modern historians realize, or should realize, that they themselves are media, no less distorting than their sources. But the realization that no certainty is possible about the "thing in itself," must not lead to despair or historical "deconstruction." What we seek is not "the objective truth," independent of the subjective viewpoint of any beholder, but it is also not a purely personal reading.[50] Historians seek a common ground for discussion—a negotiated means by which to tell better testimonies or interpretations from weaker ones. Even Thomas— providence notwithstanding—maintained that a rigorous examination of witnesses' testimonies is indispensable. Clearly, some media are more fallible than others.

The historian must not only evaluate his sources, but tell the reader by what criteria he evaluates them. Like all first principles, such criteria are often arbitrary, or at least unprovable. Further-

49. For a longer discussion of Thomas's and Hostiensis's views on canonization, see Kleinberg (1989, pp. 197–98).

50. "We may actually say that an anthropologist 'invents' the culture he believes himself to be studying, that the relation is more 'real' for being his particular acts and experiences than the things it 'relates.' Yet this explanation is only justified if we understand the invention to take place objectively, along the lines of observing and learning, and not as a kind of free fantasy" (Roy Wagner 1981, p. 4).

more, in some cases the historian relies on no general principles at all, but on his vague intuitions, applicable to specific cases only. By stating them explicitly, the historian exposes the seams of his interpretive gown to the critical gaze of the reader. Whether stated or not, methodological articles of faith are at work in any historical analysis. They are less harmful when they do not masquerade as impartial observations.[51]

To save Peter's *Life* of Christina, I would suggest a combination of the credulous and lying witness strategies. Demonic assaults and trials were a fundamental element in Christina's inner life. She must have told numerous such stories to Peter, who took them to be true in the absolute sense. Moreover, there were other people in Stommeln who were willing to swear that they were witnesses to similar occurrences. Being convinced of the historicity of events attested by so many witnesses, Peter decided to relate some of the stories he had heard as if he were there, in order to give them an eyewitness-authority. His narrative attempted to describe how real persons would behave in such circumstances: with a mixture of horror, compassion, and good spirit in the face of adversity.

Agobard of Lyon relates a firsthand encounter with a product of the process I have ascribed to Peter—a man so convinced of the truth of what he tells that he tells it in the first person. Agobard writes that he has frequently heard talk about the *tempestarii,* magicians who control storms and lightnings, but that he never met a person who claimed to have seen them with his own eyes. When he was told that such a person existed, he went to see the man and questioned him about the magicians. At first the man repeated his story, but when Agobard warned him with threats of divine retribution to say nothing but the truth, "the man affirmed that what he said was true, giving the name of the [magician], the time, and

---

51. In his *Sacred Biography,* Thomas Heffernan devotes most of the first two chapters to a critique of what he calls "empiricist biography." The positivists, he argues, fail to realize that no account is *the* true account—or an accurate reflection of reality. That is true, of course, but it does not solve our problem. Accounts which claim seriously to reflect reality (and it is not always easy to say just how literal this claim is) must be considered, among other things, vis-à-vis this claim. Different levels of credibility can and should be assigned to them, if their interpretation is to make any sense at all.

the place. He admitted, however, that he himself was not present at that time."[52] The man was so totally convinced of the truth of what he was relating that his absence seemed merely an insignificant detail. His information was as good as if he were there himself.

This explanation has one difficulty: Peter wrote his *Life* while Christina and many of the other characters portrayed were still alive. Would not some of them challenge Peter's version of things? After all, he could not be certain that they would all be happy with the roles they play in his narrative.

Perhaps we can find a clue to a solution in Peter's *On the Virtues of Christina*. Peter begins this composition with a poem. In it he proclaims his intention to describe his subject's virtues "in disguised words" (the title of the work with its explicit reference to Christina was added later), so as to render the detractors harmless.[53] We know that this book was the only part of his work that Peter sent to Stommeln. It is possible that Peter's avoidance of explicit references to people and places in *On the Virtues* was meant to defend Peter not only against avowed critics of Christina, but also against knowledgeable readers. The *Life,* intended for a Swedish audience, could be less cautious. We do not know how the second book arrived eventually in Stommeln. My guess is that after Peter's death, it was sent from Sweden to Stommeln by Peter's confreres and was combined with the letters already there to make one volume.

Does this solve all the difficulties in Peter's *Life* of Christina? Probably not. In fact, I may have woken up sleeping dogs readers were quite willing to let lie. I have certainly brought upon myself the suspicion of being a positivist (only positivists want to know what really happened), but at least the reader knows: Here I stand. Unlike Luther, I could have done otherwise.

52. Agobard of Lyon, *De grandine et tonituris* 7, in his *Opera,* edited by L. Van Acker, *C.C.CM* 52:8.

53. Peter of Dacia, *De gratia naturam ditante sive de virtutibus Christinae stumbelensis,* edited by M. Asztalos (Stockholm, 1982, p. 83).

IV

THE PASSION OF CHRISTINA
OF STOMMELN

HE reader has by now acquired some familiarity with Christina of
Stommeln, but she deserves further study. Her importance does
not stem so much from her success as a saint—of the four cases I
examine, she was the least successful—but from the extraordinary
wealth of information that has reached us about her, and, perhaps
more important, about her biographer. Sainthood consisted of a
number of concentric circles. At the center stood the saint. Surrounding the saint were people of different levels of intimacy and
emotional investment in him or her. The person who was often the
closest to the saint and who played a crucial role in the saint's career
and in his or her posthumous reputation was, at least for women,
the confessor/biographer (see Coackly 1991).

Peter of Dacia not only wrote Christina's first *Life*, he was her
most important follower. One could say that after a certain point
she performed mainly for him. The anonymous author of her second *Life* writes that shortly after the news of Peter's death reached
Stommeln, all of Christina's supernatural phenomena stopped.[1]
He has nothing to say about the remaining twenty-three or
twenty-four years of her life. Nothing was recorded: no visions, no
miracles, no saintly deeds. To say nothing about the saint's last
years and to make no mention of the impact that the saint's passing
away had on contemporaries is an unprecedented and inexcusable
gap in a hagiographical work. Did she experience no more incidents of this kind after Peter's death, or was there no one interested
in hearing about them? Either way, it is evident that after Peter's
death, Christina's public sainthood quietly evaporated. A later
scribe added at the end of book 1 in the manuscript the standard
note alluding to "many posthumous miracles," but the note describes only one, the cure of Count Dietrich of Cleves of paralysis

---

1. Peter died in 1289, Christina in 1312.

71

in 1339.[2] Between the years of 1289 and 1339, Christina ceased to be considered "worthy of memory."

Peter played the role of audience in many of Christina's saintly situations. He was also very active in spreading her reputation, both in Stommeln and in other places. His *Life*, the exceptionally personal nature of which I have discussed in the previous chapter, offers a rare look at the complex emotional relationship that developed between the participants in the saintly dialogue: the saint and the intimate devotee. The impersonal tone of most *Lives* makes such a consideration impossible. Peter's *Life* illustrates how the private language of affection and dependence was translated into a public discourse, wherein socially meaningful roles were assigned to the players.

Christina was born c. 1242 in Stommeln, a village approximately eighteen kilometers northwest of Cologne, to a family of prosperous peasants.[3] She had two sisters and two brothers. When she was ten years old, she dedicated herself to Christ, and when she was thirteen she left her parents' house without their permission and joined a community of Beguines in Cologne. In Cologne, Christina experienced various demonic attacks and heavenly consolations, but was not accepted as a true saint by the local Beguines. Their hostility probably led to her return to Stommeln three or four years later. Christina lived for awhile in her parents' house and at times in the local Beguinage. The continual demonic attacks eventually made life with her unbearable for her family and she moved into the parish priest's house, where he lived with his mother. It was in the priest's house that she first met Peter of Dacia.

Peter was born on the island of Gotland in the Baltic sea, sometime between 1230 and 1240.[4] In 1266 he was sent by the Dominican order in Sweden to the *studium generale* in Cologne. He first met Christina in December of 1267 and visited her thirteen times in all before leaving for Paris in the spring of 1269. He spent a little

2. Peter of Dacia, *De gratia naturam ditante sive de virtutibus Christinae stumbelensis*, edited by M. Asztalos (Stockholm, 1982), pp. 188–89.

3. A short biographical sketch can be found in Paul Nieveler (1975, pp. 76–97).

4. For Peter see, Jarl Gallén (1946, pp. 225–44); Monika Asztalos's introduction to Peter of Dacia's, *De gratia naturam ditante*, pp. 9–10; and Nieveler (1975, pp. 58–75).

more than a year in Paris, studying theology under Thomas Aquinas. In 1270, he returned for a visit to Cologne and Stommeln and then departed for Sweden. He held the office of lector in Skänninge until 1277, when he was transferred to Västerås, first as lector and then as prior. In 1279, Peter again visited Christina in Stommeln. Upon his return to Sweden in 1280, he was appointed lector to the Dominican house in Visby. In 1286, he became prior of Visby and was elected *socius* to the provincial prior for the general chapter of Bordeaux in 1287. Peter probably visited Stommeln one last time in that year. He died shortly after he returned to Visby in 1289.

Except for the fact that Christina's tribulations ended after Peter's death, we do not know much about her last years. It seems that she lived the rest of her life (in the Beguinage?, in her own house?) without any special events. The task of recording her experiences was not resumed by the schoolmaster (who had acted as her secretary on Peter's request) or by anybody else after Peter's death.

Our primary source of information about Peter and Christina, the so-called *Codex Iuliacensis* (after the town of Jülich where it was kept until 1973) is divided into three books (Nieveler, 1975, pp. 15–28). The first, "De virtutibus Christinae," is a scholastic theological discussion written by Peter on the workings of grace, with Christina as its focus and main example.[5] The second book includes Peter's account of his encounters with Christina, letters from Peter to Christina and to other people regarding Christina, letters from Christina to Peter, and letters of various people to Peter and to Christina. It also includes a description of Christina's early career written by Stommeln's priest, John, a friend and follower of Christina. The third book was written by a local schoolmaster, also called John, at Peter's request. It is an account of various tribulations endured by Christina between 1280 and 1287. All three books were written while Christina was still alive.

In addition to the *Codex Iuliacensis*, there exists in a manuscript now held in Vienna another *Life* written a few years after Christina's death (Nieveler 1975, pp. 34–37). The posthumous *Life* adds only little to the material contained in the *Codex Iuliacensis*. Its main importance is that it tells us about Christina's

5. This part of the codex was edited by Monika Asztalos in *De gratia naturam ditante*.

last years. All in all, this is an impressive dossier. It contains three contemporary accounts of the saint and sixty-three letters, fourteen dictated by Christina herself. It is not often that we have so much information from so many sources about one saint, especially as modest a saint as was Christina.

PETER'S first encounter with Christina, recorded in Sweden eleven years after the event, provides the key for an understanding of his devotion to her and of their subsequent relationship. It also gives us a taste of Peter's talent for realistic description and dialogue.

The Dominicans of Cologne fulfilled various pastoral duties in the city itself and in the neighboring villages. The foreign students of the *studium generale* often accompanied the local friars in these activities. On one occasion Peter joined a certain Brother Walter to hear the confession of a noble lady who was very sick. While Walter was hearing the lady's confession, Peter was approached by a Beguine who stayed in the same house. When Peter told her he had come from Cologne, she said: "Would that you were in our village and saw the marvels that are worked there in a certain young woman [*puella*]" (Christina, p. 240). It so happened that the next evening Walter went to visit the parish priest of Stommeln in whose house the very same young woman was staying.

In the poorly furnished house, Peter saw a sad family (*familiam tristem*) and a young woman, whose face was covered with a cloak, sitting somewhat apart. When she rose to greet Brother Walter, a demon suddenly pulled her backwards and struck her head against the wall with such force that the whole wall shook. At the sight of this, everybody in the room was greatly troubled—everybody but Peter. "I alone," he writes, "was filled with extraordinary joy, consoled internally, and raised to an amazement of the soul" (Christina, p. 240). His sudden joy took Peter by surprise. He tried to understand it, but found nothing in the external circumstances that could justify such happiness.

Embarrassed by his reaction and fearing it might be noticed by the others, Peter restrained himself with some difficulty and engaged in conversation with the priest and his mother. Meanwhile, as Walter was talking to Christina about the patience of Christ and the saints, the demon kept banging her head violently against the wall behind her and against a chest on her left-hand side. Peter was astonished that in spite of the violent beating Christina did not sigh or groan, but remained absolutely silent, showing no sign of impatience or pain. After watching in silence for awhile, Peter, incapable of repressing his emotions any longer turned to Brother Walter and said:

Dearest father, I do not know if you have noticed that the demon gravely afflicts the maiden that sits beside you. It would be better if you sat farther away from the wall and the chest, and put some pillow between her and the said obstacles, so that should he push her again, she would be supported by softer objects. (Christina, p. 240)

Peter's suggestion was accepted and the head-banging stopped, having lost some of its effect. But the demon did not leave Christina in peace. Fresh, bleeding wounds appeared on both of her feet. Peter approached Christina from time to time during the night to get a better look, and whenever he looked there seemed to be more wounds than before.

Walter retired to bed and Peter was given permission to keep vigil with Christina during the night. Two candles shed light over the small dark room, where seven people kept guard over Christina all night long. No one dared sleep for fear of the devil's wickedness and ferocity. Peter took Walter's place beside Christina and sat in silence for a while. Then, he writes,

[Christina] turned to me and said: "What is your name?"
"I am called Peter," I said.
"Good Brother Peter," said she, "talk to me a little about God, for I shall willingly listen, though by reason of my urgent need I cannot listen very closely, for which I am sorry."
In response to her and the others' request, though my German was imperfect, I recounted two edifying (I thought) exempla taken from the *Lives of the Brothers:* one on how the Blessed Virgin taught a certain Carthusian to serve and love her, and the other on how a certain friar of the Order of Preachers was freed of fifteen years in purgatory, because of a mass celebrated by an older friar, his close friend. (Christina, p. 241)

Christina sighed again. She drew from inside her sleeve a long iron nail covered with blood and flesh, and then another, even more horrible to behold, from the other sleeve. The demon had been wounding her with these. Peter asked for the nails and treasured them as holy relics. When the night was over, Peter returned to Cologne, exalted and dazed with joy.

When morning came, I returned to Cologne whence I had come; but I do not know whether in my whole life until that hour I felt such disposition of my heart, so that I would then have done nothing more willingly than celebrate a mass of the Blessed Virgin for all the divine gifts and the working of graces. . . . O happy night! O blessed night! You were for me the beginning of divine illuminations which know no difference of night and day. O sweet and delectable night in which for the first time I was given to taste how pleasant the Lord is! This is the night in which I merited to see for the first time my Lord's bride. (Christina, p. 241)[6]

Why was Peter so ecstatic when he left Stommeln after that fateful night? He seems to suggest that the spontaneous and perplexing feeling of joy that he felt at the sight of the first demonic attack was somehow explained by subsequent events. But even if we believe that Christina was really assaulted by a demon, and showed courage and patience, Peter's exultation seems hard to understand. Something about the events in the room had the impact of turning Peter from an observer of an afflicted, possibly possessed woman to a follower of a saint, but what?

People approach the saint with certain preconceived ideas of what constitutes sanctity. Every encounter with a saint involves an effort to establish whether there exists a correspondence between the observers' expectations and the actual person they see before their eyes. Peter tells us what he was waiting for: from as far back as he could remember, he took pleasure in listening to the stories of the saints and martyrs. One desire was dearer to him than others:

That He would show me one of His saints, by whom I would be taught plainly and surely the life of the saints not only by words, but by deeds and examples; to whom I would be linked and associated by love of the heart; by whose virtues I would be informed; by whose devotion I would be inflamed and raised from the melancholy [accidia] that afflicted me from youth . . . by whose example all my doubts would be removed, especially in that which pertains to the lives [or Lives] of the saints. (Christina, p. 239)

6. Peter uses words strongly reminiscent of the Easter Vigil liturgy. It shows the depths of his excitement, since he compares it to no less an event than Christ's resurrection. I am grateful to Richard Kieckhefer for drawing my attention to the model Peter was using.

For a long time, Peter writes, he remained unsatisfied. The Lord in his mercy,

has shown me many persons of both sexes, in whom He had often glad-dened my heart. He had not, however, satisfied the desire of my longing, nor calmed the passion of my heart. The more diligently I considered [such persons], the more I wished to contemplate. The more I saw, the more I wished to see, because in none of them did I find what I was looking for. And therefore I was left starving with desire [*famelicum*]. (Christina, p. 239)

When Peter entered the priest's house, he was not yet sure what to expect. All he knew was what the Beguine had told him, namely that something marvelous might be forthcoming. Peter prudently decided that "whatever unusual or marvelous things I might see I shall be completely silent, not knowing of what value such things be considered among those present" (Christina, p. 240). He was aware of his status as an outsider. Marvelous phenomena are open to different, sometimes conflicting, interpretations. It was best to keep quiet until, from the reactions of the others, he could learn the appropriate frame of reference: is she treated as possessed, sick, mad, a saint? More specifically, what is the nature of each particular act or phenomenon? In the event, however, Peter was unable to re-main prudently aloof for long. As soon as the demon first assaulted Christina, he was overwhelmed by an inexplicable feeling of joy. From that moment on he no longer reserved his judgment, but saw in everything that happened in the room a corroboration of his faith.

His strong emotional reaction tells us something about what he missed in other holy people. They left him cold. The demonic at-tack was a confirmation that he was in the presence of the more spectacular aspect of sanctity: not pious behavior, not long hours of prayer and acts of charity, but drama: pain and blood, heroism, and most important, direct contact with the supernatural.[7] A passage from one of Chrysostom's sermons springs to his mind: "Terrestrial things must yield, when heavenly things are pro-

---

7. In a letter from Paris, Peter complains that although he is surrounded by the most dazzling learning and piety (Aquinas was one of his teachers), he feels spir-itually cold. It was only when he celebrated mass that he felt some relief, and it was the direct contact with the divine that raised his spirits (Christina, p. 267, but con-sult Paulson's reading, p. 104).

claimed; natural things must be silent when supernatural powers [*virtutes*] speak" (Christina, p. 241). When on his next visit Peter saw Christina's stigmata, he exclaimed: "I saw the thing I desired from childhood. I know not whether, until that hour, I have seen a thing so devout and so beautiful, and which delighted and edified me that much" (Christina, p. 243).

During the first night, Peter got ample proof of Christina's "warm" sanctity. Perhaps if he had been more patient, he would have learned a little more about the value others outside the room assigned to Christina's actions. The Beguines of Cologne, with whom she had stayed for three or four years, were unimpressed with her asceticism, raptures, and demonic attacks. Some considered her insane or an epileptic, some a fool (*fatua*).[8] "The Beguines [of Stommeln]," continues the priest in his account of her early life, "ridiculed all of her actions: all of her prayers, every favor she asked for [*quidquid de veniis quesivit* could also mean her pleas to be forgiven]—they despised everything. Thus within her house and out of it she found no one to console her. In everything she did, they said that she was feigning sanctity" (Christina, p. 237).

This does not necessarily mean that had Peter known all of this beforehand he would not have become an admirer of Christina. He could have thought that the Beguines were unkind or led astray by the devil. The important point is that when he met Christina he was not yet tarnished by the skepticism of others. The people in the room with Christina were all believers. They served to heighten the impact of events on the young Swede. Their reverence and their fear were silent corroboration of Christina's authenticity. But, although Peter does not mention it, there must have been verbal communications as well. As he was watching Christina converse with Brother Walter, the other people in the room must have told him great and wonderful things about the holy maiden.

The only one who behaved differently was Walter. He was the only person to get any sleep, and he remained surprisingly calm in the immediate presence of the demon. Peter tells us that he continued to talk quietly to Christina, while she repeatedly banged her

8. Cf. L. Reypens, ed., *Vita Beatricis: De Autobiografie van de Z. Beatrijs van Tienen O. Cist. 1200-1268,* 2.16.157 (Antwerp, 1964), p. 106: "Quippe fatuitatem estimantibus, erectis sursum obtutibus, illam, tamquam deliram, celos [indesinenter] aspicere."

head against the wall. However, Peter did not imitate the detachment of his older confrere. His disapproval of Walter's equanimity erupted in the form of irony. His implicit rebuke—"Dearest father, I do not know if you have noticed, that the demon gravely afflicts the maiden that sits beside you"—reflects a criticism and an implicit claim to be better able to take care of Christina. Already Peter felt more committed than the priest who knew her "from childhood."

Let us now examine more carefully Peter's first conversation with Christina. When Walter went to sleep, Peter, all excited, took his place beside Christina who very appropriately and piously asked him to talk to her about God. Instead of talking about God Peter told her two stories from the *Lives of the Brothers*. Because Peter does not simply do as Christina asks him (and it is not for lack of willingness to talk about lofty matters with her[9]), the stories reflect Peter's preoccupations at that moment. We are fortunate to possess the collection of *Lives* from which Peter took his stories. We can know what he told Christina on that first night.[10] The first story concerns

a certain monk of the Carthusian Order, old, learned, and very devoted to the Blessed Virgin, often asked her with great fervor to tell him how to make his service pleasing to her. When he prayed in church one day, it seemed to him that the Blessed Virgin sat in front of the altar, and approaching her with reverence and fear he asked with tears that she teach him how to do what is pleasing to her. But she, watching him and smiling, said: "What is done to a beloved do to me, if you want to accomplish this wish." Said he: "What is that, lady?" She answered: "She is loved and praised and honored." Then, lying prostrate on the ground, he said: "Lady, teach me to praise you, and love you and honor you." While he dissolved in tears, she answered: "Go to the friars, and they will teach you." And when he said: "Lady, there are many orders of friars, to which of them do you send me?" She said: "Go to the Friars Preachers, because they are my friars, and they will teach you."[11]

---

9. On a later occasion Peter relates that Christina asked "ut de Deo ei aliquid dicerem." He responded with a discussion of the seraphim's love of God "secundum Dionysium" (Christina, p. 243).

10. Gerard de Frachet, *Vitae Fratrum Ordinis Praedicatorum*, edited by B. M. Reichert, *Monumenta Ordinis Fratrum Praedicatorum Historica* 1 (1986).

11. *Vitae fratrum* 1.6, pp. 41–42.

The story has an obvious lesson: If you want to be close to the Blessed Virgin you must seek the Dominicans' advice and guidance. The identity of the monk is significant. Not only does he belong to one of the most highly acclaimed religious orders of the day, but he is also old, learned, and pious. Nevertheless, he is sent by the Virgin to learn from members of the parvenu Order of Preachers. There is a message here of triumphant youth, perhaps reflecting the story of Christ teaching the elders in the temple. Peter himself was a young foreigner who had little beyond his habit to commend him. By telling her this story, he implicitly suggested to Christina that she could profit from a Dominican's guidance and that youth is not necessarily a disadvantage. By challenging Walter (who knew Christina for many years), Peter told her that in spite of his youth and inexperience he "loved better."

The second story cannot be identified with certainty. There is no story in the *Lives of the Brothers* that mentions fifteen years reduced from a friar's penance, but Peter must have had in mind one of the episodes in a series of tales dealing with the responsibility of living friars for their dead brethren. In all these stories, Dominican friars celebrate mass to relieve their brothers from a certain period of time in purgatory.[12] What matters in this story is the concept of friendship and mediation. Peter offered guidance—the traditional role of the father-confessor and spiritual director—and expected friendship and mediation in return.

Shortly before Peter left Cologne to pursue his studies in Paris, the following conversation took place:

"Brother Peter," [said Christina], "since you are going to depart from me, I wish to ask you about a certain intimate secret. Tell me, if you know, the reason for our mutual love [*dilectionis*]." Wondering what she meant, I answered: "I believe God to be the mover and originator of our love [*caritatis*] for each other and our familiarity." Said she: "I do not doubt this answer, yet I am asking whether you have received some manifest proof and special grace beyond that." [As Peter did not answer[13]], she said: "I

12. *Vitae fratrum* 5.7, pp. 287–90.
13. Peter suspected that her question referred to the small red marks he discovered in his left hand during the seventh visit (Christina, p. 248). The signs were given to him, he thought, "ut memor essem personae, in qua Dominicae passionis expressissima videram vulnera." As Peter was not certain that this was what she referred to, he preferred not to answer. Nothing in Christina's subsequent words indi-

know that the time of our separation and of my desolation is near, there-fore I shall tell you the secret which I would not have otherwise disclosed. Do you remember that when you first came to me with Brother Walter of blessed memory, around dusk, when I first saw you, I leaned for a while near you on a cushion?" I said: "I remember." Then she said: "At that time the Lord appeared to me and I saw my Beloved, and I heard Him say to me: 'Christina, do you know this man, next to whom you recline, and do you discern his propositions [*condiciones*]?' As I said: 'Lord, I have not known this man before in the flesh, and have never seen his face with my corporeal eyes,' the Lord added: 'Consider this man diligently, because he is your friend, and will be, and he will do much for you. But you too will do for him what you will do for no other mortal. Know also that he will be with you in the life eternal.' And this is why, brother Peter, I love you and am your friend." (Christina, p. 268)

The cushion, Peter's first (indirect) contact with Christina, serves her as a sort of emotional signpost in her recollection of the beginning of their relationship. She understood Peter's implicit "propositions" in his stories, for as Christ told her, their relation-ship is to be an exchange of spiritual services. Peter "will do much for her" (in this life) and Christina, in return, will do things for him she will do for no other mortal—spiritual favors, one assumes, that will procure for him a place in the life eternal.

We have another demonstration that Christina transferred her loyalty to Peter. In December 1268 Christina's father went to Col-ogne to seek Peter's help. He feared that his daughter's demonic attacks would bring ruin to the family. Greeting Peter on behalf of Christina in the acceptable manner of addressing a priest, her father said: "Christina, your daughter, greets you." But Peter observed that the man was "unable to hide the bitterness in his voice, since it showed in his face and movements," and he tried to reassure him. "Do not say this," he replied, "she acknowledges you as her father." (Christina, pp. 249–50). Apparently Brother Walter was not the only one who had to make way for Peter.

Their conversation reveals something else as well. When asked by Christina what the cause of their love for each other was, Peter responded with a conventional and impersonal reply: it is God

---

cates that she knew about the marks. Peter told her about them himself in his fifteenth visit (Christina, p. 278).

who is the *actor et auctor* of their *caritas*.[14] Christina saw things less abstractly. The source of her love is not the philosophers' mover, but the Beloved who speaks to her in very concrete terms: it is this man beside her, whom she had not yet "known in the flesh," and whose face she had not seen before "with her corporeal eyes," that will serve her and be served by her and with whom she will dwell in the life eternal. While Peter was translating his experiences with Christina into conventional-impersonal language, Christina was moving in the opposite direction.[15]

Can we say, then, that on that first night Peter found in Christina an embodiment of everything he expected to find in a saint? The answer is probably negative. The first encounter satisfied a deep craving in Peter, but it also caught him by surprise. His strong emotional reaction confounded his planned reserve. He did not reserve judgment until he had studied Christina properly and therefore now faced a *fait accompli*. When the first night was over, Peter still knew very little about Christina, yet he was now certain that she was a saint. He had to modify the rest of his expectations of saints to fit Christina and, where this was emotionally impossible, to adjust Christina to his expectations.

Peter now set out to translate Christina's actions into symbolic terms that would make her closer to his ideal of sainthood and edify readers and listeners (Christina, p. 268). Unlike ordinary people whose actions are rarely significant beyond their own personal sphere, the saints produce a surplus of meaning. Their minutest actions, their every word, bear hidden meanings that await the avid interpreter.[16] Female saints especially were often considered passive channels of symbolic material, a notion that the saints them-

14. Peter develops the theme of his love for Christina as a theological issue in a letter he sent her after his departure (see Christina, p. 280).

15. *Dilectio* and *caritas* are both quite common in reference to spiritual love. It is interesting, however, that Peter (who, it should be remembered, translates the exchange from German) makes a distinction, when they were both apparently talking about the same thing. In a later reference to their relationship, Christina confesses that her love for Peter made her fear "quod de hoc mihi aliqua tribulatio tentationis deberet pro tempore insurgere" (Christina, p. 278).

16. Cf. the letter written by Matteo Guidoni, prior of the Camaldolese of Florence, to Thomas "Caffarini" concerning St. Catherine of Siena (see chapter 3, p. 46).

selves were often willing to accept. Thus Blessed Alpais of Cudot, a female visionary who lived ca. 1155–1211, maintained that:

What they [her visions] assert, or what they signify, or what the purpose of many of them is, in what fashion they seem to happen or to be sent to me, I do not know very well. Whatever the truth of the matter, I know this one thing, . . . that what I tell you is what I see, and that what I see is what I tell you.[17]

Realizing that here was a saint in need of interpretation, Peter shouldered the task of making Christina meaningful with all the enthusiasm of a young theologian. The abundance of signs baffled him at first, but not for long. Likening Christina to God's coin bearing his image and inscription, he writes:

I see the inscription on the coin, I read and reread, but I am overwhelmed with wonder [*prae admiratione stupeo*]. Because of the abundance of figures, I cannot read all the way through [*perlegere non sufficio*[18]], because of their loftiness and subtlety I cannot understand, because of the truth of it all [*prae continentiae veritate*] I dare not doubt.[19]

Peter resorted to his books, where answers were available to all questions. "Although I did not know it through experience, I knew it through Scriptures," he writes.[20] He explains the meaning and significance of her experiences in mystical and philosophical terms (Christina, pp. 260–61, 264–65).

Monika Asztalos, who edited Peter's letters and his philosophical *On the Virtues of Christina,* comments that "Pierre utilise Christine comme un manuel théologique" (1986, p. 162). In *On the Virtues of Christina,* the "spiritual sense"—the meaning— became so all-important that the "literal sense" almost disappeared. Peter sent part of it to Stommeln. When it was translated for Christina by the schoolmaster, she wondered why Peter had never told her about that woman—so thoroughly unimportant be-

---

17. *Vita B. Alpaidis, AA.SS.,* 3 Nov., p. 205.
18. The *AA.SS.* has "sustineo."
19. Christina, p. 261. Cf. Paulson, p. 79.
20. Christina, p. 261. See also p. 280, where Peter writes: "Quamvis autem praedicta in scriptis legerim, numquam tamen ea sic datum est corporaliter et spiritualiter intueri sicut in status vestri varia dispositione."

came all the individual traits that would have allowed her to recognize herself (Christina, pp. 286, 288).

Once, standing before the closed doors of the church, Peter and his friend, Albrandinus, heard a singing so sweet that they judged it more divine than human. They entered the church and found Christina lying on the floor in ecstasy. When they listened carefully, it seemed to them that the voice was coming from Christina's heart.[21] Peter returned to the friary and began to wonder about the voice that he heard. Having considered the matter, he came to the conclusion that the voice was none other than the voice of jubilation "in accordance with the way in which the Gloss on the second verse in *Jubilate* [Psalm 99:2] explains."[22] It is the sound of joy without words in which the just sing their praises of God's wonderful works. It is a jubilation that shall be crowned. Just as Christina bore in her body the signs of the Passion, she expressed in all her acts (to the keen observer) the truth of the inspired pronouncements. As Jesus does things "so that the prophecies may be fulfilled," so do the saints authenticate (and are at the same time authenticated by) "that which is written." Philip of Clairvaux, observing Elizabeth of Erkenrode in ecstasy, noted that she jerked her head convulsively from side to side "as if she expounded for us the Gospel's: 'The Son of Man has nowhere to lay His head'" [Matt. 8:18].[23]

Thus far we have looked at the relationship of Peter and Christina mainly from Peter's point of view. We saw how, having been convinced (quite irrationally at first, according to his own testimony) that Christina was a saint, Peter strove to make her conform to nonpersonal, learned, canons of sanctity. In his letters and in his personal conversations with Christina Peter tried to teach her how she should behave and what she should be. But Christina had

---

21. Cf. Vito of Cortona, *Vita Humilianae de Cerchis, AA.SS.*, 19 Mai., p. 394. Thomas of Cantimpré resorts to the same interpretation in his *Life* of Christina the Astonishing. He calls the melody emerging from Christina's body "harmoniae jubilo" (*Vita S. Christinae mirabilis* 6, *AA.SS.*, 24 Jul., pp. 656–57). It is hard to know whether Peter knew Thomas's work or simply thought in the same way.

22. Christina, p. 249. Cf. *Glossa Ordinaria* Ps. 99:2; and Augustine, *Enarrationes in Psalmos* 99.4 *C.C.SL* 39.2:1394. Peter uses both.

23. Philip of Clairvaux, *Vita Elizabeth sanctimonialis in Erkenrode*, p. 370.

her own concept of her relationship with Peter and her own spirituality that was quite different from Peter's.

I cited earlier a conversation between Christina and Peter in which Christina gave her own version of their first meeting. She returns once more to that meeting during Peter's 1279 visit to Stommeln. Peter had been away from Stommeln for nine years. He received reports from Germany that Christina was in great need and had to sell the family property. She had also complained in a letter about her loneliness and begged him to come, saying that there were things she could tell no one but him (Christina, p. 277).

Peter arrived in Stommeln in September 1279. He spent his time with Christina and with his friends in Cologne. One afternoon, Peter and his companion Folquinus preached to a gathering of Beguines and other friends. Peter noticed that when Folquinus talked about a certain miracle of St. Agnes, Christina showed signs of joy and said: "I listened to that exemplum with great pleasure." Peter asked her why she felt such joy and she replied: "Because I recognize in us a certain similarity to that story." Peter implored her to tell him more, and after much persuasion, she said:

I will tell you a secret which I have never told a living soul. From my childhood I have known you,[24] and recognized your face and your voice. And so much have I loved you above all other men, that I feared greatly, lest with time a tribulation of temptation would arise for me from this. Never in my prayers could I remove your person from my mind, rather I always prayed for you as well as for me. And in all my tribulations I had always had you for a companion. And when for a long time I implored God to tell me whether he was the cause of it, I was finally assured of this on St. Agnes's Day. For in communion I was given a visible ring, clearly marked in my finger. And when you first greeted me, and I saw you for the first time, I distinguished your voice and distinctly recognized your face, and I was much amazed and gladdened.[25]

Peter did not see the ring, which was apparently visible only to Christina, but she told the priest, John, about the ring and he described it to the schoolmaster. The ring was not painted but in-

24. The *AA.SS.* has "in spirit," which was added between the lines (Paulson, p. 157).
25. Christina, p. 278. My translation is based on Paulson's reading (Paulson, p. 157).

scribed in the flesh, and on it was written the name of Jesus in, at times Hebrew, at times Greek, and at times Latin, characters.[26]

With time Christina adjusted Peter's historical role to correspond to his growing importance in her life. If in her first version of their encounter it was Christ who introduced Peter to her, in her second version she had known Peter *ab infantia*. Her love for him preceded Christ's introduction. Christina had to implore Christ to assure her that he was indeed the *auctor et actor* of her love for Peter.

But even more important is the context within which Christina placed Peter. The miracle of St. Agnes that triggered Christina's reaction and her revelation, which for the second time she describes as an intimate secret, offers more clues to an understanding of her state of mind. The episode is short and worth quoting in full.

A certain priest of the church of Saint Agnes, called Paulinus, began to be tormented by a dreadful temptation of the flesh; and as he had no wish to offend God, he besought the sovereign pontiff to allow him to take a wife. But the pope, who knew his goodness and his simplicity, sent him a ring set with an emerald and told him to address the request to a beautiful image of Saint Agnes which was depicted in his church. When the priest asked the image for permission, it suddenly held out its ring finger, and having taken the ring, it withdrew the finger. Immediately the temptation disappeared. It is said that this ring can still be seen on her finger.[27]

This story, Christina said, bears a certain resemblance to Peter and herself (Christina, p. 278). Might it not manifest Christina's projection of her own attraction onto Peter? Was she not the one who needed relief from temptation and sublimation to a spiritual marriage (the only one that Peter was interested in)? This interpretation is given further corroboration later in the text. A few months after her conversation with Peter, Christina told John the schoolmaster of a dream she had. She saw Peter assisting her (we are not told in what). He had a most beautiful golden ring on his finger. It

---

26. For the invisible ring given by Christ to Catherine of Siena, see Raymond of Capua, *Vita S. Catharinae Senensis* 1.7, *AA.SS.*, 30 April, pp. 890–91; see also Herbert Thurston (1952, pp. 130–40).

27. Jacobus de Voragine, *The Golden Legend*, translated and adapted by G. Ryan and H. Ripperger (London, 1941), p. 113. I have corrected the translation according to Jacobus de Voragine, *Legende sanctorum* (Venice, 1516), fol. 36 v°.

was set with a precious stone, in which was written: "Jesus Christ is our [*amborum*—belonging to the two of us] eternal faith" and other things which Christina refused to reveal (Christina, p. 284). Can there be any doubt that it is the same ring and that it has finally ended on the right finger? While others only saw a saint—an Agnes—in her, she identified with Paulinus, burning inside and condemned to be healed by a chaste spouse.

Peter certainly fulfilled his part of their original "deal" as he understood it. He had been an eager admirer and a faithful impresario. He had made her an object of devotion of a large group of students from Cologne. At her request, he arranged for her brother, illiterate though he was, to be accepted into the Dominican order. To the best of his ability, Peter granted all her wishes. He would never, said Christina, interpret her words and her actions perversely, but always "turn everything into good" [*omnia in bonum convertistis*] (Christina, p. 272). But it is exactly Peter's "turning everything into good" that blinded his eyes to anything but his image of her as a *sponsa Christi*.

When we examine the bulk of Christina's visions and letters, it is striking to discover that there is almost nothing in them of the nuptial imagery, so prominent in Peter's letters and lofty *Virtues of Christina*. Although she does have "beautiful visions," it is her trials which she dwells upon in great detail (Christina, p. 307). Even in quantity, the hordes of demons in her visions outweigh the few good spirits. From childhood on, she was haunted by revolting images of spiders, snakes, and toads creeping into her food, worms filling her drink, and demons defiling and beating her (Christina, p. 237). The entire account of John the schoolmaster for the years 1280 to 1287 recounts monotonously one demonic assault after the other.[28] If Christina's visions are not completely without consolation and joy, these all but disappear in the imagery of destruction, rejection, and defilement.

Peter's account of his second meeting with Christina, for example, is a blend of ecstatic theater and a horror tale. It took place

---

28. Christina, pp. 294–348. See, for example, pp. 306, 307, 308–9, but there are similar descriptions on nearly every page. See also the schoolmaster's letters, for example, pp. 283–84.

about two months after the first meeting.[29] This time Peter arrived with Brother Gerardus, master of students in the Dominican house in Cologne. Shortly after lunch, somebody sang for them the hymn, "Jesu dulcis memoria," in Latin, and then in German. Upon hearing this, Christina went into a trance. Her body became rigid, her breathing almost indiscernible, and she seemed to have lost all signs of life. Peter wept with joy; he felt the divine presence at arm's reach, at last.[30] After a while, Christina began to talk to the Beloved in terms of endearment, breaking from time to time into bursts of laughter that shook her entire body. She then resumed her speech, vilifying herself and glorifying God. Next, Christina began to cry bitterly; she recommended her friends and benefactors and asked forgiveness for her enemies and detractors. When she returned to her senses, she refused to talk about her experience. However, when Peter asked her how she fared during the interval between his two visits, she was more talkative. (Remember that this was the first time she had talked to Peter at any length.)

Eight days before Purification, when I was praying after Compline before my bed, I heard the sound of a toad, and I felt the presence of a demon. At first I was scared by its voice, but, regaining my courage, I remained in the same place, continuing my prayer. I heard it coming closer to me, then I felt it enter my clothes. After that I sensed it slowly climbing over my members, until finally it placed itself over my chest; it was so big that it covered almost all of my chest. Its nails pressed my flesh so hard that it left deep wounds after it. Thus, wherever I went, it remained there for eight days. . . . This was no small hardship for me. (Christina, p. 242)

On the eve of the above-mentioned feast, Christina realized that God wanted to free her from her ordeal. She grabbed the toad, disconnected it from her chest, and threw it on the floor. The demon fled vanquished, but the wounds he inflicted on her took four weeks to heal. Here the account of the second visit ends abruptly.

But what does this episode mean? Clearly Peter did not know. Unlike the ecstasy, which is symbolically rich, and which constantly

---

29. Christina, pp. 241–43. It must be remembered that Peter, as a student in Cologne, was not at liberty to go to Stommeln as often as he wished. He writes that he returned on the first opportunity (Christina, p. 241).

30. Christina, p. 242: "Fateor, dum haec fierent prae gaudio flebam. . . . Divinam praesentiam in hoc facto sum veneratus."

evoked in Peter biblical allusions, Christina's story lacked meaning beyond itself.

There are numerous accounts of diabolic assaults in John the schoolmaster's report. One after the other almost identical incidents are reported. It is hard for us to understand why such tedious repetition was thought necessary. If the incidents were similar, why not be satisfied with only one and an indication that there were more of the same? But for the schoolmaster such literary considerations were out of place. If an event happened a thousand times, it should be recorded a thousand times. The saint's tribulations are never without value, because they belong to the class of inherently meaningful events. They had a place in Christina's economy of salvation, part of a world in which the saints' suffering was never wasted. Every new torture could release numerous souls from purgatory, souls that one found pleasure in simply counting.

But Christina's tribulations seemed to lack specific meaning, or if they had such meaning, Peter did not know what it was. He, and her other biographers, reproduce Christina's horror stories without comment. Rather than attempting to understand Christina's own spirituality—a spirituality laying great emphasis on violent, repulsive, negative images, laden with sexual suggestions—Peter preferred to emphasize in his reconstruction of Christina his own spirituality.

But can *we* not find meaning in Christina's stories? Peter saw all of Christina's accounts as external and objective. The demonic aggression was seen as coming from the outside, and for him they had nothing to do with Christina's motives. For us, Christina's story of the demonic toad does demand an explanation. In our interpretive universe it contains strong sexual allusions.

In the Middle Ages, snakes and toads were held to be demonic creatures, associated with sexual lust (*luxuria*).[31] In the account she dictated to the priest, Christina relates an incident involving a snake who crawled over her, entered her body, and stayed there for eight days. When it departed, it left in her body large quantities of

---

31. On toads and frogs, see *Lexikon der christliche Ikonographie* 2 (Rome, 1968), pp. 676–77, s. v. Kröte. See also Frederic C. Tubach (1969, #1562 and #4888); Jean-Claude Schmitt (1979a, p. 428); and *Vita B. Idae de Nivella* 12 in, Chr. Henriquez, ed., *Quinque prudentes virgines* (Antwerp, 1630), p. 231.

its filth (Christina, p. 271). In a story that Christina recounted later, a number of toads crawled all over her. One of them fastened its mouth to Christina's and spewed the vilest venom into it (Christina, p. 301).

Such stories are not unique. They make their appearance in other saints' *Lives* with similar connotations. The devil, in the form of a snake, crawled into Benvenuta Bojani's bed and pressed himself to her naked body until, after a while (note again the interval of time), she threw him against a wall.[32] Of Umiliana de Cerchi we are told that "a [demonic] serpent wrapped his tail around her feet, and leaned his head against her cheek . . . When she went to lie down, she wrapped her clothes around her feet, and tied them with a belt so that the serpent could not enter from below, at her feet, and get to her nude body."[33]

Christina's images, like those of other female saints, are a combination of passion and guilt. Sex is demonic, and yet there is always a passage of time before the monstrous aggressor is removed from the saint's naked body. To the image of penetration, or the threat of penetration, Christina's accounts add images of defilement and contamination through the venomous emissions of the Satanic agents—a negative mirror image of other female saints' sense of healing and rejuvenation through the consumption of miraculous heavenly substances, especially the Eucharist. Christina's passions also surfaced in the form of more explicit sexual fantasies. A demon told her that it was sinful to live in celibacy, that God wants all to live in matrimony, that all her suffering is meaningless. Every night for six weeks the demon appeared to her with a woman and a child. He and the woman copulated in front of her, and the woman said to Christina: "There is no joy greater than the joining of a man to a woman and that which a woman has with a child." At these words Christina was greatly (*mirabiliter*) tempted. Later her guilt was expressed in an obsessive fear that demons would ruin her reputation and accuse her of bearing an illegitimate child.[34]

32. *Vita Beatae Benevenutae Bojanae, AA.SS.,* 29 Oct., p. 155.
33. Vito of Cortona, *Vita Humilianae de Cerchis, AA.SS.,* 19 Mai., pp. 390–91. I use Elizabeth Petroff's translation (1979, p. 46).
34. Christina, pp. 269–70. Christina told the priest about another temptation in which she felt a strong attraction to a man of ill repute. She imagined how the man came to see her and tried to seduce her. When she resisted, he threatened to

As for the themes of violence, death, and revulsion that recur in Christina's accounts, it has been suggested that John the schoolmaster invented some or most of the stories that appear in the third book of the *Codex Iuliacensis*. By multiplying the demonic tribulations, he made them the center of Christina's spirituality (Thurston 1928, p. 291). I see no reason to accept this view. John the schoolmaster's descriptions are entirely consistent with what Christina herself told Peter and the priest on numerous occasions. If the schoolmaster altered her visions in any direction it was to make them more positive, as Peter's account of his fifteenth visit to Christina suggests. Peter and Brother Folquinus came from Cologne to see Christina and found her lying in bed, looking very weak. When Peter inquired as to the cause of her weakness, she told him a demon had torn all the skin from her back and inflicted such terrible wounds upon her that it was a wonder she managed to survive. For some reason, Peter directed the same question to John the schoolmaster. His answer was very different. The schoolmaster offered a positive explanation for Christina's state: Christina, he said, took communion recently and entered a state of such devotion and rapture that she has not yet returned to her usual self (Christina, p. 278).

In the account of her early life, Christina relates that her demonic temptations began after two years of constant meditation on the Passion (between the ages of thirteen and fifteen). Her first temptation was a strong urge to commit suicide (Christina, p. 237). A later period of meditation on the Passion ended with a similar temptation (Christina, pp. 237–38). The rest of her account consists of a procession of torments: snakes and toads infested her food and drink, demons beat her, tore parts of her body, covered her with excrement, filled her with doubts about the Eucharist, God, the Passion, and the value of chastity.

Once she began to relate her temptations, Christina mentioned only two appearances of Christ. In both he appeared briefly at the end of a tribulation to deliver her from her suffering and fears. On

---

rape her, brandishing a knife. Christina grabbed the knife and stuck it into her thigh. "Hoc fecit ea intentione, ne cor eius perverteretur si violentiae aliquid facere voluisset, quia poenam corporis sensit" (p. 271). On a similar temptation of St. Francis of Assisi, see Thomas of Celano, *Vita secunda Sancti Francisci* 2.82, *Analecta Franciscana* 10 (1926–41), 199.

one occasion he appeared as a child in the hands of the priest to remove her doubts about the Real Presence (Christina, p. 237); on another he told her she will not die of a wound, commended her for choosing him for a spouse, compared her to St. Catherine, and finally healed her wound and disappeared (Christina, p. 271). The Virgin appeared to Christina once in a dream, but she too only came to heal Christina's wounds (Christina, p. 271).

Her letters, irrespective of the person to whom she dictated them, reveal the same prevalence of evil over good. In none of them does Christina engage in more than the briefest dialogue with Christ. We are told that she enjoyed heavenly joys with the bridegroom, but she is never specific. John the schoolmaster tells Peter in one of his letters that he learned about Christina's dreadful tribulations from her own mouth, while she was in ecstasy. In her conscious state she would never talk about her experiences to him, he writes (Christina, p. 286). These, then, were supposedly the things that came directly from Christina's inner soul, unhindered by shame or the will to please.

The powers of good play a relatively minor role in Christina's stories—no more than about a page out of the twenty-two pages (in Paulson's edition) dictated by her to the priest.[35] Christina's meditations about the Passion, in spite of their supposed importance for her, are very vague in comparison with the demonic assaults. Good is secondary and posterior to evil in Christina's world. The despair Christina relates that she felt after her first period of intensive contemplation about Christ's Passion and the demonic assaults that followed immediately in its trail may suggest that she was more deeply impressed with the negative aspect of the drama of salvation. In Christina's world, relief from evil comes only at the very last moment, as an anticlimax, almost, to the drama of redemption through suffering and humiliation.

But were Christina's stories a faithful reflection of her psyche at all? In other words, Christina might have been giving Peter (as well as other admirers) what she thought he and they expected of her.

---

35. Paulson, pp. 109–31. The Bollandists, instead of reproducing the priest's notebook (*quaternus*) in its entirety where it appears in the manuscript, moved the parts relating to Christina's childhood to the beginning of their edition and later stories to where they thought they would fit chronologically.

Since Peter was very eager to hear new stories, perhaps she felt pressured to tell them, even if at some point she ceased to experience them. For Peter, Christina was a source of information he wanted to transfer to future generations and in the process immortalize himself as well (Christina, pp. 281, 356). It is clear he did not think she had any control over her experiences and so did not tell her which ones she should produce. He simply wanted to record as many of them as he could get. On one occasion, when Christina seemed slow in providing wonders, he complained to his local companions: "You have as much time as you wish, but I am going away, and I do not hope to return to this place and this person in this life.[36] It grieves me much, therefore, to be defrauded of that consolation which I hope to receive here" (Christina, p. 255).

On his way back from his 1279 visit to Stommeln, Peter wrote to John the schoolmaster, urging him to record faithfully in writing (*in charta*) all the great things that God worked through Christina, "for the memory of mortals is very frail" (Christina, p. 354). In his answer, the schoolmaster stated that he was driven by Peter's devotion—so "eager to rekindle his pious avidity by ever new and divine miracles" (Christina, p. 290). Christina promised Peter exclusive rights (*praerogativa*) over her visions, but he was yet unsatisfied.[37] He felt she did not tell him enough and urged her to reveal more (Christina, pp. 360, 361). Christina, however, in a letter already mentioned, stated her disappointment that although she had written Peter two letters "full of divine miracles (*plenis divinis miraculis*)," he had failed to act on behalf of her brother (Christina, p. 292). In the exchanges between her and Peter, Christina's revelations were goods in high demand. If Peter was so eager to get them, why could she not use them to get things from him in return? (Nieveler 1975, p. 99).

One is reminded of the nails that Christina claimed were demonic instruments and that her head-banging stopped when it lost its effect. On other occasions, too, Christina showed that she was not without a sense of drama. Once when Peter sat beside her, she suddenly needed to spit so she had to remove her veil, thus re-

36. The text has "in hac die," but Paulson is probably right that "hac vita" was intended (see Paulson, p. 60, n.5a).

37. Christina, p. 266. Typically, she then recounted demonic assaults.

vealing her bruised face to Peter (for examples, see Christina, pp. 244, 248, 254). "Est-ce vraiment la pure Providence qui amène Christine à lever son voile?" wondered Pierre Debongnie, "Serait-il impie de soupçonner que cette pieuse femme savait ménager ses effets?" (Debongnie 1936, p. 48).

Even her accounts of her private experiences are not without problems. Christina told John the schoolmaster how she converted seven murderous bandits in a forest, three hundred miles from Cologne. After their conversion, they went to the nearest town to find a priest who would hear their confession. They were apprehended by the townspeople, who were unaware of their change of heart, and quickly executed (Christina, pp. 331–33). An almost identical story is attributed by Salimbene to the Franciscan preacher Bertold of Ratisbon.[38] The story is almost certainly apocryphal. Bertold was the kind of man about whom legends were told already in his lifetime. We do not know whether Salimbene and Christina had a common source, or whether Christina was familiar with the Bertold legend. The latter possibility is quite likely, for Bertold was active in Germany only a few years earlier (he died in 1271).

What matters, however, is that Christina appropriated a story she had heard and incorporated it into her own corpus. Is this a case of unconscious "internalization" or of spiritual plagiarism? Do her almost identical accounts of demonic attacks indicate an obsessive mind or an exhausted imagination, unable to supply the demand?

It seems to me unlikely that all of Christina's supernatural phenomena were authentic; but I also find it hard to believe that they were all faked. Christina's ecstasies are described in detail on a number of occasions.[39] Like other saints, she had her share of doubting Thomases. Brother Albrandinus, who was at first skeptical, was convinced that she was really in a trance by the rigidity of her body (Christina, p. 248). More skeptical persons pricked her arm while in ecstasy, and a certain Beguine wounded the calf of her leg with a pair of scissors (Christina, p. 278). Christina remained insensitive

---

38. Salimbene de Adam 1966, 2:816–18. Christina's bandits were converted by the sight of her patient suffering, Bertold's through a sermon.

39. For particularly detailed descriptions of ecstasies, see Christina, pp. 242, 321.

and rigid, although when she regained consciousness, she complained of great pain.

It seems, then, that Christina's ecstasies were real enough. It would be reasonable to assume that she experienced at times very vivid visions which she considered real in the absolute sense. Even if she made up some of her stories, they still reflect her inner world. Where exactly the spontaneous ended and the premeditated began is hard to say. Oscar Ratnoff, a physician who studies psychogenic purpuras, relates how he once asked a stigmatic patient whether she might have brought on the stigmatic wounds by injuring herself.

Her answer was enigmatic. "I've asked myself one hundred times whether I rubbed or stabbed myself. I had at times trouble being able to distinguish the truth and know it was the truth."

Thus this patient summarizes the question of whether the stigmata are conversion reactions or self-induced, and leaves it unanswered. As Walshe pointed out, the difference in psychodynamics is slight, although of course the mechanisms involved are grossly different. (Ratnoff 1980, p. 210).

As always we are left with uncertainty. But the reality of the paramystical phenomena is only secondary in importance for our purposes to the significance the saints' contemporaries assigned to them. Catherine of Siena's stigmata were, from an empirical point of view, nonexistent. She showed no visible marks on her body but was nevertheless accepted by many as a stigmatic. Christina had visible wounds which could be used to corroborate her claims for sanctity (or the claims others made for her). We have seen that Peter found Christina's claims entirely convincing. But did others? The people of Stommeln displayed various degrees of interest in Christina. The most committed to her was a small group of followers that spent much of their time with her. They included her sister Hilla, her niece, also called Hilla, a Hilla von Berg who was also Christina's relative, the Beguines Hilla of Ingendorp and Alice, the latter's niece Engilradis, the priest, his mother and his sisters Gertrud and Hadewige, and finally John the schoolmaster (Christina, pp. 259, 352). To this group must be added Godfrey, prior of the Benedictine house at Braunweiler. Although he was not part of Christina's entourage, he seems to have been very devoted to her (Christina, pp. 273, 351).

It is impossible to say how committed individual members of

this group were to Christina and how long they stayed with her. John the schoolmaster, for example, did not continue to serve as Christina's secretary after Peter's death, thus raising some doubts as to the strength of his earlier devotion. The priest's mother accused Christina after her son's death of wasting the family's property (Christina still lived with the priest's family at that time). It is likely that both she and her daughters left Christina's circle. Whether others maintained their faith in her to the end remains unknown (Christina, p. 277).

As for other villagers, they seem amazingly indifferent to the presence of a saint in their midst. Christina's family suffered great hardship when her father lost his wealth serving as surety for a loan between Jews and Christians. After the father's death, the family house collapsed. Christina received no assistance from the community. She complains in a letter to Peter that she is totally without the help of benefactors and comforters. There is no one in the village, she writes, in whom she can confide (Christina, p. 277; see also p. 274). When she wanted to obtain things for her brother or for John the schoolmaster, she had to ask for Peter's intervention from far-away Sweden.[40]

Worse than indifference, there was also hostility. The Beguines of Cologne, as we saw, refused to accept Christina's claim for sanctity, considering her mad or sick rather than holy. Some Beguines from Stommeln accused her of being an impostor (Christina, p. 237). The local Franciscans were hostile, too. Christina twice mentions in her visions that they have preached against her.[41] Again, one can only guess the reason. It might have been simple skepticism; it might have been hostility toward a protégée of the Dominican competition. It is also possible that her claims to have received the stigmata antagonized the Franciscans, who at that time still insisted on the exclusivity of their founder's stigmatization (Vauchez 1968, pp. 610–12).

The Dominicans of Cologne were, it seems, rather lukewarm toward Christina. Although Peter arrived in Cologne in 1266 (see Christina, p. 254), he only found out about Christina in December

40. Christina, p. 290. The Dominican prior at the time, Ingeldus, refused to see Christina or help her brother (p. 292).
41. Christina, pp. 302, 318. *Vita anonymi*, p. 381.

of 1267. By that time, Christina had been "spiritually" active for at least twelve years. When Peter and his Italian friend Albrandinus asked their prior for permission to go and visit her, the prior replied:

I have heard so many marvelous things about this young woman, that I would have gone gladly to see her with you, if I had the time. But you, dearest, who are young, and come from far-away countries, go and see marvelous and edifying things, which in time you could tell for the edification of others in your countries, even in old age.[42]

It is a polite answer. The prior, Hermann von Havelbrecht, encourages the young men to accumulate edifying recollections for old age, while, at the same time making a distinction between them and himself. He could afford to be more selective. Indeed, he had heard marvelous things (perhaps from Brother Walter, who, it would be remembered, was Christina's confessor from childhood), but they were not such that would make him take the short trip to Stommeln and see this young peasant girl with his own eyes.

Apart from the already-mentioned circle of followers, it seems, then, that most of Christina's admirers were outsiders in Stommeln, students attending the school in Cologne. Many were also not German. Of the twenty-one names of Dominican students (including Peter) that are mentioned in connection with Christina, ten were Scandinavian, one Italian, one Polish, one Flemish, one English, and one Hungarian. Six were German, but not from Cologne. She was the friars' saint, the subject of devotion for a group of people who were not sensitive to local attitudes. As we know that Peter had heard nothing about Christina before their first meeting, it is evident that he himself was responsible for Christina's success among the students in Cologne. The incidence of so many Scandinavians among Christina's followers suggests where Peter's influence was the greatest.[43]

The problem with a following of students was that they soon went back to their countries, and without Peter's enthusiastic promotion, the new generation of students did not catch on in quite

---

42. Christina, p. 250. People always go to the saint "ut aliquid aedificatorium possemus vel videre vel audire" (Christina, p. 249).

43. For a discussion of Christina's international following, see Quetif and Echard (1719, 1:407–13).

the same way.[44] Without Peter, even an old devotee like Brother Gerardus grew cold. He became subprior in Cologne, but although it was only about an hour's ride from Stommeln, he now visited Christina only rarely. It was too inconvenient, he told Peter, who came all the way from Sweden to see Christina, "for many of the people who used to accommodate the friars are now dead."[45] There were not very many devotees of Christina who would help visitors. Peter's influence on the locals must have been limited. As a student he could not come to Stommeln very often. During the eighteen months of their acquaintance, prior to his departure for Paris, Peter visited Christina in Stommeln thirteen times and stayed for about a day each time.

Thus, while the unlettered villagers remained skeptical, the young theologians were enthusiastic. Part of the explanation might lie in the fact that the villagers were probably more conservative than the literati and preferred to direct their devotion toward miracle-working relics or healing preachers like Bertold of Ratisbon. The young Dominicans (and the Dominican Order in general) were more open to the sanctity of women and to the affective type of spirituality typical of the Beguines of that age. But the reaction of the Beguines themselves could not be attributed to misogyny or religious conservativism. Perhaps we should not look for cultural reasons. The Beguines had spent much more time with Christina and knew her better than any of her learned friends. They were simply not convinced that Christina's reported experiences were authentic.

44. Cf. the case of Arcangela Panigarola (1468–1525). "La Panigarola," writes Gabriella Zarri, "deve il suo culto al gruppo francese che frequentava il monastero. Dissoltosi il cenacolo con la perdita di Milano da parte del re di Francia, la monaca visionaria torna nell'ombra" (1980, p. 386).

45. Christina, p. 278. See G. H. Martin (1976, p. 167). It would have taken a man about four hours to walk the eighteen kilometers between Stommeln and Cologne.

V

THE MAKING OF LUKARDIS
AND THE DISSOLUTION
OF DOUCELINE

W E WILL now shift the emphasis from the saint and her biographer to the larger community, from what motivates individuals to what helps establish social consensus. The saints to be discussed were both more popular than Christina. Lukardis of Oberweimar (1257–1309) gained the admiration of her monastic community; Douceline of Digne (1214–74) was considered a saint not only by her own community of Beguines, but by large segments of the population of Marseilles.

The two women also display different types of social rapport between saint and community. The first type, of which the *Life* of Lukardis is an example, can be called co-operative; the second, described in the *Life* of Douceline, can be called detached. As I wish to highlight modes of audience collaboration in the creation and authentication of sanctity, I will discuss the co-operative type at greater length than the detached type. In both types of rapport, however, the audience is equally active, although in very different ways, in the formation of public sainthood.

The *Life* of Lukardis of Oberweimar as we now know it was written as a result of an unexpected misfortune.

The nuns hoped that the honorable men in Christ, Brother Henry and Brother Eberhard, Dominican confessors of the said servant of God, to whom great and most profound things were revealed in confession, would diligently collect them in writing in a tract. As the entire convent pressed upon them to write down some of the things that they knew and could tell, Brother Eberhard, moved by piety, ready and willing, promised to consent to their wishes as soon as possible. At least one of them would have done it, had they not both, shortly afterwards, been taken from our midst.[1]

1. *Vita venerabilis Lukardis,* in *Analecta Bollandiana* 18 (1899), 363 (hereafter cited as Lukardis).

99

But why was this such a loss? Why would the friars be the nuns' first choice? Surely there were nuns in the community who knew Lukardis better than the friars whose contacts with her were, after all, limited. Moreover, reading the *Life* that was subsequently written, it is evident that even without the confessors there was no scarcity of visions and revelations. What bothered the nuns was not the accuracy or the fullness of the account. These were not the first considerations in writing a saint's *Life*. The most important function of the first *Life* was to convince readers of the sainthood of the *Life*'s subject.

There were important advantages to having the female saint's *Life* written by her confessor. The confessor was one of the few men allowed to have frequent intimate contact with the saint. He knew her *in foro conscientiae*—presumably her most true self—and, as a priest (often a member of a religious order), he had an eye to what was worth remembering. It was implicitly assumed that a priest, as a representative of the religious hierarchy and a man, would be less easily misled by pretenders, heretics, and lunatics than, say, a layman or a woman. The confessor would remember the right things and present them in a way that would best serve the saint.

We are not given the name of Lukardis's biographer, but he was neither her confessor, nor a man of great authority. In a sense, the sisters had good reason to be concerned by the death of Lukardis's confessors. As a piece of promotion, the *Life* was a failure. Lukardis's cult did not spread, she was not canonized, and the *Life* itself, surviving in a single manuscript, had very little, if any, impact. For the historian, however, the *Life* of Lukardis is a fortunate finding. The writer had to rely mostly on the accounts of Lukardis's sisters, who recorded some of her words and deeds (Lukardis, p. 363). (The abbess and a nun who served Lukardis for her last [?] seven years were probably his main sources [Lukardis, p. 361].) What matters is that the writer did not interview Lukardis, nor did he have any privileged information.

Thanks to the biographer's limitations, we are allowed to look at a saint from a different angle. Too often in saints' *Lives* the saint is so sharply in focus that all others around him or her almost disappear. Thus, the production of sainthood is presented as a personal process involving only the saint and her calling. All others in the process (with the exception of the writer/eyewitness/confessor) are seen as a passive audience. But, as I hope to show later, the saints' reputation and self-image depended on the efforts of their intimates. Without followers to appreciate and make public the saint's merit, the saint would remain anonymous. Lukardis's biographer shows her through the eyes of her community—his only source of information. Other writers could produce works where the saint's private experiences totally dominate. They would reproduce page after page of visions, but tell us almost nothing about the saint's most intimate audience. In Lukardis's *Life,* the community's input was allowed a more prominent role than is usual in most female saints' *Lives* written by men. It is as if the anonymous apprentices in a master painter's workshop were allowed to sign their names next to their individual contributions and one realized that what looked like a smooth surface is in face a mosaic made of many small pieces.

Shared Sainthood: Lukardis and Her Sisters

Lukardis was born around 1262,[2] probably in the city of Erfurt (Lukardis, p. 311). She entered the Cistercian convent of Ober-weimar near Weimar around 1274 when she was twelve years old.

2. The exact chronology is very hard to establish. It is clear that 1276 could not have been the date of her birth, as Wieland and the Bollandists had assumed (Lukardis, p. 310). The writer says that her suffering, not her life, lasted thirty-three years (p. 313). Lukardis died in 1309, and we are told (p. 318) that she bore the stigmata for twenty-eight years, that is, from around 1281. However, we are also told that for ten years she lived "in variis passionibus," and then, for eleven more years "tamquam paralytica" (p. 314). After the eleven years of lying "quasi contracta," she was healed of her contractions by a vision of the Virgin (p. 320) and entered a state of "flaccid paraplegia" (see Edward Shorter 1986, pp. 559–64) with intermittent periods of remission. The following tentative chronology can be suggested: Lukardis's ailments began around 1276. After three years, she had a vision of the suffering Christ (1279), and two years later received the stigmata (1281). Seven years later (1288) the violent contractions and running were replaced by "spastic paraplegia," which lasted eleven years. She was then healed by the Virgin (1299) and lived for the rest of her life in a less painful type of paralysis. It is unlikely that Lukardis was appointed "magistra infirmarum" as a candidate or a novice (see Micheline de Fontette 1967, pp. 47–49). Assuming that in addition to the one-year novitiate another year had passed before Lukardis was put in charge of the infirmary, Lukardis was probably between fourteen and fifteen years old when her problems started, half a year after her appointment (1276). She was born, therefore, around 1262.

101

We know very little about her family. Her mother died shortly after she entered the convent. She had a sister who brought her the news of their mother's death and who is not mentioned again in the *Life*. Lukardis was a serious and pious girl, and the abbess appointed her to the office of *magistra infirmarum* (Lukardis, p. 312; see also p. 362). Being in charge of the infirmary required strength and industry, and Lukardis must have had both. But half a year later, her inconspicuous existence came to an end with the onslaught of a series of strange and debilitating ailments.

Lukardis suffered from the pains of kidney stones, from fevers, and fainting spells. Her hands were so badly contracted that the cane with which she supported herself had to be fastened to them with pieces of cloth. At times it seemed as if her hands were being beaten by a mysterious force, so that her fingers struck each other, sounding like pieces of wood. "When she lay in bed, her legs would sometimes fasten together underneath her, and her head would be thrown back, her belly and chest uplifted, so that she formed the shape of a very curved arch." She spent long hours standing on her head and shoulders, feet up in the air. She would often run violently, sometimes in circles, sometimes straight on, indifferent to obstacles that stood in her way. She displayed great restlessness, and would sometimes revolve in bed "like a roast before the fire." All this was highly unusual—"unknown even to the most learned doctors" (Lukardis, pp. 312–13).

One must be extremely cautious in attempting to identify in past descriptions the symptoms of what we now consider psychological disorders, but one cannot help noting the striking similarity between the medieval description and what in modern psychoanalytic terminology is known as conversion disorder or, more commonly, hysteria.[3] The contracted limbs, the fainting spells, the compulsive behavior, even the famous back arching of Charcot's *"arc en cercle"* are all there. Among Lukardis's contemporaries there were also some who suspected that her afflictions might not be organic in nature: "She was thought by certain simple strangers to be

3. See Edward Shorter (1986, p. 556) for a similar case in the nineteenth century. As Lukardis's biography and other evidence show (cf., for example, Pierre-André Sigal 1985, pp. 239–43), hysterical paralysis did not make its first appearance in the nineteenth century.

troubled by some spirit" (Lukardis, p. 312). We are not told who those strangers were and what, besides this observation, made them simple. What matters is not the name we give to Lukardis's ailment, but that it left conventional medicine baffled, and therefore called for spiritual—initially, at least, unsympathetic—explanations. Thus, at a fairly young age, Lukardis became ill with an incurable, somewhat suspicious infirmity. She ceased to participate in the normal routines of the community and began living the life of an invalid.

The life of the chronically ill in a monastic community could be bleak. From being in charge of the welfare of others, Lukardis became dependent on her sisters' charity. She had no special friend to tend for her out of personal affection, nor was one appointed to look after her. She often found herself lying alone in the dark, hungry and thirsty (Lukardis, p. 313). In visions she had during that period, the Virgin Mary offered her a refreshing drink and the child Jesus fed her a roast chicken (Lukardis, pp. 313, 334). This was not spiritual nourishment—the biographer ascribes no symbolic significance to it—but food to fill an empty stomach.[4]

For three whole years Lukardis suffered without attracting the attention of the community.[5] Her few visions were not of the kind likely to arouse the interest of the other nuns. They reflected her personal anguish and could not easily be given universal significance. In a religious community such visions were hardly unique. As long as the community attached no spiritual value to Lukardis's suffering, she was little more than a burden.

"As a religious problem," writes Clifford Geertz, "the problem of suffering is, paradoxically, not how to avoid suffering, but how to make of physical pain, personal loss, worldly defeat, or helpless contemplation of others' agony, something bearable, supportable—something, as we may say, sufferable" (Geertz 1973,

---

4. In the *Life* of Gertrude van Oosten, we are told how God woke up a peasant and commanded him to bring Gertrude some bread and cheese (*Vita Gertrudis ab Oosten, AA.SS.*, 6 Jan., p. 350). Gertrude's biographer, like Lukardis's, attaches no symbolic interpretation to this miracle. The issue of food symbolism and its importance for women has been dealt with extensively in Caroline Bynum's *Holy Feast and Holy Fast*. Bynum does not always distinguish between the cravings generated by an empty stomach and those coming out of a full heart.

5. For my suggested chronology of Lukardis's life, see note 2.

p. 104). In a medieval religious milieu, suffering inevitably brought to mind the suffering par excellence—Christ's Passion. The Passion was a pervasive metaphor in late medieval society. It was anywhere and everywhere: in art, in literature, in the crucifixes that hung in nuns' dormitories and cells, in the liturgy, and in the *Lives* of the saints. Lukardis, seeking to give meaning to her suffering, turned her thoughts to the Passion. She asked God in her prayers to be allowed to participate in Christ's suffering. She then had a vision of Christ nailed to the cross, all covered with blood. Lukardis collapsed at his feet, and he said to her:

"Rise up and help me." By this she understood that she must help Him not only by the memory of His Passion, but by diligent co-suffering. Having regained her powers somewhat at Christ's words, she answered timorously: "How can I help You, my Lord?" And raising her eyes, she saw His right arm loosened from the cross, miserably hanging down, by which it seemed to her that the pain of the suffering Christ was greatly intensified. The beloved servant, approaching with much pain, tried to tie the arm to the cross with a silken thread, but could not succeed. With groans, she began then to lift His arm with her hands, and to support it. Then the Lord said to her: "Attach your hands to My hands and your feet to My feet, and your breast to My breast, and thus shall I be helped by you and it will be lighter for me." Having done this, in a moment, the servant of God felt internally the most piercing pain of the wounds in her hands, feet, and breast (though the wounds were not yet visible to the eye). (Lukardis, p. 314)

In their embrace, Lukardis's pains were given direction and meaning. Her pains were to be the pains of the Passion and, like the Passion, her own ordeal was redemptive and vicarious.

The vision was a turning point in Lukardis's life. Immediately after she had it, Lukardis announced her symbolic claim to sanctity through redemptive suffering.[6] She began to strike violently with her finger the place of the stigmatic wounds in each palm and in the breast. With her big toes she likewise tried to bore into the places of the wounds in her feet (Lukardis, pp. 314–16). This pattern of behavior lasted for about two years. After two years, Lukardis had another vision of Christ. This time he appeared to her in the form of a delicate youth. He told her that he wanted her to suffer with

6. On illness as a recurring theme in the *Lives* of female saints, see Elizabeth A. Petroff (1986, pp. 37–44).

him; with her consent, He pressed his right hand to hers, where a visible wound appeared. Ten days later, a second wound appeared on her left hand and, then gradually, the three other wounds. Later, the bleeding scars of Christ's flagellation and his crown of thorns also appeared on her body.[7]

Lukardis had successfully externalized her internal feelings. The pain she focused on the stigmatic spots became "visible to the eye." The community, at last, began to show interest in her anguish. Lukardis's private pains were now expressed in a culturally meaningful idiom. In response to a question on how she bore such pains without complaint, Lukardis confidently positioned herself in the context of the drama of salvation.

Do not wonder at this. For God, whom it pleased that this passion would be shown externally in my body, in memory of His Passion, mitigates it in my soul by the wondrous sweetness of His consolation. (Lukardis, p. 316)

Lukardis's pains followed a temporal pattern. Every Sunday night her pains began to decrease and scabs formed over her wounds; every Friday the pains increased, and fresh blood flowed from her wounds. Thus, the resemblance to Christ's Passion was further enhanced. Now that her sickness had achieved religious significance, Lukardis requested, and received, permission to communicate more often than the others. At first she communicated every Sunday and feast day, then on Fridays also, and daily during Lent (Lukardis, p. 317). Lukardis was set apart. She was no longer an ordinary invalid, but a holy sufferer, having an intimate relationship with the divine. Her frequent communion symbolized this exceptional and privileged condition.[8]

Being set apart is a necessary condition for any aspirant for sainthood. In a religious community this might not be easy. A

7. Lukardis, pp. 315–16. For the crown of thorns, see Lukardis, p. 353. It is interesting that this last phenomenon appeared at the suggestion of her attendant. She asked Lukardis whether now that she had all other marks of the Passion, the crown of thorns should not appear also. A short while later it did.

8. On the saint's public proclamation of his or her claim see Jean-Michel Sallmann's excellent article, "Il santo e le rappresentazioni della santità: Problemi di metodo" (1979a, p. 598): "[Once the claim has been made] La società non si sbaglia: sa di aver a che fare con un santo, e lo venera come tale nel corso della sua vita."

layperson could suddenly assume a more religious persona by increasing her pious activity, renouncing her wealth, or entering a religious order, for example. This activity would draw attention to the actor as being sharply distinct from others. But a religious had to outdo her companions in an environment that was already ascetic and often did not encourage free religious enterprise.[9] Monastic communities, especially such conservative bodies as the Cistercians, could be firm in discouraging individualism. Lukardis's feeble attempt at additional piety shortly after she had joined the community met with strong disapproval. We are told that the first time she had gone into the choir, she stopped and prostrated herself in front of the altar, her arms spread like a cross. The abbess sharply rebuked her and ordered her to behave according to the rule (Lukardis, p. 311). After that we are not told of any special ascetic practices of Lukardis until she became ill.

Stigmatization bypassed the communal checks on religious individualism. The stigmata, unlike excessive asceticism, could not be stopped by authority. They were an objective, visible sign of divine grace that others could not ignore. Lukardis, it must be understood, was not thought to have fabricated her stigmata. For the stigmata to appear, it was necessary that she have the second vision of Christ, announcing their arrival. This divine intervention separated Lukardis's actions from what we conceive as their result. It was assumed that Lukardis's wounds would not have appeared through her efforts alone. The appearance of the stigmata, then, was seen as categorically distinct from Lukardis's acts preceding its reception.

The community began to regard Lukardis as a saint and see her within the context of saintly expectations. The nuns observed her more keenly than before and engaged in a process of purposeful interpretation of her actions. On one occasion, for example, Lukardis was seen by a certain nun floating above the ground. She told her friends about it, only to be told that they had seen nothing unusual (Lukardis, pp. 331–32). Why is this incident recounted as a miracle? On the face of it there is no reason why it should. The

---

9. See Thomas of Celano, *Legenda S. Clarae virginis* 17, edited by F. Pennacchi (Assisi, 1910), p. 25: "In all these things [ascetic practices], since there were others in the convent that did the same, she [Clare] does not perhaps merit special praise."

nun saw something, conferred with the others, and found that she was mistaken—Lukardis had not floated in the air. But since Lukardis was already recognized as a saint, things took a different course. The nun's vision was not considered an optical illusion, nor an arbitrary statement (after all, she could say whatever she wanted as long as no proof was required). Instead, it was assumed that the visible manifestations of Lukardis's sainthood were but the tip of the iceberg (Lukardis, p. 340). Others could catch an occasional glimpse of it, but this did not mean that they would all be able to see each manifestation. If only one nun saw this wonder, it was because she was granted a special favor and the others were not. Of course, this exceedingly favorable interpretation could only be possible if the person was already considered holy.

The reader will note that Lukardis was not really part of this marvel at all. She neither did nor said anything. At times the marvelous was attributed to the saint in spite of her explicit denials. One of the nuns peeked into Lukardis's room and saw four beautiful ladies. One of them, more gloriously clad than the others, sat close to Lukardis, who held the lady's child in her hands. The beautiful child, wearing a green tunic, lovingly held Lukardis's face in his hands. The nun ran to the infirmary and asked who Lukardis's guests were. She was told by the other nuns that there were no guests present in the convent. The nun declared that such guests were indeed present in the saint's room and that she would return there to see if she knew any of them. She went back to Lukardis's cell and found her alone, reading her psalter. To her inquiry, the saint replied that she had had no guests, and as the nun could see, she was alone (Lukardis, p. 335; see also p. 322).

Anyone reading the nun's description would recognize (as was indeed intended) the Virgin accompanied by three saints and the child Jesus. Even the portrayal of the child in Lukardis's arms, looking up at her face and playing with her chin, is a well known iconographical motif. It is evident that we are dealing here with a vision of the nun that is transferred to Lukardis. Lukardis's denial was seen as a pious lie, an act of humility, not to be taken seriously.[10]

---

10. Odo of Novara once refused to perform a cure, but his refusal was interpreted as an actual cure or as a curative formula pronounced "quasi ironice." See Odo's process of canonization, "Documenta de B. Odone Novariensi ordinis Carthusiani," *Analecta Bollandiana* 1 (1882), 329.

The nun had thus produced a vision which would contribute to Lukardis's prestige. The nun's name, as those of most other "contributors," is not given, and with good reason, for the miracle was not to be attributed to anyone but Lukardis.

The saint's control over her collaborators' activity was rather limited, although she was supposedly the beneficiary (and benefactor) of such activity. Every attribution of the miraculous to the saint committed her to a specific type of spirituality. The supporters were actually shaping the saint in their image while claiming to be no more than witnesses to her powers. Even the saint's explicit denials were ineffective as we have just seen. In most cases, however, the saint gratefully accepted that the price of affirmation was serving as a legitimating agent for her supporters.

Consider the following case, where Lukardis did not explicitly affirm a "contribution," but could be seen to accept it implicitly. One Friday, Lukardis was afflicted by unwonted pains. Asked by her attendant whether these were the usual Friday pains, Lukardis responded in the negative. What these new pains were she did not know. The nun then said to Lukardis: "Lukardis, blessed sister, bear your pains patiently, and offer your suffering in sacrifice for the salvation of the faithful, living and dead." Lukardis did not answer, but she raised her eyes to heaven as if to say *(quasi diceret)*—and here comes the attendant's interpretation—"I offer to Your mercy, almighty Father, my suffering with patience, for the salvation of all living and dead faithful."[11]

Lukardis's pains worsened and she began to dig compulsively into her wounds with her finger. A group of other nuns was called to assist her and a few days later one of them had a vision that expressed in symbolic terms Lukardis's vicarious suffering. She saw the entire convent celebrating mass on Christmas. On Lukardis's chest lay an enormous, heavy chalice. Two beautiful youths appeared and stood in front of the pulpit with their faces toward the community. Then, a most impressive, long haired and bearded figure and, later, four youths joined the two. They all gazed at the

11. The process could be reversed. The saint might suggest to another person that a particular revelation was in order. When the vision was subsequently reported, both saint and medium would gain affirmation. See, for example, Thomas of Cantimpré, *Vita Lutgardis, AA.SS.,* 16 Jun., p. 202.

community. The bearded figure approached Lukardis and took the chalice from her. He removed her entrails and poured them into the chalice. He took the chalice to the altar and lifted it up most devoutly. And the nun was given to understand that the figure was Christ, and the chalice was the chalice of his Passion. Christ was offering Lukardis's suffering to God the Father for the salvation of "the entire human race" (Lukardis, pp. 342–44).

Of course the concept of the salvific role of Lukardis's suffering was not first suggested by the nun. Lukardis's role as a stigmatic already implied it, but the two nuns went beyond that notion to an elaboration that surpassed Lukardis's own.

A more active collaboration took place between Lukardis and one of the more pious nuns in the convent. The nun, Agnes, was not allowed to take communion as often as she wished (or as often as Lukardis). Once, perhaps because of the priest's negligence, Agnes was unable to communicate. She prayed to God with great agitation of spirit; then she heard the voice of God telling her that he is always present for those who love him. He ordered Agnes to approach Lukardis and cling to her so that she would be able to catch the saint's breath in her mouth.

Agnes used a pious ruse. As she suffered from weak eyesight, she asked Lukardis to blow on her eyes. Lukardis consented, and Agnes was able to catch her breath in the process. She immediately felt the taste of the host as if it were put in her mouth by the priest. The taste filled her with sweetness and grace. Her inner eyes were opened and she saw the great and wonderful things that God worked for her friend. She saw in Lukardis's heart a great feast, and it seemed as though the entire Holy Trinity celebrated mass, "as she later assured many." Lukardis, on her part, saw in Agnes's heart how great the latter's merits were and how saintly her prayers and her works. "Thus, those two saw each other as if looking at a mirror, and illumined by the light of divine knowledge, they knew wonderful and marvelous things" (Lukardis, pp. 337–38). It is significant that Agnes "assured many" of this exchange of compliments. In advertising their experience, the reputations of both would be served. Lukardis was clearly more prominent, but Agnes too had "saintly works and prayers" that were publicly recognized by Lukardis, so much so that unlike other nuns who remained anonymous, Agnes was deemed worthy of being mentioned by name.

The saint could also appropriate miracles that were not offered to her. On one occasion, Lukardis simply joined in another nun's vision, authenticating it, yet reducing the latter to a minor role. It was revealed to a nun that the whole convent would be destroyed by fire. In time the convent had indeed caught fire, but only the refectory was consumed. When told about the matter by two nuns, Lukardis reacted: "It is true, for God decided that this should be so, and it was not hidden from me, but through my prayers God spared our church" (Lukardis, p. 346).

One is struck by the fervent spiritual activity in the convent. It seems that there was always somebody having a vision or receiving a divine message in some other way. All those visions, holy dreams, and sometimes trivial, sometimes momentous, revelations, were more than just corroboration of Lukardis's sainthood; they were an assertion of the nuns' own spiritual value through a chosen medium. In a vision a certain religious describes Oberweimar as a spiritual garden where many trees bear fruit. Lukardis was the most important plant, but not the only one (Lukardis, p. 348). As Lukardis was the local holy woman, it was through her that the nuns' spirituality was expressed. Though not significant enough to claim personal contact with the divine, the nuns could achieve contact through Lukardis. By reaffirming to one another Lukardis's sainthood, the community asserted its own worth, since the presence of a saint in their midst was a source of great pride and comfort to the community. They were deemed worthy of hosting one of God's elect. When the community announced the universal significance of its saint (bringing salvation to "the entire human race" [see Lukardis, pp. 337–38]), it was also expressing its own (Cf. Bynum 1987, pp. 83–84).

The economic and civic aspects of a saint's presence in a community have often been emphasized (the saint was a source of income and political power),[12] but the sense of spiritual sharing has not. The nun who saw into Lukardis's heart could find consolation for her own frustration through Lukardis. She received heavenly

12. See, for example, Michael Goodich (1982; 1983); Patrick Geary (1978); André Vauchez (1981); and Gabriella Zarri (1980).

hosts that filled her with consolation. After a later conversation with the saint, Agnes was said to have experienced the joy that the Baptist felt inside his mother's womb during the Visitation (Lukardis, p. 339). The insignificance of daily life, the drudgery of an uneventful existence, was redeemed by the meaning that the very presence of the saint gave even to the common and the trivial.

The saint existed on two planes. She was part of the daily and earthly, but as her raptures manifested, she was also living on a more exalted plane. Through the saint, the community had a taste of that nobler existence.

On the vigil of the Ascension, St. Douceline was rapt in ecstasy. In this state, she sang heavenly songs in an incomprehensible language and walked as if she was part of a procession. The sisters followed her, carrying lighted candles, full of joy and ineffable consolation. "[They felt] that they took part in the joy of the heavenly court, and followed the marvelous procession, that they all believed the saint saw in heaven."[13]

Cooperating

The harmonious picture depicted in the *Life of Lukardis* was certainly not universal. Not all saints were treated with such tender affection. Lukardis's sisters refer to her as "carissima, benignissima, felicissima, nostra praedilectissima." When it looked as if she had recovered, the nuns applauded her and lovingly touched her cheeks. When some tables collapsed in the refectory, making a great noise, the nuns sent someone to hurry and soothe Lukardis in case she had been frightened (Lukardis, p. 332). Not all communities hosting a saint were so warm. As we shall see, the community could be rather indifferent to the saint's personal needs. But whether the community's attitude was affectionate or not, the saint and any community that recognized his or her sainthood were in collaboration.

Christian saints were expected to play an impossible role. They were denied the right to advertise themselves too explicitly, for one of the most important attributes of the true saint was humility. But total humility—a complete refusal to co-operate with potential

13. *La vie de Sainte Douceline: Texte provençal du XIVᵉ siècle,* edited and translated by R. Gout (Paris, 1927), pp. 143–46.

admirers—would result in anonymity. This may not be important in the church triumphant; all that matters to God is perseverance in righteousness to the end. But if the saint was to play a social role in the church militant, his or her sanctity had to be seen and socially recognized (Kleinberg 1989). Saints needed, therefore, to advertise both their claim and their proof without seeming too assertive.[14] Thomas of Cantimpré, while praising Margaret of Ypres for revealing the content of her revelations only to her confessor, criticizes other religious women for being like chickens who "make a great noise as soon as they lay an egg."[15]

Saints could not publicly praise themselves, but, like all Christians, they could publicly denounce themselves. Extravagant self-denunciation was interpreted as having the opposite of its literal meaning and, in effect, as being a claim to sainthood.[16] Such acts were considered instances of pious exaggeration (the saint fusses about his or her tiny transgressions) or holy lies (the saint denies his or her miracles), which further demonstrated what the saint denied (he or she is a saint). Saints expressed great reluctance to divulge self-laudatory information, such as revelations, while eventually conveying it. Sometimes they related such stories in secret to a confidant, who would then (regardless of the saint's wishes) pass it on.[17] Often the saints were "forced" to communicate such information by their devotees' incessant pressure. Even

14. The expectation that the holy man not seem too eager to be recognized as such is common in other cultures. The holy man's behavior needs to be seen as spontaneous and unrehearsed (see Franz Boas 1930, 2:11).

15. Thomas of Cantimpré, *Vita Margarite de Ypris*, 27, in Gilles G. Meersseman, "Frères Prêcheurs et mouvement dévot en Flandre au XIIIᵉ siècle," *Archivum Fratrum Praedicatorum* 18 (1948), pp. 119–20.

16. Giunta Bevegnati, *Vita Margaritae de Cortona* 2.38, AA.SS., 22 Feb., pp. 310–11. The prototype for many subsequent acts of ritual self-degradation (certainly in the Franciscan tradition) is found in the various *Lives* of Francis of Assisi (see Rosalind B. Brooke, ed. and trans., *Scripta Leonis Rufini et Angeli sociorum S. Francisci: The Writings of Leo, Rufino, and Angelo Companions of St. Francis*, 39 [Oxford, 1970], pp. 157–59). The episode in which Francis orders a friar to lead him with a cord around his neck and to denounce him as a glutton appears also in Celano's first *Life* (c. 52), and in the *Speculum perfectionis* (c. 61).

17. *Vita Beatae Benevenutae Bojanae*, edited by Johannes F. de Rubeis (Venice, 1757), pp. 41–42. In many narratives the saint would relate certain things on the condition that they be made public only after his or her death.

when the saint was willing to reveal his or her secrets, it was assumed that there was much more that remained unknown.[18]

The implicit messages the saints were transmitting were quite different from the explicit ones. After the Virgin cured her of her spastic paralysis, Lukardis got out of her bed and went to the nuns' choir.[19] The nuns, seeing Lukardis walk without support, solemnly sang the "Te Deum" in gratitude for her recovery. When this was later mentioned to Lukardis (she was apparently in a state of trance or semi-trance during the event), she reproved herself saying: "What have I allowed to be done for me? Am I a saint?" [*numquid sum sancta?*] (Lukardis, pp. 320–21). Clearly, Lukardis recognized in the community's behavior an ascription of sainthood.

Explicitly, Lukardis rejected the ascription of sainthood to her, yet only a short while earlier she performed a healing according to the canons of saintly performance. A cure was solicited and Lukardis took it upon herself to obtain it through the authoritative use of a sacred formula. One of the sisters suffered from dropsy and was so swollen that she could not walk and had to be carried on a stretcher. She asked Lukardis to cure her of her ailment. Lukardis took the nun's hand, raised it, and said: "In the name of our Lord Jesus Christ, rise and come with me." The nun who until then had had to be carried by six of the sisters, rose and, aided only by Lukardis, went back to the infirmary.[20] Jeanne Favret-Saada commented on role-acceptance among French peasants in the Bocage: "[others place the magician] in the position of subject, supposed to be able [to perform the task] and the magician himself must acknowledge he is in it, and accept what it implies in terms of personal commitment to a discourse (Favret-Saada 1980, p. 19). Lukardis made a commitment to the discourse suggested by her community (by agreeing to work miracles) and, whether she admitted it or not, played the role of a saint.

18. See, for example, Lukardis, p. 363: "Et sic, ut aliqua colligerent quae scripta sunt, ab ipsa subtiliter extorserunt." See also pp. 319, 324, 340. Cf. *Vita fratris Abundi,* fol. 1r. The writer interviewed the reluctant saint and "nihil erat quod importunitate mea, etiam invito, non extorquerem."

19. See above, n. 2.

20. Lukardis, p. 321. Cf. *Il processo per la canonizzazione di S. Nicola da Tolentino,* edited by N. Occhini, (Rome, 1984), pp. 222–23.

Unlike the saint, the saint's followers were not bound by the constraints that limited the saint's freedom of action. They could make for their saints all the claims that the latter were unable to make themselves. They could praise them to high heaven, and denounce their detractors, using language and means considered unacceptable for the saints themselves. A passage cited by Erving Goffman in his *Relations in Public* can demonstrate the role of intermediaries in everyday life. The context may be different, but the dynamics are similar.

I bought the shoes and made Gretel's day. "Oh, I'm so happy for you," she said. "I know just what you'll go through tomorrow when everybody sees them. Everybody'll say, 'Oh, they're cute.' Just you wait. You'll have such fun."

I am obliged to elaborate here. You see, "everybody" knew I was going shoe-hunting because I said so at lunch. When Gretel got home she would telephone the report on our trip, thereby alerting all eyes to my feet. When I would arrive at school in the morning, if the new shoes were found on me, appropriate comments would be made. Thus did it happen the next morning—and all day long—that everybody did indeed examine my shoes and say, "Oh, they're cute." They also said, "Oh, let's see them Oh, how tough." One girl told me that she loved my shoes without looking at them. She knew just from hearing about them that she loved them.[21]

Buying shoes is naturally very different from being a saint. What is common to both is the intermediaries' creation of consensus (over the suitability of shoes or the sainthood of a person), even before the audience had an opportunity to examine the visual evidence. Because the saint was so restricted in what he could say about himself, his reputation depended on the advertising of his virtues by his followers. If the saint's admirers did their duty, then by the time the saint made his personal appearance, everyone—like the girls in the episode just quoted—knew where to look and what to see.[22]

21. Lyn Tornabene, *I Passed as a Teenager* (New York, 1968), p. 144; cited in Goffman (1971, p. 68).

22. In some cases, the saint's dependence on intermediaries was almost total. St. Lutgard, for example, was a Flemish-speaking nun in a French-speaking convent. She relied for her communications on the services of a bilingual nun who acquired, as one could imagine, great importance. On the failure of a Moslem holy man for lack of preparation, see Michael Gilsenan (1982, pp. 132–39).

Sometimes the saints' followers intervened after the saint's appearance to make sure that the best possible interpretation of events would be accepted. Consider the following episode from the *Life* of Catherine of Siena. Catherine went to visit the body of St. Agnes of Montepulciano. As Catherine knelt before the body and lowered her head to kiss the saint's foot, the foot raised itself to Catherine's lips and then gradually returned to its original position.

When Raymond of Capua arrived at the convent the next day, everyone was talking about the miracle. Some of the eyewitnesses, however, attributed it to demonic intervention rather than to the power of God. As this was a Dominican convent under Raymond's jurisdiction, Raymond could exercise his authority in Catherine's favor. He summoned all the nuns and by interviewing the supporters first, established a consensus on the fact of the miracle. Then he called up one of the most vociferous critics and asked her whether it had all happened as the others said.

At once she said quite voluntarily in front of everyone that everything had indeed happened as the others had said it had—but then she went on to say that the blessed virgin Agnes had had a quite different intention in performing this miracle from the one we imagined her to have had. "Dearest sister," I answered her, "we are not interested in your idea of what Agnes's intention was: you are not her adviser or secretary! All we want to know is whether you saw the miraculous raising of the foot." And she said she had.[23]

Raymond realized that here the initial position of the saint's opponents was one of implied accusation—the miracle was the work of the devil. It is not clear whether they implied that the miracle was in fact a demonic illusion or a physical event of his doing. The point is that by a combination of implicit threat (Raymond was the nuns' superior and also a known devotee of St. Catherine) and social pressure, Raymond managed to bring the skeptical nun to concede the miraculous nature of the event.

The skeptical nun gave up her claim that it was a demonic act. She conceded that it actually happened and that it was St. Agnes, not the devil, who accomplished it. At this point, the battle was lost for the skeptics' cause. Since she conceded that the miracle oc-

23. Raymond of Capua, *Vita S. Catharinae Senensis, AA.SS.*, 30 Apr., p. 935.

curred and that it was not a demonic trick (for an accusation of demonic deception, like accusations of heresy, had to be taken seriously), Raymond could refuse to hear what she had to say. If what was necessary was an interpretation, the nun had no authority to offer one after his had been pronounced. Raymond was quite certain that he already had the interpretation that best suited his (and Catherine's) needs.

Given her opening position, the nun's interpretation was likely to be problematic. If heard, it could prolong the state of confusion that Raymond wanted to dispel—what if her interpretation was for some reason more convincing than his own? To guarantee that the nun had no second thoughts, Raymond imposed a penance on her for her "calumny." The others were "to be given an example" and obediently accept the version of events that was now official.

In a small religious community, it was highly important that the whole community eventually support the saint. It would be very difficult for the saint to face an audience of outsiders without the solidarity of the entire community. This solidarity, however, was usually achieved gradually, as all members of the community were not convinced simultaneously. Thus, before the saint's "team" became a "team" it was itself an audience.[24] In other words, after an initial period when the saint acquired her first followers, there followed a transition period during which some members were more willing than others to accept the saint's claims. These persons helped the saint perform before an audience that might eventually become part of the team. The devoted members, faced, at least initially, the danger of being branded fools, if not worse, in the event that the saint's status was successfully challenged. Their personal investment in the saint made them eager to find corroboration for their approval, on the one hand, and anxious to prevent the saint's "exposure" as a fraud on the other.

An episode from Lukardis's Life demonstrates this process. Lukardis was regarded as a paralytic, or at least as extremely weak—hence she could not participate in day-to-day activities. One day, she wished to visit the chapel of the Virgin, but being unable to do so on her own, was carried there by two fellow nuns and left alone.

24. I am borrowing the term used by Erving Goffman (1959, chapter 2, "Teams," pp. 77–105).

After a while, she was visited by the Virgin and the baby Jesus, and "against the right and the nature of all her powers," she rose to her feet and stood up.

Meanwhile, a certain nun, a special friend of the servant of God who had followed her for a long time, silently opened the chapel door somewhat, and peeked in secretly. Seeing her stand, she wondered beyond measure that one so weak could rise and stand by herself. She closed the doors and secretly left, forbidding others to come near. She feared that if they saw her thus standing, they would conclude that she could rise and stand whenever she pleased (Lukardis, p. 318)

This incident must have happened at an early stage in Lukardis's saintly career, for her shifts between periods of powerlessness and relative strength were later accepted by the community as miraculous. Indeed, they were published as such to enhance Lukardis's reputation (Lukardis, pp. 320–21). The nun's caution is an indication of the transition period, when Lukardis's status was still precarious. We are told that at first there were nuns who complained about Lukardis's frequent communion (Lukardis, pp. 320–21). It was necessary to justify this practice with the help of visions of other nuns that confirmed God's support for Lukardis's privilege (for the visions, see Lukardis, pp. 317, 349).

The transition period was fairly short and nontraumatic in Lukardis's case. But there were doubts, and self-doubt too. Like other saints, Lukardis was not certain that her visions were divine in origin. The devil, it is well known, can transform himself into an angel of light (2 Cor. 11:14). Lukardis revealed her doubts to some nuns, but they would not reassure her. She was probably looking for solidarity as much as theological certainty. It is likely that a show of faith in her from her sisters would have done much to alleviate her insecurity. But as this did not come, Lukardis remained troubled. Her attendant urged her to seek the advice of Henry of Mühlhausen, a Dominican who served as the saint's spiritual advisor. Henry tried to allay Lukardis's doubts, but without success. He then asked the abbess to be present in Lukardis's now periodic "rising." She agreed, and Henry observed how Lukardis, usually unable to move, rose and remained standing for a long time. The friar ascended the pulpit in the nuns' choir and delivered an excited sermon. Then, he led all the nuns to the chapel where Lukardis was still standing. He prostrated himself and prayed to God, shedding many pious tears. When Lukardis laid herself in bed again, he approached her and reassured her in the most absolute terms that God's, not the devil's, works were revealed in her (Lukardis, pp. 330–31).

All this was very impressive. More important, it was public. Henry, himself a man of a saintly reputation, added his authority to that of Lukardis and her supporters. He impressed upon the community his own conviction in her sainthood by publicly and unequivocally committing himself. Lukardis's doubts were removed because the doubts around her were dispelled.

Even more important for an aspiring saint than the approval of a person of authority could be the encouragement of an already established saint. A saint was seen as an expert in recognizing other saintly talents. Thus people who gained her approval benefited from her prestige. This explains why so many friends of saints acquired a saintly reputation. The saint could, for example, direct patients to somebody of a lesser reputation. Francis of Assisi sent a possessed friar to St. Clare for treatment, and she herself referred a child to her mother, who was then a nun in the same community. This created a certain ambiguity as to who was really responsible for the cure: "Clare asserted that the child has been healed by the merits of her mother, while the mother turned the praise to her daughter, declaring that she was unworthy of such an honor."[25] It seems likely that both parties would enjoy an increase in reputation.

An interesting example of a symbolic initiation of one saint by another is recounted in the *Life* of Beatrice of Nazareth (c. 1202–68). Beatrice was sent as a young girl to La Ramée, where Ida of Nivelles (1199–1231) was already an acknowledged saint. Ida recognized Beatrice as a bride of Christ and promised her future glory.[26] Beatrice was uncertain. She asked for a sign of grace, for divine reassurance. Ida agreed. On the coming Christmas, she promised, Beatrice's wish would be granted. Christmas day passed, though, without the promised sign. Beatrice was disappointed.

25. Thomas of Celano, *Legenda S. Clarae virginis* 33, edited by F. Pennacchi (Assisi, 1910), p. 46.
26. L. Reypens, ed., *Vita Beatricis:* De Autobiografie *van de Z. Beatrijs van Tienen O. Cist. 1200–1268* (Antwerp, 1964), 1.10.50–51, pp. 42–43.

She blamed her own sins for the failure, but Ida reassured her and predicted success on the eighth day of the Octave of the Nativity. Beatrice spent her days in a state of tense expectation and, somewhat earlier than predicted, she had a vision of the Trinity.[27] In a sense, Ida ordered Beatrice to have a vision. When it eventually came, after much psychological preparation, it initiated Beatrice into the role of a visionary and eventually a saint.[28] There could be no fear of demonic deception in a vision predicted by a saint. Ida's praise of Beatrice together with the latter's new confidence in her status created such a reputation of sanctity that Beatrice feared she might succumb to vainglory.[29]

The saint, then, was a friend, a medium, and a protector. It is related in the *Life* of Lukardis that a nun saw the convent of Oberweimar in a vision as a big house floating on endless waters under pouring rain. A voice told the nun that the house (an allusion to Noah's ark) was safe as long as Lukardis was in it. After her death, the community would have to invoke God for protection from trouble and tribulation (Lukardis, p. 346). Without the reassuring presence of the saint, there was no certainty that God would spare his servants.[30]

In everyday reality, however, it was often the saint, especially the female saint, who needed some very real protection. Treated as a curiosity by some, and as a walking reliquary by others, the saint could find it hard sometimes to protect her privacy and even her person. Both were seen as not entirely hers. It was acceptable, even laudable, to spy on the saints.[31] For as the hagiographers again and again reminded their reader, the candle must not be hid under a bushel basket [Matt. 5:15](Van der Essen 1923, p. 335; Van Uytfanghe 1989, 1:159 n. 16). Saints were not supposed to have back-

27. Ibid., 1.10.55, p. 46. It is a sign of the account's authenticity that the vision occurred earlier than expected, although the author does not comment on it in the text. Cf. *Vita B. Idae de Nivella,* 8 and 10, in *Quinque prudentes virgines,* edited by Chr. Henriquez, pp. 219, 225 (Antwerp, 1630).

28. For another instance of commanding a person to have a vision, see *Vita Julianae corneliensis, AA.SS.,* 5 Apr., pp. 458–59.

29. Reypens, ed., *Vita Beatricis* 1.12.61, p. 50.

30. Cf. *Vita B. Idae de Nivella* 12, p. 226.

31. See, for example, *Vita Julianae corneliensis,* p. 454. See also Jean-Michel Sallmann (1979b, p. 863).

stage behavior; they were expected to be constantly saintly. Saints could not excuse themselves by saying that they were not aware of being watched. It was assumed, furthermore, that they would try to hide their sanctity, adding humility to their catalog of merits, but depriving others of *their* rewards. This pious selfishness was not tolerated by spectators who did their best to catch the saint in *flagrante sanctitate*. As for their bodies, the saints were seen as mere custodians of their miracle-working flesh. The saint's relics (pieces of clothes, blood-stained material, for example) could be torn away from the saint with or without his or her permission. When the followers of St. Romauld learned of his intention to move to another place, they planned, *"impia pietate,"* to kill him to avoid losing his body.[32]

Lukardis, as we saw, was willing to share her sanctity with her community, but she was deeply troubled by the curiosity of outsiders. After her first miraculous recovery during Lent, Lukardis developed a personal ritual, which she performed every Friday, and daily during Lent. From Nones to Vespers she would stand erect, her arms outstretched in the form of a cross, one foot placed on top of the other. Some time after the ritual commenced, she would emit a sound the others interpreted as Christ's dying words on the cross.[33]

Once, during the second Sunday in Lent, a powerful noble came to the convent with his retinue to see Lukardis. The noble asked to see her, but was told that strangers and secular people were not allowed to watch her during the "performance." The refusal aroused the noble's curiosity, and he insisted on seeing Lukardis, particularly in that state. The abbess, unable to resist the powerful man's wishes, went to Lukardis and asked her with anguish to consent to the man's request. Lukardis, who was always timid, blushed deeply, but obeyed her abbess. Then the noble approached "not alone, as he should have, but pompously, with his entourage." He moved her hands and touched her legs and her feet. Finding her feet joined

32. Peter Damian, *Vita B. Romualdi* 13, in Fouti per la storia d'Italia, edited by G. Tabacco (Rome, 1957), p. 35.

33. Lukardis, p. 328. The ritual bears a marked resemblance to Philip of Clairvaux's account of his visit to Elizabeth of Erkenrode. See Philip of Clairvaux, *Vita Elizabeth sanctimonialis in Erkenrode,* pp. 362–79 in *Catalogus codium hagiographicorum bibliothecae regiae bruxellensis,* vol. 1 (Brussels, 1886).

together so that the wounds matched each other perfectly, he tried to separate them with all his power but could not. In the crowded room, full of curious men and women, the intimacy of Lukardis with God and with her sisters was shattered. She felt such great shame that she became gravely sick and was given Extreme Unction. For almost a year afterwards, she felt that she had lost God's grace. She recuperated slowly with the help of her sisters, through small reassuring rituals and their physical aid in reenacting her Passion play. Until she could once more rise on her own, the nuns had to support her for the duration of her ritual. After the incident with the nobleman, no stranger was permitted to approach Lukardis during the time of her ritual (Lukardis, p. 328).

Outside intervention often came in this obstructive way: insensitivity to the saint's wishes, inquisitive hands violating the privacy of body and person. Often an atmosphere of public spectacle prevailed in the visits of powerful outsiders to the saint. For Lukardis, however, the invasion of the outside world was an exception. The community of Oberweimar did its best to protect her from the world, proclaiming her virtues without exposing her in person to its *impia pietas*. Other saints were not so lucky.

I will now turn to a saint whose life reflects a different type of relationship with both the smaller community of the house and the larger community of the outside world.

Losing Control: St. Douceline

Douceline (d. 1274), sister of Hugh of Digne, was the founder of two congregations of Beguines, one in Hyères and one in Marseilles.[34] Her Provençal *Life* was written in the late thirteenth century by her successor, Philippine (Felipa) de Porcellet.[35] Philippine was the head of an important religious community, a member of one of the wealthiest families in the region, and intimately familiar with Douceline.[36] Had she been a man, there is no doubt that she could have added weight to the *Life*. Yet Philippine preferred to re-

34. On Douceline, see Claude Carozzi (1975; 1976).
35. See R. Gout, ed. and trans., *La vie de Ste. Douceline: Texte provençal du XIVᵉ siecle* (Paris, 1927), pp. 10–16.
36. See J.-H. Albanés, *La vie de Sainte Douceline fondatrice des Béguines de Marseille* (Marseille, 1879), pp. xxv–xxxix; Martin Aurell (1986, pp. 165–69).

main anonymous. A woman who was not herself a saint could not contribute much to a *Life*'s authority. The fact that the *Life* was written in the vernacular is further indication of limited ambitions. Vernacular *Lives* were aimed at a local, lay readership; such readership could not significantly alter the saint's official status. If we consider the biography's dissemination a rough index of success, the *vida* of St. Douceline was not successful. In spite of the saint's fame, her *Life* survived in a single manuscript.[37]

Like Lukardis's, Douceline's *Life* is not a professional work. It is an account given by a member of the community, probably not intended for more than a limited audience. The community was wealthy enough to afford the services of a professional Latin writer but it chose not to do so (Aurell 1986, pp. 167–78). If the picture that emerges from the two *Lives* is different, it is not because the writers' narrative strategies were different, but because the patterns of relationship in Marseilles and Oberweimar were different.

Douceline was a strict and authoritarian figure. "When it came to reprimanding and chastising," writes her biographer, "she was very terrible and of great authority" [*en repenre e en castiar era mot terribla e de gran auctoritat*]. There was not a sister that did not tremble before her.[38] Douceline forbade the sisters to look at men. One day, she saw one of the sisters, a girl of seven years, watching some men working near the house. Douceline beat her so hard that she began to bleed. Whoever was caught talking about men was severely punished. The sisters were afraid to talk to each other even about their relatives.[39] In this and in other matters, Douceline clearly exercised strict control over her community.

But there was a weak spot in Douceline's control, for Douceline was an ecstatic. She spent long and fervent hours in meditation and prayer, and her mind reacted by separating itself from the world of the senses. For two whole years she succeeded in hiding her ecstasies, until they could no longer be kept secret. Hearing any talk of God, she would immediately fall into an ecstasy. Whatever she was doing, a devout word, a sweet sound, a sparrow's song

37. See Salimbene de Adam (1966, 2:804).
38. Gout, *La vie de Ste. Douceline,* pp. 90–91.
39. Ibid., pp. 86–88.

122

could trigger her ecstasy, and she would pass into a different world.[40] The picture that emerges from the *Life* of Douceline is not one of spiritual co-operation. Douceline does not seem to have been interested in letting her community actively participate in her spirituality. It is significant, for example that while she practiced absolute poverty in the Franciscan spirit, she did not permit her sisters to do the same, preventing from the outset their being as holy as she was. Her ecstasies likewise did not call for participation, but for amazement and admiration; nor did she often relate what she saw while in ecstasy. Douceline, in short, was holy apart from her community, not with it.

But while her subordinates could be kept at a distance by obedience, it was more difficult to compel outsiders to remain passive. Her frequent ecstasies left her at the mercy of her spectators. To better assure themselves of the reality of her raptures (*per plus fort a probar*), people pricked her with awls, jabbed needles between her fingers and fingernails, and stabbed her with a chisel.[41] Charles of Anjou, more formidable than mere commoners, more ruthlessly pious, subjected her to a loftier test. By his order, molten lead was poured over Douceline's feet.[42] Douceline successfully passed all these tests; she remained immobile and serene. But when her ecstasies were over, she suffered great pain. After her ordeal in Charles's court, she was sick and could not walk for a long time.

There was also the loss of privacy. As Douceline's ecstasies became less controllable, she could not prevent "even seculars" from seeing her in that state. When she went into ecstasy during mass,

---

40. Ibid., pp. 116–17. Cf. Jaques de Vitry, *Vita Mariae Oigniacensis, AA.SS.*, 23 June., p. 548. The cardinal describes a woman who could have twenty-five ecstasies a day. The *Life* of Colette of Corbie relates that any mention of the Holy Name triggered an ecstasy in the saint. Her friends had to be careful not to mention divine matters, if they wanted to discuss more worldly matters with her. *Vita B. Coletae, AA.SS.*, 6 Mar., pp. 575–76. Other mystics also reported an inability to control their reactions. See Margery Kempe, *The Book of Margery Kempe*, chap. 57, edited by S. Brown Meech (Oxford, 1961), pp. 149–54.

41. Gout, *La vie de Ste. Douceline,* pp. 114, 126; see also p. 108. Cf. Gregory Lombardelli, *Vita B. Aldobrandescae 3, AA.SS.*, 26 Apr., p. 475.

42. Gout, *La vie de Ste. Douceline,* p. 115.

the crowd rushed toward her, eager to touch her, until there was real danger to her life.[43] Douceline, so afraid of men, so careful to avoid any contact with them, was unable to avoid being handled by men as she gradually lost control over herself. She decided to stop attending public sermons, conventual masses, and masses on high feasts to escape being seen.[44] When she was among people who spoke of God and felt an ecstasy coming, she tried to wound her own hands to distract herself. Once when a Franciscan from Paris talked to her about God, she fell into an ecstasy. It was then discovered that her hands were covered with cuts and bruises from needles she kept under her sleeve in a futile attempt to avoid losing control.[45]

But the faithful would not easily give up their rightful edification. The countess of Provence wished to see Douceline in ecstasy. She asked Douceline to grant her this favor and was refused. The countess then brought a "good friar" who talked very ardently about the Lord in Douceline's presence. Douceline's bruised hands could not protect her from such a "great sentiment." The countess had her way, and, indifferent to the saint's wishes, she and her children knelt before her and kissed her hands.[46] The once proud ruler of her community, who had almost total control over her own and others' lives, was turned into a mere object, a devotional toy. She could be manipulated at will because, once possessed by God, she was no longer in sole possession of her person.[47] Forced into an ecstasy by the count of Artois, Douceline complained to her daughters in these bitter words: "Unfaithful sisters, why did you allow this, to make a spectacle of me? How could you commit such wickedness, such great treachery?"[48]

Lukardis's lot was happier than Douceline's. Her community was more successful at protecting her from outside intrusions. What matters, however, is not whether Douceline's sisters could have protected her better or not (she seems to have thought they could). More significant is that the two *Lives* reflect two different

43. Ibid., pp. 118–19.
44. Ibid., p. 120.
45. Ibid., pp. 122–23.
46. Ibid., pp. 124–25.
47. Ibid., pp. 124–25; see also p. 127.
48. Ibid., p. 130.

social situations, but one basic dynamic. In Oberweimar, Lukardis performed almost exclusively for her "team." When the transition period was over, it was only the intrusion of an outsider that disturbed the harmony surrounding Lukardis. She was not expected to prove herself again and again, because all significant others were already convinced. There was no violent grabbing of spiritual favors because Lukardis was available and willing to share.

Douceline's trials at the hands of the crowd were a prolonged transition period. There were always new people who needed to see for themselves whether what they had heard was true. Douceline's admirers were not allowed to share her sanctity in the same way as Lukardis's. The occasions when they could play an active role in her spiritual exercises were rare. They resorted to taking by force what she refused to give willingly.

BUT in both the tranquil atmosphere of Oberweimar and in the hectic commotion of Marseilles, the same processes were taking place. The aristocrats who forced Douceline to have painful public ecstasies and Lukardis's loving sisters who offered her their visions were after the same effect. They were shaping the image of their saint. Lukardis, who was more co-operative, became the focus of visionary activity, of a spiritual trade; Douceline, who tried to relegate her admirers to a passive role, was made an object herself, forced in spite of her protests to perform before unwanted audiences. Their spectators were confirming for themselves and for others that they had not been mistaken, that God himself had manifested their heroines' holiness. The aristocrats who abused Douceline had no doubt in her sainthood. Like a child, she was given assignments she was certain to perform well, so that the spectators would be proud of her and of themselves. The devotees of both saints were announcing by word and by act that this was *their* saint.

VI

ST. FRANCIS OF ASSISI AND THE
BURDEN OF EXAMPLE

FRANCIS of Assisi (1181–1226) had an immense following, much greater than the saints I have examined in previous chapters. As the founder and first leader of an important religious order, Francis's concept of sainthood and his actions as an admired saint had far-reaching implications for his order. His influence can be felt on every aspect of medieval religious life from his time on. Nevertheless, Francis was no less dependent on the collaboration of his audience than his more humble counterparts. His position made this interaction more complex: Francis was looked upon as a model in a way that the three women were not. But the dynamics of the saintly situation, the co-operative nature of public sainthood, were the same.

The story of Francis's life was written many times. I want to start with the story of one episode from the saint's life as it appears in three different sources. First, as it was told by his friends, then by his first official biographer, Thomas of Celano, and last by one of Francis's successors as minister general and his second official biographer, St. Bonaventure.[1]

The earliest version (1246) comes from the collection of anecdotes told by his companions Leo, Rufino, and Angelo:

Once a minister of the friars came to St. Francis, who was then staying in the same place [Greccio], to celebrate Christmas with him. When the friars of the house had laid the table specially on Christmas Day with beautiful white clothes which they had acquired, and glass vessels for drinking, in

---

1. The literature on St. Francis is huge and constantly growing. The reader can consult the bibliography in *St. Francis of Assisi: Writings and Early Biographies, English Omnibus of the Sources for the Life of St. Francis,* edited by M. Habig (Chicago, 1973). For some of the more recent scholarship, see Duncan Nimmo (1987, pp. 45–47, n. 114). For a discussion of the sources, see Stanislao da Campagnola (1981, pp. 67–123; Raoul Manselli (1980, pp. 3–57); and Nimmo (1987, pp. 78–95). The "question franciscaine" is by no means settled.

honor of the minister, it happened that St. Francis came down from his cell to eat. When he saw the table put up on a dais [*in altum positam*] and so elaborately laid, he secretly went and took the hood of a poor man who had come there that day, and the staff which he carried in his hands. He quietly called one of his companions and went outside the door of the hermitage, without the other friars of the house knowing. Meanwhile the friars came in to the meal, chiefly because the holy father sometimes used to prefer it so: when he did not come at once at mealtimes, and the friars wished to eat, he wanted them to go in to the table and eat. His companion closed the door, staying inside near him. St. Francis knocked at the door and he at once opened to him. He came in like a pilgrim [*peregrinus*—here in the sense of wayfarer, stranger] with the hood on his back and a staff in his hands. When he came before the door of the building where the friars were eating he cried out like a beggar saying to the friars: "For the love of the lord God give alms to this poor sick pilgrim." The minister and the other brothers recognized him at once [*statim*]. The minister said: "Brother, we also are poor like you. Since there are many of us, the alms we eat are necessary to us; but for the love of God on whom you have called, come in and we will give you of the alms which the Lord has given us." When he entered and stood before the friars' table, the minister gave him the dish from which he himself was eating and likewise bread. Taking it he sat down on the ground near the fire facing the brothers who sat at the table on a dais. He said to the brothers sighing: "When I saw the table laid with honor and elaborate care I thought this was not the table of poor religious who go daily from door to door. For it is our duty, dearest brothers, to follow the example of humility and poverty in all things more than other religious, because we were called to this and have professed this before God and men. So now it seems to me that I sit like a friar." The friars were ashamed [*verecundati*], perceiving that St. Francis spoke the truth and some of them began to weep bitterly, thinking how he sat on the ground and that he had wanted to correct them in so holy and fair a way.[2]

---

2. Rosalind B. Brooke, ed. and trans., *Scripta Leonis Rufini et Angeli sociorum S. Francisci: The Writings of Leo, Rufino, and Angelo Companions of St. Francis* 32 (Oxford, 1970), pp. 144–47. (Unless otherwise indicated I am using Brooke's translation.) Brooke's edition is the most readily available, but it is not without its critics (see the works discussing the sources in the previous note). Most of the controversy concerns Brooke's reconstruction of the hierarchy of sources, not her reading of the manuscript. The reader may want to consult Bigaroni's edition that reproduced MS. 1046 of Perugia *in toto* (see Marino Bigaroni, ed., *"Compilatio Assisiensis" dagli scritti di fr. Leone e compagni su S. Francesco d'Assisi* [Assisi, 1975]). Whatever their disagreements, all scholars agree that MS. 1046 is the earliest witness to the friends' stories. I have refrained, therefore, (unless there was a special reason for doing so) from citing

Here is the same story as it appears in Thomas of Celano's *Vita secunda*, published in 1247:

It happened one Easter that the brothers at the hermitage of Greccio prepared the table more carefully than they usually did with white linen and glassware. Coming down from his cell, the father came to the table and saw that it was placed high and decorated extravagantly [*vane*]. But he did not smile at the smiling table. Stealthily and little by little [*furtim et pedentim*] he retraced his steps, put on the hat of a poor man who was there, and taking a staff in his hand, he went out. He waited outside at the door until the brothers began to eat; for they were in the habit of not waiting for him when he did not come at the signal. When they had begun to eat, this truly poor man cried out at the door: "For the love of the Lord God," he said, "give an alms to this poor, sick pilgrim." The brothers answered: "Come in, man, for the love of him whom you have invoked." He immediately entered and appeared before them as they were eating. But what astonishment [*stuporem*], do you think, the pilgrim caused these citizens [*civibus*]?[3] The beggar was given a dish, and sitting alone on the floor [*solo solus recumbens*], he put the dish in the ashes. "Now I am sitting as a Friar Minor should sit," he said. And to the brothers he said: "We should be moved by th examples of poverty of the Son of God more than other religious. I saw the table prepared and decorated, and I knew it was not the table of poor men who beg from door to door." This series of actions proves that he was like that other pilgrim who was alone in Jerusalem on that day. He made the heart of the disciples burn within them no less while he spoke [cf. Luke 24:18; 32][4]

The third version is taken from St. Bonaventure's *Legenda maior* (1263):

One Easter Sunday he was staying at a hermitage which was so far from the nearest house that he could not easily go begging. Then he remembered Him who had appeared to the disciples walking on the road to Emmaus

---

later works such as the *Speculum perfectionis*, the *Actus B. Francisci*, and Celano's *Vita secunda* when the same story appears in the *Scripta Leonis*.

3. I am not sure why Thomas uses this term here. Perhaps he wanted to contrast Francis, who is a "peregrinus" in this world, to the brothers, who by succumbing to the material became true citizens of it.

4. Thomas of Celano, *Vita secunda Sancti Francisci* 2.31.61, in *Analecta Franciscana* 10 (1926–41, pp. 167–68. I based my translation on Placid Herman's in *St. Francis of Assisi: Writings and Early Biographies, English Omnibus of the Sources for the Life of St. Francis,* edited by M. Habig (Chicago, 1973), pp. 414–15. My version is more literal.

that very day in the guise of a pilgrim [*peregrinus*], and he begged an alms from the friars themselves, like a pilgrim and a pauper. When he had received it humbly, he spoke to them, telling them how they should pass through the desert of this world like strangers and pilgrims, and like true Hebrews celebrate the Lord's Pasch continually in poverty of spirit, the Pasch that is the passage from this world to the Father.

And because in begging for alms, he was moved not by greed, but by true liberty of spirit, God, Father of the poor, seemed to take special care of him.[5]

This last version, published seventeen years after the first, is considerably different. In fact, had we not known Celano's version, we would probably find it difficult to recognize the friends' account as the source of Bonaventure's version. Celano's version seems on first sight fairly close to the friends' account, but a closer look reveals a critical change in tone and in meaning. In what follows, I will try to show that Bonaventure's adaptation represents a continuation and accentuation of Celano's approach to the text, though, due to the writers' dissimilar goals, it delivers a very different message.

We do not know what actually took place in Greccio. The friends' account is the closest source that we have to the historical event. Not only was it written by eyewitnesses, but it was not meant for publication. Its language and style are simple and straightforward. The friends intended it to serve as raw material for the person chosen by the order's authorities to write the saint's second official biography. In their letter to the order's minister general, Crescenzio of Jesi, the friends express their satisfaction with the way the existing legends relate events from the saint's life. They suggest, however, that had the episodes contained in their collection been known to the saint's biographers they "would not have passed them by, but would have adorned them with their eloquence to the best of their ability and left them for the memory of posterity."[6]

Thomas of Celano was the person chosen to write the saint's second biography. As a professional writer, it was assumed he would

5. Bonaventure, *Legenda maior* 7.9, in *Analecta Franciscana* 10 (1926–41, p. 590; my translation is based on Benen Fahy's in *St. Francis of Assisi: Omnibus of Sources,* pp. 685–86.

6. Brooke, *Scripta Leonis,* p. 88.

be better qualified than the eyewitnesses to narrate the saint's story in a way both pleasing and edifying. This stands in contradiction to the Isidorian theory of historical authorship, often repeated without much conviction by medieval writers. According to Isidore, eyewitnesses are the best historians, since all the historian needs to do is recount truthfully the events of the past.[7] But the events of the past conveyed messages that the eyewitness did not always see clearly. Francis's friends accepted the need for a higher authority when they praised existing legends—of which Celano's *Vita prima* was the most important. The eyewitnesses' role was to tell what happened; the professional writer's was to reduce the "noise" in their account so that a clear message could get through.

The first difference one notices between the friends' version and Celano's is the time of the events: in the former, Christmas; in the latter, Easter. This looks rather insignificant. It has been suggested that Thomas either confused the dates or corrected a confusion in the source.[8] The main point of the story, after all, is not the exact time of year, but that the festivity had been the occasion for extravagance by Francis' standards. However, this alteration is more significant than it seems at first sight. As we shall see, it exposes to us the professional hagiographer at work.

Celano builds his version of the episode around the themes of example and imitation. Francis sets an example for his friars to follow, while he himself imitates Christ at the same time. This moral circuit is whole on one side and broken on the other. Francis is a faithful copy of Christ, but the friars start with a failure—they were not naturally faithful imitators of Jesus. They need Francis as a medium and their success in the future is not guaranteed. This structure rests on the identification of Francis with Christ. The encounter of the Disciples with the resurrected Christ on the road to Emmaus consists of the same elements of nonrecognition, rebuke, then recognition. This is why the setting of the scene is changed to Easter.

But this is not the only change. Perhaps the most significant alteration is the total disappearance in Celano's version of the friars'

---

7. Isidor of Seville, *Etimologiae*, 1.41 Cf. Beryl Smalley (1974, pp. 22–25).
8. See Bigaroni, *Compilatio Assisiensis*, p. 199, n.122.

active role playing. Francis's performance in the friends' account consists of two levels of collaboration. First, Francis requires the help of his unnamed companion. Francis had together with him in Greccio a number of friends who accompanied him in his travels. He told one of them about his plan and made sure that the friend opened the door for him, presumably to avoid the possibility that the friars would not hear Francis or would ignore the pleas of a beggar while they were eating.

Second, as soon as he entered the house dressed as a pilgrim, he was identified by the visiting minister and the rest of the brothers. And, of course, it would be strange had they not recognized him just because he was wearing a hat and holding a staff in his hand. It is unlikely that Francis thought they would not; the drama that followed was a symbolic statement—edifying theater, not a real attempt to deceive the friars. The friars immediately (*statim*) recognized Francis, but they did not "call his bluff," as no bluff was intended. Instead, having realized the purpose of the show, they played along. Their words as well as Francis's are formal statements, not natural dialogue. Because of the importance of the drama, it is the visiting minister, not the local friars, who took the lead. The minister's reply—"Brother, we are also poor like you. Since there are many of us, the alms we eat are necessary to us; but for the love of God on whom you have called, come in and we will give you of the alms which the Lord has given us"—hardly fits the reality of the situation. The friars were not as poor as they claimed. The description of the fine vessels and the presence of poor people in the house (with whom, one assumes, the friars shared their food) suggests that the friars had a certain measure of surplus (if they were destitute they would surely have exchanged their vessels for food).

Furthermore, when the minister finished his speech, he gave Francis food from his own dish, hardly normal practice. Other beggars did not, apparently, enjoy the same treatment. Real beggars who were fed by the friars, like the one whose hat and staff Francis borrowed, did not eat with the friars, but elsewhere—probably in the kitchen. It is hard to believe that Francis was unaware of not being treated like an ordinary beggar. He sought to teach his brethren by example that they must not eat in what he saw as luxury and extravagance. When he sat on the floor rather than at the table, it was clear to everyone present that Francis was giving them a lesson as their spiritual leader.

Celano, by removing all trace of the friars' co-operation, gives the episode a much sterner tone. The little conspiracy with the companion is removed. Francis alone enters the arena, and he alone acts in it. The friars are no more fellow actors in a ritual drama, but underlings caught red-handed. Francis is not given the very best dish—that of the visiting minister—but just a dish. He then not only sits on the ground, but places his dish in the ashes, thus adding as ascetic element to his action.[9] Only when he starts to speak is he recognized by the brothers, who react with great "astonishment." Francis's detachment from the others is emphasized by the stress on his loneliness in Celano's account. Sitting alone on the floor (*solo solus recumbens*), Francis expresses an inverse relation between his spatial inferiority (he is sitting below all the rest) and his moral superiority (he alone behaves as a friar should).

Francis's rebuke is not mitigated, as in the original, by a friendly address (dearest brothers). The brothers are now admonished to follow the example of the Son of God, not simply the example of humility and poverty. Celano's conclusion, as I have argued, connects all the threads by comparing Francis to Christ on the way to Emmaus. This serves Celano's purpose of presenting the saint as an *alter Christus* whose relation to Christ is more than an *imitatio*—it is a *conformitas*.

In his version of the same story, Bonaventure follows the lead of Celano. For him also the central aspect of this episode is Francis's *imitatio Christi,* only he moves one step ahead of Celano and projects this notion onto Francis himself. In Celano's narrative, Francis only mentions Christ in his admonition to the friars to follow the ideal of poverty. The observation of Francis's *conformitas Christi* is external to the event. It is the narrator who compares Francis to Christ on the road to Emmaus. Bonaventure relates the story as if the notion of the biblical analogy arose in Francis's own mind. His begging is presented as an effort to imitate Christ and is

9. Celano added a touch of asceticism in other places. In the *Vita prima,* in the famous conversion scene before the bishop, Francis disrobes and remains naked. In the *Vita secunda,* he has a hair shirt beneath his clothes.

not followed by a criticism of the brothers. All reference to Francis's playacting disappeared in Bonaventure's *Legend*. There is an allusion to Christ appearing to the disciples in the guise of a pilgrim, but there is no hint that Francis also disguised himself as one. We are simply told that he begged an alms "like a pilgrim."

In Bonaventure's account, Francis's sermon is more important than his example. Unlike Celano's version, there is no emphasis on the difference between Francis's actions and the friars'. His begging, the center of the two previous accounts, is presented as merely preliminary to his words. The message itself is abstract; it invokes a frame of mind, not action. The saint lectures the brothers about the friar's existential status: they must not be citizens of this world, but of the next. It is also significant that Bonaventure changed the circumstances of Francis's begging from the friars. No longer is it a deliberate role playing; instead, it is presented as the result of external constraints: the hermitage was isolated and he could not easily go begging (*commode mendicare non posset*). This naturally takes the sting out of the story. These alterations of the original add up to give Bonaventure's story a different significance. Action is deemphasized, and ideas, severed from their concrete situations, are brought to the fore.

I chose to begin with a demonstration of the hagiographer's craft, because it shows us which elements get lost in the process of turning the saints from individuals in specific circumstances into universal models. All the stories agree on one point: Francis was consciously teaching by example. What the friends' story retained and the others' blurred was the active co-operation of Francis's audience. The success of Francis's lesson depended on the collaboration of the friars. Had they refused to pretend not to recognize the saint, the whole lesson would have been impossible. As we shall see again and again below, Francis was constantly assigning roles to his companions and larger audiences in the various edifying dramas that he was staging throughout his life. Sainthood is a joint effort, not a one-man act.[10] But first we must examine the issue of saintly example.

---

10. Cf. Philip of Clairvaux, *Vita Elizabeth sanctimonialis in Erkenrode*, 1;367–68. While Elizabeth reenacted the Passion of Christ, her attendants constantly produced and removed props that she needed for her performance.

In previous chapters I have had a great deal to say about audience participation in the saint's performance, but little on the issue of saintly example and saint-imitation. It was not an important element in the *Lives* I have discussed so far. The three saints I examined were seen as holy sufferers and visionaries and not so much as the subjects of imitation. But for some saints, example and imitation ruled much of the rapport they had with their followers. They were essential factors in Francis's life.

All saints were expected to serve as exemplars. Saintly example was part of the saints' role as mediators between God and men. Unlike Christ, the saints were not perfect, and thus being like them was conceivable.[11] The propagation of the saints' fame was justified only because they were to set an example, to stimulate, and to edify. But different saints chose to focus on different aspects of the repertoire of perfection. Some chose a way of life that even ordinary human beings could emulate, however imperfectly. Others chose to serve as an example in a less direct way. Because the life they chose was too extreme, not their actions, but the motivation behind their actions was to be imitated.

In the Middle Ages, writers distinguished between *imitanda* (things that should be imitated) and *admiranda* (things that should be wondered at) (see Kieckhefer 1984, pp. 12–14; Bynum 1987, pp. 336–37, n. 82). These elements could, and usually were, present simultaneously in the same saints. What exactly was to be wondered at and what to serve as a model was open to debate; both the saints and their audience had views as to which was which. However, the elements in the saints' lives that fell under the category of admirable were to serve more as demonstrations of God's power, while the elements that fell under the other category were seen as lived moral lessons.

On the whole, medieval female saints tended to belong more to the admirable than to the imitable pole of the spectrum. Women were not allowed to assume pastoral duties as men could, so the type of evangelical model that began in the twelfth century to be adopted by men was rarely available to them. St. Clare, for example, shared Francis's evangelical ideals, but though he originally dressed her in the Minor's habit, he soon confined her within the

11. Ambrose of Milan, *De apologia prophetae David ad Theodosium Augustum* 2.7. (*PL*: 854).

convent of San Damiano. In a convent, a woman's audience was limited. The highly structured life prevented innovation in action and tended to direct women toward a less action-oriented spirituality. The following discussion of saintly example should be seen as more pertinent, though not exclusive, to men.

The emphasis on the saints as models for action, as exemplars to be literally imitated, became more prominent in the twelfth century (see Bynum 1982, pp. 102–6; also 1979). The new concept of sainthood was of a spiritual struggle, often beginning with a conversion and continuing with a public effort within society.[12] The saint was seen as a model and an *agent provocateur*. The old saint inspired in his beholders admiration and confidence; the new saint the more intimate feelings of guilt and shame.

Francis was the "new" saint par excellence, and shame, as we have seen above, was a very important element in his rapport with his audience. By doing what was right, often by overdoing what was right, the saint could shame his audience into repentance. Francis was habitually stressing the contrast between his own and others' behavior to put his audience to shame.

Consider the following story. Once when he had just started to recover from the quartan fever, he remembered that he had eaten a little meat during his illness.[13] He summoned the people of Assisi to the piazza and ordered them to wait for him there. Then he went back to the church of San Rufino with Brother Peter Catanii. He took off his tunic, put a cord around his neck and ordered brother Peter to lead him naked before the people. Accompanied by weeping friars, he addressed the people assembled in the piazza:

"You believe me to be a holy man, and so do others who, on my example, leave the world and join the Order and way of life of the brothers. But I confess to God and to you that in this sickness of mine I ate meat and broth cooked with meat."[14] Nearly everyone began to weep with pity and compassion for him, especially because it was then very cold: it was wintertime and he was not over the quartan fever. They beat their breasts, accusing

12. Bynum argues that women were less likely to adopt the model of religious conversion than men (see Bynum 1984, pp. 105–24).

13. Celano's first *Life* (19.52) indicates that he had eaten chicken meat.

14. In Celano's *Vita prima* (see previous note) the absurdity of the accusation is stressed even more as Francis commands the brother leading him to announce: "here is the glutton who has grown fat on the meat of chickens."

themselves and saying: "If this holy man, whose way of life we know, accuses himself with such shame for the justifiable and manifest needs of his body, who, through excessive abstinence and austerity which he has used against his body from the beginning of his conversion to Christ, we see live in the flesh as if already dead, what shall we wretches do, who through our whole lives have lived and want to live after the wishes and desires of the flesh?[15]

Note how all of Francis's actions work to increase the impact of his lesson. He begins by creating heightened expectations in his audience. Francis does not simply appear in the piazza. First he summoned the Assisians and preached to them (we do not know the content of his sermon but it was probably related to what was to follow). Then, without a word of explanation, he ordered the crowd to wait for him and departed to prepare the main act of the drama. His reappearance, naked and trembling with a rope around his neck, must have shocked his spectators.

The sobbing brothers and the facial expression of Peter Catanii all told the audience that something important was forthcoming. Then came the lesson itself—a verbal gloss on the symbolic gesture the audience was already witnessing. Francis started by reminding the listeners who he is—he is a man considered a saint. By his example (*meo exemplo*), he had moved people to the way of salvation. The situation, as his audience could not fail to realize, is paradoxical. Francis, a religious leader and a saint, is led as a common criminal in the traditional ritual of degradation. Now comes a moment of great tension, for Francis is about to explain this paradox to his audience. "I confess to God and to you," he declared, "that in this sickness of mine I ate meat and broth cooked with meat." This is the key utterance in the whole drama. Francis prepared the way by beginning his confession with the mitigating circumstances ("in this sickness of mine"). Now that he revealed his "sin," it was immediately recognized as trivial to the point of absurdity.

The audience realized that there was no real need for penance here. His nakedness, the rope, the cold weather, the sobbing friars all fell into place. But they fell into the wrong place. If anyone deserved to stand there with a rope around his neck, it was they, not

---

15. Brooke, *Scripta Leonis* 39, pp. 158–59. I revised Brooke's translation in a number of places.

Francis. Francis shamed them while setting himself apart. A man in whose eyes such a trifle is a sin great enough to justify public humiliation must be a saint. The performance calls upon the viewers to follow the teacher, but at the same time manifests the enormous gap that still separates them.[16]

The element that dominates Francis's concept of example-setting is his literalism (see Bynum 1982, pp. 105–6). When Francis gave his inspired example, he expected it to be followed to the letter, at least by his brethren. Francis did not believe in interpretations and glosses. Christ's words and actions were clear, and so were his. It was enough to watch him carefully to know exactly what to do. In his testament Francis forbade his brothers "to interpret the Rule or these words [the testament], saying: 'This is what they mean.' But just as the Lord inspired me to speak and write the Rule and these words simply and clearly (*simpliciter et pure*), so you too must understand them simply and without gloss (*sine glossa*) and observe them with holy labor (*sancta operatio*) to the end."[17]

Francis's literalism stemmed not only from his belief in the univocity of the divine message—a belief that only a century earlier was condemned as heretical (Wakefield and Evans 1969, p. 133)—but from his conviction that inspired acts and words can be seized directly and intuitively, without the need to incorporate them into a comprehensive, consistent system (De Beer 1963, p. 158). Each act could be imitated faithfully and fully without concern for its compatibility with other acts (a concern that the gloss—"this is what they mean"—responds to).

There is a revealing story in one of Bonaventure's letters. A copy of the New Testament once came into Francis's hands. As there was only one copy and many friars, he divided the volume into separate sheets and gave each friar a portion (Bonaventure 1898, 8:334). This act expresses a belief that each portion is meaningful in itself and that it is not necessary to have the whole for a correct understanding of the parts. If something is sacred, then surely it contains

---

16. On the power of religious drama to provoke strong emotional reactions among the viewers see William A. Christian Jr. (1982).

17. *Testamentum S. Francisci* 4, in Kajetan Esser (1976, p. 444). Cf. the story of the confrontation between Francis and the ministers. Christ says to Francis and the ministers: "Volo quod Regula sic observetur ad litteram, ad litteram, ad litteram, et sine glossa, et sine glossa, et sine glossa" (Brooke, *Scripta Leonis,* 113, p. 286).

no contradictions and would cause no difficulties for those who approach it with the right spirit.

Francis represents the culmination of a new spiritual and social trend. From the twelfth century on, there was a feeling that the Gospel and the *Lives* of the saints could and should be copied literally. The story of St. Alexis, for example, was probably told many times in medieval cities and taken, as it was meant to be taken, as hagiographical romance. It was to be admired and imitated in spirit, not in the letter. But when Waldo (or Valdo) decided to renounce his goods and imitate Alexis and Christ, he acted on an urge to respond directly to the saintly example. Francis likewise seizes a text, or an event, and without worrying about its relative value or meaning vis-à-vis other texts, declares it to be *the* message, at least for a while. He then carries it out with abandon to the extreme.

Francis expected from his followers literal and uncritical imitation. There is a story in the friends' account concerning one Brother John.

He indeed was of such simplicity that he believed himself bound by every single thing St. Francis did. So when St. Francis stood in a church or in any remote place for prayer, he wanted to see and look at him so that he might copy all his gestures [*ut eius se gestibus omnibus conformaret*]. If St. Francis bent his knees or clasped his hands to heaven or spat or coughed he did the same. St. Francis with much delight [*multa letitia*] started to remonstrate with him about such acts of simplicity.[18] He replied: "Brother, I have promised to do all that you do. So I want to do all that you do." St. Francis could but marvel to see such purity and simplicity in him. For he began so to perfect himself in all virtues and good qualities that St. Francis and the other friars marveled greatly at his perfection. Not long after, he died in this holy perfection. Therefore St. Francis used with much delight [*cum multa letitia*], both inward and outward, to tell of his manner of life among the friars and used to call him, not brother John, but St. John.[19]

Of all his virtues, John's effort to imitate Francis was his most important claim to glory. We are not told in what else he excelled. It

18. Brooke translates "letitia" as "amusement," possibly because of the criticism that follows. However, Francis seems to be happy with John's intentions and only questions his excesses. The word "letitia" always means delight or joy. Cf. further down in the same passage.

19. Brooke, *Scripta Leonis* 19, pp. 122–23. I made some minor changes in Brooke's translation.

would seem as if Francis was at first critical of John's behavior, but it should be noted that his supposed criticism was made "with much delight." Francis was happy with John's spirit. He might have wondered only whether the friar was not imitating the insignificant and accidental together with the essential. But John's answer, that he simply refuses to use his own discretion to tell them apart, satisfied Francis. More than that, it convinced him that Brother John was a saint. For the famous Franciscan simplicity was exactly that: reacting directly and wholeheartedly to things *sine glossa*.[20] For Francis, imitation was the culmination in action of a state of mind. As we saw, Francis's official *Lives* attempted to move away from action to words and ideas.

Francis's idea of sainthood was totalistic. One was a saint in whatever one did. Unlike other religious leaders, Francis did not accept a separation between the role of saint and the role of leader. Bernard of Clairvaux could complain that the pressing demands of the church did not allow him to fulfill his duties as a monk.[21] But for Francis there was no part-time sainthood. There could be no contradiction between the ideal of sanctity (as it was expressed in his teachings to his friars) and the needs of the church. Hence his refusal to moderate his Rules to meet practical needs. If only the good would be done, without any thought for the (mundane) future, God would provide whatever his faithful might need.

As a model for others, Francis wanted to be, and was, constantly in the public eye. This meant that he could never relax the demands upon himself. He was always and everywhere to set an example of righteous behavior. Even when he was not seen, he had to behave according to the standards established by his public behavior. "I want to live before God in hermitages and other places," he says to his friends, "in the same way that men know and see me in public. For if they believe me to be a holy man [*sanctum hominem*] and I do not live the life which befits a holy man, I would be a hypocrite."[22] Erving Goffman noted that, "when a performer guides his private

20. See, for example, Brooke, *Scripta Leonis* 86, p. 236.
21. In his youth, Bernard was less compromising than he later became. William of St. Thierry writes that when the saint heard a monk snoring loudly or sleeping restlessly he would accuse him of sleeping "carnaliter et saeculariter" (*Viat prima S. Bernardi*, PL 185:239).
22. Brooke, *Scripta Leonis* 40, pp. 160–61.

activity in accordance with incorporated moral standards, he may associate these standards with a reference group of some kind, thus creating a non-present audience for his activity" (Goffman 1959, p. 81).

In a sense, this entails a contradiction. The saint is supposed to react directly to situations, instead he is always thinking in terms of how others would react to his performance and regulating it by their assumed reaction. Either the pastoral duty, the duty to edify, was stronger than personal, psychological considerations, or perhaps Francis was not aware of the difficulty. The fact remains that Francis consciously and conscientiously performed for the sake of others, especially after he had resigned his post as the minister general, when he could no longer use his institutional authority, but only his moral authority as a recognized saint.

The necessities which he denied his body in food and clothing so as to give his friars a good example . . . were so many and so great that we who were with him could not possibly recount them all. In this it was always St. Francis's chief and greatest care, especially after the brothers began to multiply and he himself gave up the office of superior, to teach the friars more by works than by words [*magis operibus quam verbis*] what they should do and what they should avoid.[23]

Francis turned his life into a continuous exemplum. All saints live a role to some extent, but the larger the saint's audience and the higher the saint's didactic aspirations, the more demanding this role becomes. Having to perform constantly is a terrible burden. Even the most intimate moments are marred by the perpetual knowledge that private acts would be divulged by eager admirers. Every act could teach a lesson and so every act was a struggle to teach it properly. This can be a painful process: "Do not the brothers think that a little indulgence is necessary to my body?" asks the aching Francis. "It is because I need to be a model and example [*formam et exemplum*] to all the brothers that I want to use and be content with wretchedly poor food and things that are not dainty."[24] It is touching to read how, shortly before his death, Francis asked his friend, the lady Jacoba, to indulge him with things

23. Ibid., 85, pp. 236–37; see also 38, p. 156.
24. Ibid., 2, pp. 90–91.

that were dainty. He asked her to bring him cloth the color of ashes for a shroud and some marzipan cookies.[25]

The death scene was a climactic moment for the saints. It was the most important "passage" (*transitus, migratio*) in their lives, and it deserved to be adorned by the proper rites of passage. We do not know if all saints succeeded in properly performing their last drama. The stereotypical description of the death scene in may *Lives* makes it hard to be certain (Lauwers 1988). Francis's, however, was an impressive, carefully directed death scene.

As his death was approaching, Francis was accosted by certain friar with these words:

Father, your life and behavior have been and are a light and a mirror, not only to your friars but to the universal Church of God, and your death will be the same. . . . You may know in truth, that unless God sends His medicine from heaven to your body, your sickness is incurable and you have little time to live, as the doctors have now said. I tell you this to comfort your spirit, that you may rejoice always in the Lord inwardly and outwardly, especially that your friars and others who come to visit you may find you rejoicing in the Lord, since they know and believe that you will shortly die, so that in the memory of those who see this and others who will hear of it after your death, your death may be inscribed, as your life and behavior have been for all.[26]

The friar's exhortation was a reminder to Francis that neither his life nor his death belong to him. His audience expected him to behave like a saint and it was his moral duty to do so. The saint had to renounce the private and the trivial (his private fears, his pains) for the sake of the exemplary and the ceremonious. Life and death, words and acts, need to be forcefully inscribed on the slippery surface of people's memory. The saint has an obligation to mold his or her life into mnemonic units, and the best way to achieve this effect was through ritual performance.

Francis's death scene shows that he heeded the friar's counsel. He conducted it as a sacred drama in which he was the director and the star. Feeling his death approaching, Francis asked the brothers to lay him naked on the ground. "I have done what was mine to

25. Ibid., 101, pp. 268–69.
26. Ibid., 100, pp. 264–65.

do," he said. "May Christ teach you what you are to do."[27] These words have the sound of last words, for Francis handed the responsibility for the friars over to God. But death was slow in coming. While Francis was waiting for the end, his guardian reminded him that the tunic the saint used to wear was given to him by the guardian. The saint had no ownership with regard to it, and the guardian now forbade him to give it to anyone.

As often happened, the spectators were not content with being passive. If they were imaginative, they could contribute their own symbolic act to the drama. The guardian's act was deemed worthy of recording and recollection, because it fit the spirit of the event as Francis orchestrated it. Actions and words that did not contribute to the dramatic effect, that had no poetic value, could be forgotten.

At some point it must have become apparent that Francis would take longer to die than expected. It can be deduced from the text that he was again dressed up, and a second stage in the drama began. This time the message was Francis's conformity with Christ. He blessed the brothers and asked that the description of the Last Supper be read to him from the Gospel of St. John. He asked bread to be brought in and distributed pieces thereof to the friars. Again the timing was not perfect, for it was not the right day of the week. Although it was not a Thursday, "he said to the friars that he thought it was a Thursday."[28]

With all the important rituals played out, he spent his last days in waiting. To the brothers, he said: "When you see that I am brought to my last moments, place me naked upon the ground just as you saw me the day before yesterday."[29] To the last moment, Francis was faithful to his duty to inscribe his death as he tried to inscribe his life, "in the memory of those who see this and others who will hear of it after [his] death."

As long as he lived, Francis could try to control people's interpretations of his ideas and instructions. For, though they did not explicitly challenge his ideas, people everywhere had their own way of understanding them. In his absence, all kinds of freedoms were

27. Thomas of Celano, *Vita secunda* 162. 214, p. 254.
28. Brooke, *Scripta Leonis* 117, pp. 290–91.
29. Thomas of Celano, *Vita secunda* 163.217, p. 255.

taken by his confreres.[30] But as long as he lived, Francis could rectify aberrations by pronouncing to the offenders the authoritative interpretation of his ideas. As long as he was around, he alone determined which interpretations were legitimate. If he insisted on something, it was hard to defy him to his face, but once he was no longer there, others decided what constituted a legitimate interpretation.

This situation, true for any living saint, was complicated by the discrepancy between Francis's huge success as a saint and his ineffectiveness as a leader of one of the fastest growing orders in the history of the church. Running an international organization takes administrative skills, which Francis did not have, and a willingness to compromise, which Francis refused to do. His concept of total faith in God, expressed as a refusal to "take thought for the morrow," was seen as irresponsible when it meant forbidding friars to carry provisions on long trips,[31] or sending groups of friars with no preparation at all to do missionary work in foreign countries.[32] Spontaneity can be dangerous when it means accepting postulants without any formal procedure and without a novitiate.

For a papacy that needed preachers and priests to serve as its spearhead in society, Francis's prohibiting the friars to appeal directly to the pope was folly (Moorman 1968, p. 50). It was one thing for the saint to be impractical; indeed, this was greatly admired in saints, for it was proof of their otherworldliness. But for a political leader (and the order was heavily involved in ecclesiastical politics), it was intolerable.

In 1220, six years before his death, Francis resigned the office of minister general of the order. In a dramatic gesture, he nominated his successor, Peter Catanii, and subjected himself to his authority.[33] The resignation was the result of frustrations and conflicts with the ministers. Francis lost his institutional power, but he did

30. See, for example, Jordan of Giano, *Chronica fratris Jordani* 13–15, edited by H. Boehmer (Paris, 1908), pp. 12–15.

31. See *Intentio regulae* 6, in L. Lemmens, ed., *Documenta antiqua Franciscana* (Quaracchi, 1901–2), p. 88.

32. See Brooke, *Scripta Leonis* 82, p. 232; Rosalind B. Brooke (1975, pp. 206–10.

33. Brooke, *Scripta Leonis* 105, p. 272.

not thereby lose his authority as a saint, as his relationship with his new superior, Peter Catanii, would demonstrate.

On one occasion, Francis criticized a certain brother for bringing a leper with him to the church of St. Mary of the Porziuncola. Immediately after he spoke he regretted his words. He turned to Brother Peter, who was then the minister general, and announced that he was going to tell Peter what penance he had chosen for himself so that Peter could confirm it "without any contradiction at all."

Brother Peter said to him: "Do as you please, brother." For Brother Peter had such veneration for St. Francis and was so fearful of him and so obedient to him, that he did not presume to change his orders [*obedientiam eius*] even though on that occasion and on many others he was distressed inwardly and outwardly.[34]

Francis does not speak like a man in somebody else's power. He practically orders Peter what to order him and expects this order to be carried out "without any contradiction at all." Their institutional relationship notwithstanding, Francis was a saint and Peter was not. Disobeying one's superior may in some extreme circumstances cost one his life, but disobeying a saint of Francis's caliber may cost one his salvation. Moreover, publicly humiliating the saint could not be done without either provoking great indignation or (which may be even worse) destroying the saint's prestige. Both alternatives were not particularly appealing. The saint could be convinced to compromise occasionally, but when he persisted, he usually had his way (see Moorman 1968, pp. 53–61).

A story attributed to Brother Leo relates how Francis refused the suggestion of Cardinal Ugolino's (the future Gregory IX) that he adopt an existing rule and insisted on writing his own. The cardinal made his proposal at a General Chapter in Assisi (probably in 1222). Francis led Ugolino to the assembled friars and spoke to them. The saint assured the brothers that he was acting on God's orders. God called him by the way of simplicity; he wanted Francis to be a new fool (*novellus pazzus*) in the world. Any knowledge, other than God's inspiration, would confound those who followed

34. Ibid., 22, pp. 126–27. I have revised Brooke's translation.

it. Such people would lose the right course and be punished by God. The cardinal said nothing and all the friars were afraid.[35]

There are two important elements in the story. First, Francis did not answer Ugolino directly; he addressed the simple friars, to whom high politics meant nothing, but to whom Francis meant a great deal. By so doing, he transformed a private conversation into a public exchange. Whereas it would be legitimate for the saint's intimates to argue with his private, "unofficial," persona, it would be highly inappropriate to challenge his public persona. Second, Francis emphasized the inspired, suprarational nature of his vision. If others call it irresponsible, he would be the first to agree with them. Indeed, he admits to being a fool in the world. But has not God "chosen the foolish things of the world to confound the wise" (1 Cor. 1:27)?[36]

So those who wished to make the saint's ideals more practical had no choice but to grit their teeth and wait. They did not have to wait long. Francis was only forty-five when he died in 1226. His remains were transferred four years later to the grandest, most sumptuous edifice in Assisi, the basilica of San Francesco. It was a symbolic demonstration that not even St. Francis could stop the glosses.[37] In the same year, the Bull *Quo elongati* was issued. In it Pope Gregory IX elegantly dismisses Francis's testament as a docu-

35. Brooke, *Scripta Leonis* 114, pp. 288–89. Chapters 111–16 in Brooke's *Scripta Leonis* precede the rest of the stories in the manuscript (see p. 36). They belong to a group of stories, not included in the friends' letter, probably written by Brother Leo around 1257 (see *Verba S. Francisci*, in L. Lemmens, *Documenta antiqua Franciscana*). For Francis's relationship with Ugolino, see Rosalind B. Brooke (1959, pp. 59–76).

36. On the political implications of a reputation of sanctity (in this case that of St. Bernard of Clairvaux) see, Robert I. Moore (1977, pp. 274–77).

37. Francis inspired a singular phenomenon in the history of Canon Law. Pope Nicholas III had imposed a ban on the glossing of his decree of 1279, *Exiit qui seminat* (*Liber Sextus* 5.12.3), ratifying the Franciscan Rule. Although the Bull is in itself an interpretation of the Rule, it shares with the Testament the wish to issue a final version that would be understood literally (see M. D. Lambert 1961, pp. 141–48). The ban was extended to Clement V's Exivi de paradiso (1312, *Constitutiones Clementinae* 5.11.1), which was a version of the previous decree. The prohibition was observed until 1322, when John XXII lifted it in his decree, Quia nonnumquam (*Extravagantes Johannis XXII* 14.2). On the political and legal implications of Exiit and Quia nonnumquam, see Brian Tierney (1972, pp. 97–99, 173).

ment with no binding power. The pope states that Francis had no legal authority to write such a document without the consent of the friars and the ministers. The pope then proceeded to interpret the Rule according to his own ideas.[38]

But the victory of the practical-minded was not as decisive as it looked. By constantly insisting on the heuristic nature of his actions, Francis tried to retain the status of a living saint after his death. His prohibition of nonliteral interpretations of his actions aimed at leaving those who survived him in the same situation they were in in relation to him during his life. The pope might have solved the legal complication that the testament posed, but the emotional complications were less easy to solve.

The feeling of the first generations of friars was that all of the founder's life was inspired. It was not necessary to distinguish the saintly from the nonsaintly in Francis's life, since it was saintly in its totality. We saw that Francis himself had a similar concept. The stigmata that appeared on the saint's body gave this notion a visible mark of divine approval. It must be remembered that this was the first time the phenomenon was recorded, and the impact it had on contemporaries was immense.[39] The stigmatization was the first thing that the minister general, Brother Elia, announced to the Franciscan communities together with the news of the saint's death. In the first decades after Francis's death, it was presented as a unique event, as the crowning glory of a life of *imitatio Christi* (Benz 1969, pp. 97–119).

Just two years after his death in 1226, Francis was canonized, more or less by acclamation. Although by that time the papacy was already conducting formal enquiries of applicants, there was no investigation of Francis's merits. Even the first *Life* of the saint was published after the canonization (Celano's *Vita prima* was published in 1229).

There was great demand for information about the saint from different sectors of the order. Celano's first *Life* was seen as insufficient, and just fifteen years later, in the general chapter of Genoa,

---

38. See *Bullarium Franciscanum* 56, edited by J. H. Sbaralea (Rome, 1759; repr. Assisi, 1983), p. 68.

39. The stigmatization occurred two years before Francis's death, but it became generally known only after his death.

the order called for more information. Thomas of Celano wrote his second *Life* in 1246. The greatest part of it—197 of 224 chapters—consists of isolated episodes from the life of St. Francis without a plot to connect them. It is an impressionistic tableau that reflects a belief in the value of all the saint's actions. In addition, Celano wrote an official collection of miracles (the *Tractatus de miraculis*, c. 1252–53). Within less than thirty years after the saint's death, the order produced no fewer than three official biographical works. There were also numerous unofficial biographies.[40]

When Bonaventure became minister general of the Franciscan Order in 1257, the order was already torn by a great controversy over the correct interpretation of the saint's ideal. For as institutions tend to do, the order was changing, and its temporal success was seen by some as endangering its spiritual calling. There was a feeling in certain circles that the saint's successors in the leadership of the order had no authority to reinterpret or modify the Franciscan way of life. The only authority for them was, Gregory IX's *Quo elongati* notwithstanding, Francis himself, of whom a great deal was already known by then, and who, in his own words, could be understood without any gloss.

Bonaventure understood that the only way to unfasten the grip of Francis's dead hand was to offer an alternative that would transform Francis's history into a new, less action-oriented, and less radical message. (We saw at the beginning of this chapter something of the technique by which he sought to achieve this goal.) At the same time, it was necessary to destroy the other authentic records of the saint's life. As long as they were there, they would always be more authoritative than his, since they were earlier and produced by eyewitnesses. In 1263 Bonaventure published his *Legenda maior*. In 1266 the general chapter of Paris ordered the destruction of all earlier biographies.

The decree failed. Most copies of earlier *Lives* were destroyed, but this was not enough to stop the controversy. It failed because there was an oral tradition and because there was an opposition in the order that was willing to record those stories and expected the listeners or the readers to feel bound by them. For centuries to

40. For a review of early Franciscan biographies, see Stanislao da Campagnola (1982, pp. 36–48).

come, Franciscans kept debating among themselves what exactly the founder did and what the meaning of his authoritative example was. The Observantines and the Capuchins, as well as numerous smaller groups and reform movements, tried to offer not just a purer interpretation of the Franciscan ideal, but a more faithful imitation of its founder.

Francis is an extreme example of the enormous power the successful saint can wield even over his posterity. At first, disobeying the saint might be easy, but the greater his prestige, the more difficult it becomes. Francis's success was a great asset to his order, but it also made it difficult to contradict him. By combining his prestige with an insistence on literal imitation and a delegitimation of his successors' authority to reinterpret his actions, Francis made it impossible to accomplish smoothly the necessary metamorphosis of living to dead saint—a process that consisted of forgetting the saint of reality and recreating him in his successors' image.

VII

THE BLIND SEE AND THE
LAME WALK

"Go and tell John the things which you hear and see: 'The blind receive their sight and the lame walk; the lepers are cleansed and the deaf hear; the dead are raised up and the poor have the gospel preached to them.'" —Matt. 11:4–5

THE aspirant saint made her claim known to others by visible signs: increased piety, ecstatic states, a change of dress and of everyday conduct, and almost always some form of self-mortification: in short, whatever caused the candidate to be perceived as more religious than other people in her condition.[1] The precise content of the external manifestations of a saintly claim depended on a wide variety of cultural and social expectations. What one community considered piety another considered hysteria; what was extraordinary for a king might be a monk's everyday duty. The saint's appearance in the public arena took place when certain public acts presented her to others as a saint or as a false claimant to the honor.

The initiative could be taken by the candidate himself—reenacting Francis's public ritual of self-degradation, for example— or by others assuming the role of announcers or accusers. When members of the community openly identified themselves as devotees or accused a candidate of impersonating holiness, it was a sign that he or she had begun to be seen within the context of what that community understood as sainthood. What happened when a community refused to accept the candidate's claim? What happened when the candidate refused to accept the role assigned to him by his "announcers"? What was the role of miracles in marking the beginning of a saintly career and what was the nature of the miraculous dynamic? These are the themes of this chapter.

The fate of Margery Kempe (1373–1439) demonstrates the

---

1. On the symbolic importance of dress, see Dyan H. Elliott (1989, pp. 326–31.

community's power to determine what constitutes a legitimate claim to sainthood and the variety of responses to the same phenomena. Margery Kempe is a rare instance of an unsuccessful aspirant to sainthood about whom we know a great deal. Hagiographical literature is by nature triumphalist; it tells success stories. The dropouts appear only briefly, often just to provide a contrast with their betters or to be denounced as heretics, impostors, lunatics, or fools. Margery, however, saw to it that her own version of things was recorded.

Margery relates in her book the hostility her loud crying in church provoked in Lynn. She reports that the first incident of loud crying occurred during her pilgrimage to the Holy Land, on a visit to the place of the crucifixion.She experienced a series of similar bursts of tears at other sites of pilgrimage. Her tears and general conduct must have impressed people in the Holy Land. She recounts that the friar who served as her group's guide asked one of her companions "if she were the woman of England whom they had heard said spoke with God."

This for Margery was a confirmation of the impact she was making, for she says that "when this came to her knowledge, she knew well that it was the truth that our Lord said to her, ere she went out of England—'Daughter, I will make all the world to wonder at thee, and many a man and many a woman shall speak of Me for the love of thee, and worship Me in thee.'"[2]

"The friars of the Temple made her great cheer and gave her many great relics, desiring that she would dwell still among them if she would, for the faith they had in her."[3] In fact, everyone in the Holy Land, save her own countrymen, was well disposed toward her. As for her English traveling companions, though they did not, perhaps, show her any special signs of respect, they were also not hostile toward her.

Back in England things were very different. Margery's crying and the white robes which she began to wear after her experience in the East were not well taken. "Many said that there was never a saint in heaven who cried as she did, wherefore they would con-

2. *The Book of Margery Kempe: A Modern Version,* edited by W. Butler-Bowdon (London, 1940), p. 114.
3. Ibid., p. 116.

clude that she had a devil within her which caused her that crying; and so they said plainly, and much more evil."[4] Worst of all, a friar (Margery does not identify him) repeatedly preached against her crying in his church so that eventually even her friends turned against her.[5]

But the people of Lynn were wrong. There was nothing unusual about Margery's crying. Similar behavior can be found in many earlier *Lives*. Its reported effect on other audiences, furthermore, was not unlike the effect it had on the friars in the Holy Land. Margaret of Cortona, lived about a hundred years earlier in Italy. One Sunday, while her confessor and biographer, Fra Giunta, was preaching in the church of the Franciscans, Margaret began to scream in front of all present, asking Giunta where the Lord crucified was and where he had hidden her Master. "Before such uncontrollable crying," writes Giunta, "all the men and women present began crying with devout fervor."[6]

The priest to whom Margery dictated her book was among those who turned away from her under the influence of the friar's preaching. He renewed his faith in Margery when he realized that there were canonical precedents to her behavior. He discovered episodes of unrestrained crying in the *Lives* of Marie d'Ognies and Elizabeth of Hungary, for example. As I showed in chapter 2, accepted saints could be used to vindicate a candidate whose conduct was in question. The priest apparently only became aware of this later, as there is no indication that he or Margery tried to use the saints' precedents as a defense.

What was really at stake was not a form of behavior that a particular audience found foreign and unsavory. The question was one of a claim to sainthood—made not in words, but explicit enough nonetheless. Some of Margery's supporters were saying that her crying was a special grace of God. The friar who condemned her crying was willing to reach a settlement with her: if she would ad-

---

4. Ibid., p. 156.

5. Dame Julian of Norwich was an exception (see Atkinson 1983, p. 64).

6. Giunta Bevegnati, *Vita Margaritae de Cortona* 87, *AA.SS.*, 22 Feb., pp. 320–21. In *Holy Anorexia*, Rudolph Bell offers an insightful description of how, as times change, the same set of characteristics—prolonged fasting in this case—once thought to prove sainthood can become a source of doubt and suspicion (1985, pp. 151–79).

mit that her crying was the result of cardiac ailment, or some other sickness, "he would have compassion on her, and stir the people to pray for her, and, on this condition, he would have patience with her and suffer her to cry enough, so that she could say it was a natural sickness."[7] In other words, the friar was willing to free Margery of the suspicion of demonic possession and abate the public hostility toward her, if she agreed to renounce her claim for intimacy with the divine.

Margery's crying was recognized by the people of Lynn as a claim to personal sainthood, but it was not accepted as a legitimate expression of such a claim. This does not mean that by choosing an unfamiliar expression of piety a person necessarily aroused a hostile reaction. A different person might have been accepted by the people of Lynn in spite of her crying, or the crying might have been accepted as legitimate and edifying. There were no simple rules of thumb for acquiring a saintly reputation. The relationship between the saint's behavior and the community's expectations was dialectical. If a person was a saint, then everything he or she did was saintly. If that person was not a saint then everything he or she did that resembled saintly behavior was deemed presumptuous and worthless. Margery was not a saint in the eyes of her audience.

We will never know what exactly convinced a community to accept one person as a saint, but deny another's claim, even though, on paper at least, their claims look equally strong. Why were the religious innovations of one person embraced enthusiastically by an audience, while another's were condemned? It was not just what the candidates said and did, but also how they did it that determined their communities' reactions to them. Our sources cannot convey the power of one person's performance and the weaknesses of another's. People saying the same words or making similar gestures can have a very different effect on us.

When a candidate's sainthood was accepted, it provoked an immediate impulse to make use of it. The saint was one of God's favorites. Such status implied power of the highest sort. In a world where most people felt both physically and spiritually powerless, the powerful drew a following that sought to enter a patron-client relationship with them. It was crucial to choose the right patron.

7. Ibid., p. 227.

There were good people in any community, there were even some who were exceedingly pious and ascetic. Their prospects of finding grace in the eyes of God were naturally better than those of the common man, but most of them were not sufficiently endowed with divine grace to enable them to help others. Only a handful possessed such powers and they became the focus of their communities' supernatural aspirations.

Though the possibility of a saint without miracles was not excluded, there was a general agreement in the Middle Ages that sainthood and the miraculous were closely linked. The saint who enjoyed public recognition was expected to work at least some miracles. Jesus responded to the Baptist's query, "Are You the Coming One, or do we look for another?" with the recounting of the visible effects of his power, cited at the beginning of this chapter. A person's miracles were the most decisive response to the skeptics.

The living saint's miracles did not have to be such that would be acceptable to the trained canonist examining a canonization dossier. One of the main functions of the curial examination was to separate the proved miracles that could be assumed to have really happened from the many that were mere hearsay. But hearsay and rumor were exactly the things that made the saint's reputation. "The point," as Brian Stock has suggested, "is not whether the miracle 'took place' but that people whose social affiliations can be the objects of empirical study explained their behavior in terms of it" (Stock 1976–77, p. 187). When a person began to be seen as a legitimate explanation for various beneficial effects in people's lives, it was an indication that his or her holiness had passed from the private to the public domain.

Miracles are not empirical events. Labeling an event miraculous places it within a sociolinguistic context. It is an act of classification, not description. In most cases, even in a society that does not question the reality of miracles, this label is debatable. While there can be agreement on what actually took place, there can be other explanations to it. Even if no natural explanation is available, an acceptance of the miraculous explanation is not automatic. The skeptic can admit his inability to explain the event (a rare occurrence), but argue nevertheless that it is not a miracle. More important, however, the audience can accept the fact of the miracle, but refuse to link it to the alleged saint, choosing instead to see his involvement as accidental. Finally, both the miracle and the miracle-worker can be accepted, but the latter can be accused of being an instrument of the devil rather than of God. In such a situation—as happened, for example, to Joan of Arc—the miraculous events would not only not corroborate the person's claim to sanctity, but serve as evidence against it.[8]

The dependence of the saint on his audience began before the debate on the true nature of events claimed to be miraculous. The saint's success, his very status as an intercessor depended on his services being sought out. If people refused to engage the saint in saintly situations, his ability to function as a saint was severely limited. The client's faith in the saint's ability to work miracles precedes and is a necessary condition of his actual performance. As Claude Lévi-Strauss once noted in relation to shamans: "Quaselid [a Kwakiutl shaman] did not become a great shaman because he cured his patients; he cured his patients because he had become a great shaman." The miraculous dynamic revolves around the relationship between a "specific category of individuals and specific expectations of the group" (Lévi–Strauss 1967, pp. 36–37).

When directly approached, the saint was usually expected to give his consent. He or she was requested to perform certain ritual acts, usually very simple: laying on hands, uttering a blessing, making the sign of the cross. At other occasions, however, the saint was identified as the benefactor without his or her concurrence. A fourteenth-century fragment describes a meeting between Louis IX and Bertold of Ratisbon. Louis reported to Bertold one of the latter's miracle stories: a peasant who was forbidden by his master to hear Bertold's sermon, nevertheless heard every word of it from a distance of miles. "Good sir," exclaimed Bertold, "do not believe, nor have faith in such stories that are told about me as if they were miracles."[9] Note that the saint has to be informed about his own

8. For a discussion of the verification of visions, see William A. Christian, Jr. (1981, pp. 188–203). In this section, Christian discusses particularly the case of Joan of Arc. My own impression is that whatever the formal criteria for verification of visions, they could always be manipulated. Joan's main problem was not that she lacked the appropriate proofs for the authenticity and divine origin of her voices; it was that she was anti-English. A different tribunal, using the same criteria, could come up with the opposite verdict.

9. See *Analecta Franciscana* 1 (1885), Appendix, p. 417. The miracle is related without comment in Salimbene's chronicle (Salimbene de Adam 1966, 2:813).

doings. Bertold's reaction reflects a discomfort about his inability to control his fame. As we have seen in earlier chapters, even an explicit denial was often ineffective.

There was an entire category of involuntary miracles related to the saints' bodies. The biblical prototype for this is Christ's healing of the woman with the issue of blood (Mark 5:25–34). Christ only noticed the miracle when he sensed that power had gone out of him. He did not know who the beneficiary of his power had been and had to inquire who had touched him. The saints' sacred bodies produced miracles independently of their will. Although the saints could try to deny access to their bodies, they could not control their influence once contacted.

The saints' devotees were not restricted merely to reporting the saints' miracles to others. They often played the role of the chorus in the Greek drama. They offered explanations and urged the main characters into action. Consider the following incident related in a deposition in Clare of Montefalco's process of canonization. When Clare died in 1308, the nuns performed an autopsy on her body and discovered in her heart a tiny crucifix made out of flesh and nerves and all the instruments of the Passion. A resident of Montefalco, Symon ser Gili, having been shown the heart, "started laughing and jeering, and did not display the appropriate devotion to the things that were shown to him." All of a sudden, his nose started bleeding. A relatively minor event, but not so for Symon's friends who immediately reacted to the situation. "Wicked man," they said to him, "don't you see the miracle God has made in you for the sake of this saint? How can you not have faith in her, and doubt her sanctity and these things [the miraculous instruments]? He then repented and began to believe."[10]

Symon's first reaction is that of a bystander. He had not as yet accepted the role of participant. He looked at the saint's heart and, not surprisingly, could not see the objects that were supposed to be in it. The event that followed (the nosebleed) was used by the friends to make Symon part of the miraculous dynamics. They interpreted for him the bleeding of his nose and suggested a resolu-

10. Enrico Menestò, ed., *Il processo di canonizzazione di Chiara da Montefalco,* in Quaderni del "Centro per il Collegamento degli Studi Medievali e Umanistici nell' Università di Perugia" 14 (Todi, 1984), p. 461. See also pp. 459, 485.

tion to his plight (appeal to the saint). At the same time, they insinuated that the problem was not trivial and that the future consequences of his skepticism might be much more serious than a bleeding nose.

Symon invoked the saint, and the bleeding stopped. He then (if not already at the moment of the invocation) saw what he had not seen before. The organ itself had not changed, it was still as ambiguous as it had been when he had first seen it. But, as Symon's attitude had changed from a bystander to a client of the saint, the meaning of the shapes in Clare's heart had now become clear to him.[11] It is interesting to compare a photograph of the actual heart and a picture of it made in the seventeenth century.[12] It takes a great deal of creative imagination to see the crucifix and the instruments in the photograph, but the drawing makes them as clear as the painter chose to see them.

A living saint was not just the absent third in the miraculous situation; he or she was often an important player in it. When the saint was reluctant to play along, the sympathizers could compensate for his or her inactivity to some extent, but there was a limit to what they could do. The case of Brother Nicholas of Montefeltro demonstrates both the importance of the sympathizers' role and its limitations.

Brother Nicholas was, according to Salimbene, a truly humble man who refused to consider himself of any consequence, and always rushed to serve the other friars in the community. One day a certain Bolognese lady, Marchesina, dreamed that if Brother Nicholas would make the sign of the cross over her son (who was covered with ulcers) he would be healed. The woman, who was a devoted friend of the Franciscans, approached the Guardian and requested that Brother Nicholas help her son in the specified way.

The Guardian assembled all the convent's priests and told them that, as it was not likely that Nicholas would cooperate in anything that might put him in the role of a saint, they would have to use a ruse. The friars would pretend that the lady asked that all the priests

11. See Susan F. Harding (1987), where she deals with the switch from outsider/observer to convert/participant status. It is an insightful and moving account of the process from the point of view of one who had experienced it herself (at least momentarily).

12. Menestò, ed., *Il processo*, pp. clxx–clxxii.

of the house sign her son. The Guardian would comply first, and then they would ask Brother Nicholas to do the same. This was done as planned. At first, Nicholas tried to refuse, protesting that he was totally unworthy of such an act, but when the Guardian ordered him to obey, he did, and the son immediately regained his health.[13]

Although all the elements necessary for launching a saintly career were there—popular and peer faith in the candidate's powers, general willingness to help him work miracles, and a successful public miracle—a career did not develop. Salimbene mentions two more miracles he ascribes to Brother Nicholas, but they are both private and the role of the friar in them is ambiguous. After Nicholas's death, no miracles occurred on his grave, a favor he had expressly asked of God.[14]

We do not know why the Lady Marchesina chose, of all people, to believe in Nicholas's power. He neither believed in it himself, nor did the people closest to him show special signs of devotion to him. The important thing was that when Marchesina singled him out, he seemed a reasonable candidate to his immediate circle. We have seen in chapter 2 that violence was necessary to convince the Dominicans of Forlì to accept Brother Marcolinus's miracles. Had Marchesina picked someone unacceptable to the community, she would probably have encountered opposition from the friars and perhaps been offered a worthier candidate. As it was, Nicholas was acceptable. The community was even willing to take full responsibility for his first performance.

But the potential saint's friends could only go so far without his or her collaboration. Living saints were expected to be active participants in at least some of their own miracles. Unless he began to take a more active role (agree to bless patients, touch them, and so on), there could not be much chance of a saintly career. If the saint did accept this role (or even aspired to it in the first place), past successes were used as proof and as means of advertising the saint.

One should not get the impression from the incidents I have cited that whenever the situation called for a miracle, it came about, though the authors of saints' *Lives* and almost all witnesses in cano-

13. Salimbene de Adam, *Cronica* (1966, 2:809–11).
14. Ibid., p. 810.

nization procedures would like us to think that it was so. Nor were all observers of a potentially miraculous event simply waiting to be convinced by some trifle. Many waited in vain for a sign, or dismissed it even when it came. Those who remained unconvinced, who chose to remain outsiders in certain or in all situations rarely stepped forward to tell their story. But they must not be assumed not to have existed.

There are certain beasts [writes Jacques de Vitry], not having the spirit of God in them, wise in their own eyes, who refuse to perceive anything but that which can be proved by human reason. Whatever they do not understand, they ridicule and despise. . . . They despise the spiritual as insane and ignorant and consider the prophecies and the revelations of the saints as hallucinations and the delusions of dreams.[15]

The skeptics laughed and went away. But their laughter can be heard behind the vigorous attempts of the serious to prove it misplaced. It is the silent other side of the hagiographer's triumphalist approach to the miraculous and the holy.

For some all saints were fallible; for most others, at least some saints were.What happened when a saint failed to perform? To establish failure in the miraculous sphere, there had to be a clear indication that the saint attempted to perform a miracle. A living saint could establish such a link between himself and the supplicant in an unequivocal way. In contrast, the advocates of the dead saint could always save their saint from a suspicion of weakness. Because the connection between the dead saint and the supplicant was established by the supplicant alone, the absence of results could be interpreted as a refusal by the saint to enter the contractual relationship offered by the supplicant. The only way one could know for sure that the saint consented to the supplicant's plea was if he or she granted his wish. But if the living saint promised to perform a healing and the patient did not recover, or made a prediction that did not come true, the saint could be seen as incompetent.

---

15. See Jacques de Vitry, *Vita Mariae Oigniacensis, AA.SS.,* 23 Jun., p. 549: "Sunt enim quidam animales, spiritum Dei non habentes, apud semetipsos prudentes, qui nihil volunt percipere, nisi quod humana ratione possunt convincere: quaecumque vero non intelligunt, derident et despiciunt . . . quia spirituales quosque, quasi insanos vel idiotas despiciunt; et prophetias sive sanctorum revelationes, tanquam phantasmata et somniorum illusiones reputant."

An incompetent saint was an embarrassment to his followers. Failure was laughable. It made the saint look presumptuous in attempting what was beyond his powers, or, worse, made it look as though God had forsaken him. To protect themselves from the embarrassment of failure, saints were careful to take the first safety measure of saintly performance—they were vague about details so that their performance could be saved. Predictions remained unspecific and healings were tied to the patient's faith, or the will of God, or the fulfillment of some other additional term (Davis 1980, pp. 223–38). Raymond of Capua said he had "never heard her [Catherine of Siena], in private or in public, fix a set time for the coming to pass of any future event which she ever predicted."[16] In the *Life* of Margaret of Cortona, we are told that God ordered the saint to disclose her prophecies to her Franciscan confessors. The latter, however, would only publicize those prophecies that came true *(non pandant quousque viderint adimpleta quae dicis [Margarita])*.[17]

A lack of discretion on the part of the saint could be very upsetting for his followers. When, in the beginning of his career, St. Bernard of Clairvaux promised a cure without a face-saving clause, his brother and uncle were frightened and troubled. They secretly reproached him for such an incautious promise and his brother accused him of presumption.[18] What Bernard should have made clear was that the success of the miracle depended on the patient's faith. When on another occasion, he promised a miracle, again without adding the precautionary formula, the local bishop added it for him.[19]

But there were times when the saint insisted on speaking clearly. Bernard in the two cases just mentioned refused to use the face-saving mechanisms. Catherine, too, was apparently less vague about the coming crusade she was promising than Raymond wished her to be. If the saint succeeded, the impression his or her success left was very great, but success did not always follow.

16. Raymond of Capua, *Vita S. Catharinae Senensis* 2.15, *AA.SS.,* 30 Apr., p. 943.

17. Giunta Bevegnati, *vita Margaritae de Cortona* 35, *AA.SS.,* 22 Feb., p. 310.

18. William of St. Thierry, *Vita prima S. Bernardi* 1.9, *PL* 185:1080–81.

19. Ibid., p. 312.

There were three accounts of failures attributed to Bernard in Walter Map's *De nugis curialium*. Map's book is very different from the hagiographical works that are the main source of information in this book. Although Map does not provide us with firsthand information about a saint, he does document a saint's reputation.

Map attributes the first story he relates to John Planeta, a clerk of Thomas Becket who told it in the presence of the archbishop and two Cistercian abbots. John, professing to tell a miracle of Bernard, related how he was present when a demoniac was brought to the saint in Montpellier. The patient was presented to Bernard bound. The saint commanded the demon to depart and then ordered the patient released. As soon as he was unbound, the demoniac began to throw stones at Bernard, chasing the saint through the streets until he was apprehended. "Those who were present," John noted sarcastically, "said it was very memorable *(dignum memoria)*, because the madman was gentle and kind to everyone, and only harmful to hypocrites; and it still seems to me that it was a punishment for presumptuousness."[20]

This story is followed by two stories of unsuccessful resurrection attempts. The first was related by a Cistercian abbot who witnessed it with his own eyes, according to Map. Two Cistercian abbots were praising Bernard's miracles in the presence of Gilbert Foliot (bishop of London, d. 1187) when one of them said he had once seen how the grace of miracles had failed Bernard. Bernard consented to heal the son of a man living on the borders of Burgundy. The saint with his entourage entered the house and found the boy dead. He asked everyone to leave, threw himself on the boy, prayed and rose up again, all in vain; the boy remained dead. This occasioned indecent insinuations by Map about monks who throw themselves on young boys. The abbots were humiliated and many people left the room to have a good laugh.

The last episode concerns "Walter" (probably Count William II), of Nevers. Map does not identify his source, but claims that the incident was commonly known *(publicatum est)*. He writes that Bernard came to visit Walter's tomb in the Chartreuse. The saint lay long upon it in prayer and finally cried out in a loud voice:

20. Walter Map (1983, 1.24, pp. 78–81). My translation is based on James's.

"'Walter, come forth!' But Walter, not hearing the voice of Jesus, had not the ears of Lazarus, and did not come."[21]

Map tells all three stories in an ironical mood. Planeta even parodies the hagiographical use of the label *dignus memoria* for his irreverent story. The theme of the stories is humiliation as punishment for presumption. Nobody expected every saint to raise the dead. It is not Bernard's inability to accomplish such a feat that is criticized, but his presumption in undertaking it.

The first and last episodes seem to me almost certainly fictitious; not because there were not demoniacs which Bernard failed to cure, or because he could raise the dead whenever he wished, but because the stories are unrealistic. It is strange that a demoniac who was gentle and kind to everyone would be brought bound to the saint. It is also highly unlikely that the saint's attendants would allow him to be chased through the streets by a madman with a disliking for hypocrites. As for the third episode, not even Bernard would have attempted to resurrect a person dead and buried for some time.

Map writes that Planeta's story was told after Cistercian abbots had made much of their leader's miraculous powers. Map was clearly in agreement with Planeta in feeling outraged by the Cistercians' boasts. The episodes he recounts criticize the arrogant Cistercians by sticking a cynical needle into their saintly balloon. The saint's miraculous powers were used by his admirers as confirmation of the validity of the saint's activity in general. As such, they had political implications that went beyond an objective examination of their authenticity. One was expected to accept and add to the miracles of "our" saints and cast aspersions on the saints of the opposition—or competition, as the case may be.

The second story, however, is different. We saw earlier in this chapter that Bernard could be overconfident in his miraculous abilities. On one occasion, he promised a cure, not only without using any precautionary formulas, but explicitly denying his dependence on the patient's faith.[22] It is not impossible that the same Bernard tried to resurrect a boy who had just died. Such deaths were often

21. Ibid., pp. 80–81.
22. William of St. Thierry, *Vita prima S. Bernardi, PL* 185:384.

161

illusory and the deceased could sometimes "rise from the dead." What is more interesting is the fact that it was told by a Cistercian abbot. The story itself was serious. Only Map's indecent comment turned it into a farce.

Why would a Cistercian abbot report a failure of his own hero? The abbot's story should be seen against the background of the rest of the circumstances in which it was told. The two Cistercian abbots spent much of the evening telling miracle stories that established beyond any doubt (at least in their mind) Bernard's miraculous powers. The abbot's account of an unsuccessful miracle was intended to establish his reliability as an impartial witness who relates the good and the bad. Saints who had very few miracles could not afford to fail, but Bernard could. The abbot's mistake lay in his assumption that he had a friendly audience. Map was skeptical about Bernard and unsympathetic toward his politics. If he could not do much about the miracle stories without directly challenging the abbots' authority, he was only too quick to widen the small rhetorical hole that the abbot opened for him with his story of failure.

In most cases neither success nor failure were empirically unequivocal. What mattered was the willingness of those not present at the scene of action to believe the reports of others. However, after a certain point rumors feed upon themselves and have an effect of their own. Reports of the saint's failure created an anxiety, a nervous tendency in his audience to detach itself from the saint. People were less likely to attribute miracles to a questionable saint, preferring to turn to a safer address. It was crucial for the saint's career that failures, real or imaginary, be followed by a quick success.[23] A saintly reputation could be as transient as the hopes and the fears of the people who created it.

23. After the fiasco of the second crusade, Bernard, asked to cure a boy of blindness, declared that if God was indeed his inspiration, the boy would be cured (*Vita prima S. Bernardi* 3.4, *PL* 185:1121). Bernard was trying to show that his failure did not prove that he was deserted by God—that it was in fact no failure of his at all.

VIII
EPILOGUE

The saints and their communities needed each other. The men and women who played the demanding role of saints needed the attention, the reassurance, and the support of their audiences. For the saints' followers, the saints provided a measure of confidence in an uncertain world. The devotees' ascription of ever more fantastic powers to the saints, often beyond what the saints would have claimed for themselves, reveals a deep strain of anxiety, a desperate wish to believe in happy endings to the terrible stories of their lives. The all-powerful saint, made up by the people, reassured them that in the end, when all else failed, as it often had, there was still hope. The saints' reputation was greater than any one of them. It focused the hopes and fears of an entire society.

My concern in this work has been with the saints as they were seen by others. I focused on the encounter of saint and society in the public domain. The saints' ideals and aspirations were discussed only when they were part of the social consideration of their role. It was necessary to isolate the saintly situations from the nonsaintly elements of the saints' lives. But the men and women whose performances I have studied were more than their public image. They were human beings: often frightened, often in pain, sometimes heroic, at other times petty and vindictive. "Holy folk," said the steward of the archbishop of York to Margery Kempe, "should not laugh."[1] But holy folk do laugh, and cry, and do many other things that need to be suppressed in public.

The saints' rapport with their followers was more than a client-patron, performer-impresario relationship. There is a moving passage in the *Life* of Beatrice of Nazareth: a nun, observing Beatrice sitting in a state of trance, mistook it for sleep and kept pulling at her garment until she interrupted the saint's rapture. Beatrice was heartbroken for being torn away from the heavenly bliss she had

1. Margery Kempe, *The Book of Margery Kempe* 54, p. 135.

enjoyed. She sat herself on the floor and cried bitterly. The nun heard Beatrice crying; she turned back to her, thinking that she suffered some sudden bodily pain. She sat beside her on the floor, took the saint's head to her bosom, wiped her tears, caressed her, and as best she could under the convent's regulations of silence, tried to console her.[2]

This little scene has nothing to do with Beatrice's status as a saint. The text explicitly states that the anonymous nun did not realize the true cause of the saint's sorrow. She was a human being reacting instinctively to the pain of another. But Beatrice—on whose own account the Latin text is based—remembered. She recorded the incident, even though it has no moral—no edification is achieved by it. Though she meant well, the nun actually hurt Beatrice. In a study like mine, which seeks to explain and interpret medieval sainthood, there was no place for this and similar other episodes. The situation is neither saintly nor even particularly medieval. Stories such as this show us in a straightforward and eloquent language that human beings can show kindness and compassion to one another. They need no interpretation; they need to be told. I wanted to tell at least one.

2. L. Reypens, ed., *Vita Beatricis: De Autobiografie van de Z. Beatrijs van Tienen O. Cist. 1200–1268* (Antwerp, 1964), 1.11.56, p. 47.

SELECT BIBLIOGRAPHY

Abbreviations

AA.SS.   *Acta Sanctorum*
C.C.CM   *Corpus Christianorum, Continuatio Mediaevalis*
C.C.SL   *Corpus Christianorum, Series Latina*
M.G.H.   *Monumenta Germaniae Historica*
PC   Process of canonization
PL   *Patrologia Latina*

The following abbreviations are used for the *Corpus iuris canonici:*

c.   canon
C.   causa
D.   Distinctio
De cons.   De consecratione
gl. ord.   glossa ordinaria
q.   quaestio
X   *Decretales Gregorii IX*
VI   *Liber Sextus*

Hagiographical Sources

ABUNDUS OF VILLERS

Vita fratris Abundi. Brussels, Bibliothèque Royale de Belgique. MS. 3255 (19525).

AILRED OF RIEVAULX

Daniel, Walter. 1950. *Vita Ailredi abbatis Rievall' (The Life of Ailred of Rievaulx),* edited and translated by F. M. Powicke. London.

ST. MARGARET MARY ALACOQUE

St. Margaret Mary Alacoque. 1952. *Autobiography.* Translated by the Sisters of the Visitation. 2nd ed. Roselands, Walmer.
———.1915. *Vie et oeuvres.* 3 vols. Edited by Mgr. Gauthey. Paris.

ALDOBRANDESCA OF SIENA

Lombardelli, Gregory. *Vita B. Aldobrandescae. AA.SS.,* 26 Apr., pp. 472–76.

ALPAIS OF CUDOT

Vita Beatae Alpaidis. AA.SS., 3 Nov., pp. 174–209.

AMBROSE OF MASSA

PC of. *AA.SS.*, 10 Nov., pp. 571–608.

ANGELA OF FOLIGNO

Angela of Foligno. 1927. *Le livre de l'expérience des vrais fidèles.* Edited by M. J. Ferré, translated by M. J. Ferré and L. Baudry. Paris.

ANSELM OF CANTERBURY

Eadmer. 1979. *The Life of St. Anselm.* Edited and translated by R. Southern. Oxford.

ANTONY OF PADUA

Gamboso, V., ed. and trans. 1981. *Vita prima di S. Antonio.* Padua.
Kerval, Leon de, ed. 1904. *Sancti Antonii de Padua vitae duae.* Paris.

BEATRICE OF NAZARETH

Reypens, L., ed. 1964. *Vita Beatricis: De Autobiografie van de Z. Beatrijs van Tienen O. Cist. 1200–1268.* Antwerp.

BENEVENUTA BOJANI

de Rubeis, Johannes F., ed. 1757. *Vita Beatae Benevenutae Bojanae.* Venice. Also *AA.SS.*, 29 Oct., pp. 152–85.

BERNARD OF CLAIRVAUX

William of St. Thierry et al. *Vita prima S. Bernardi. PL* 185.

BRIDGET OF SWEDEN

Collijn, I., ed. 1924–31. *Acta et processus canonizacionis Beate Brigitte.* 2 vols. Uppsala.

CATHERINE OF SIENA

Thomas Antonii de Senis "Caffarini." 1974. *Libellus de suppelmento.* Edited by I. Cavallini and I. Foralosso in Testi Caterinnniani 3. Rome.
Raymond of Capua. *Vita S. Catharinae Senensis. AA.SS.*, 30 Apr., pp. 862–967.
———. 1960. *The Life of St. Catherine of Siena,* translated by George Lamb. London.
Valli, F., ed. 1936. *I miracoli di Caterina di Iacopo da Siena.* Siena.

Celestine V/Pietro Morrone

Celestine V. 1954. "Autobiografia." Edited by A. Frugoni in *Celestiniana*, pp. 56–67. Rome.

"Procès-verbal du dernier consistoire secret préperatoire à la canonisation." [Unsigned article], *Analecta Bollandiana* 16 (1897):475–87.

Christina the Astonishing

Thomas of Cantimpré. *Vita S. Christinae mirabilis. AA.SS.*, 24 Jul., pp. 650–60.

Christina of Markyate

Talbot, Charles H., ed. and trans. 1959. *The Life of Christina of Markyate: A Twelfth-Century Recluse*. Oxford.

Christina of Stommeln

Vita anonymi AA.SS. 22 Jun., pp. 367–387.

Peter of Dacia. *Acta B. Christinae Stumbelensi.* [sic] *AA.SS.*, 22 Jun., pp. 236–367.

———.1896. *Vita Christinae stumbelensis*, edited by J. Paulson. In Scriptores Latini medii aevi Suecani 1 facs. 2. Göteborg.

———. 1982. *De gratia naturam ditante sive de virtutibus Christinae stumbelensis*, edited by M. Asztalos. Stockholm.

Clare of Assisi

Lazzeri, Z., ed. 1920. "Il processo per la canonizzazione di S. Chiara d'Assisi" in *Archivum Franciscanum Historicum* 13 (1920):439–93.

Thomas of Celano (?) 1910. *Legenda S. Clarae virginis*, edited by F. Pennacchi. Assisi.

Clare of Montefalco

Menestò, Enrico, ed. 1984. *Il processo di canonizzazione di Chiara da Montefalco*. In Quaderni del "Centro per il Collegamento degli Studi Medievali e Umanistici nell' Università di Perugia" 14. Todi.

Clare of Rimini/Clara de Agolantibus

1784. PC of. *Positio super dubio.* Rome.

Luke Wadding. 1932. *Annales Minorum*, 6th ed., pp. 394–98. The Quaracchi Fathers. Quaracchi.

Colette of Corbie

Vita B. Coletae. AA.SS., 6 Mar., pp. 539–87.

SELECT BIBLIOGRAPHY

DELPHINE OF PUIMICHEL

Cambell, Jacques. 1978. *Enquête pour le procès de canonisation de Dauphine de Puimichel comtesse d'Ariano*. Turin.

DOMINIC

Acta canonizationis S. Dominici. Edited by A. Walz. In *Monumenta Ordinis Fratrum Praedicatorum Historica* 16.2 (1935): 88–194.

DOROTHEA OF MONTAU

Stachnik, Richard, ed. 1978. *Die Akten des Kanonisationsprozesses Dorotheas von Montau*. Cologne.

DOUCELINE OF DIGNE OR OF MARSEILLES

Albanés, J.-H. 1879. *La vie de Sainte Douceline fondatrice des Béguines de Marseille*. Marseille.

Gout, R., ed. and trans. 1927. *La vie de Sainte Douceline: Texte provençl du XIVᵉ siècle*. Paris.

EDMUND OF ABINGDON

Eustace of Faversham. 1960. *Vita S. Edumundi*. Edited by C. H. Lawrence in *St. Edmund of Abingdon: A Study in Hagiography and History,*. Oxford.

EGIDIUS (GILES) OF ASSISI

Br. Leo. 1970. *Vita B. Fratris Egidii*. In *Scripta Leonis Rufini et Angeli sociorum S. Francisci: The Writings of Leo, Rufino, and Angelo Companions of St. Francis*, edited and translated by Rosalind B. Brooke, pp. 318–49. Oxford.

ELIZABETH OF HERKENRODE

Philip of Clairvaux. 1886. *Vita Elizabeth sanctimonialis in Erkenrode*. In *Catalogus codicum hagiographicorum bibliothecae regiae bruxellensis*, 2 vols., 1:362–79. Brussels.

ELIZABETH OF THURINGIA

Huyskens, Albert. 1908. *Quellenstudien zur Geschichte der hl. Elisabeth Landgräfin von Thüringen*. Marburg.

ELZÉAR DE SABRAN

Cambell, Jacques. 1973. "Le sommaire de l'enquêt pour la canonisation de Elzéar de Sabran." *Miscellanea Franciscana* 73 (1973): 438–73.

FRANCIS OF ASSISI

Bigaroni, Marino, ed. 1975. *"Compilatio Assisiensis" dagli scritti di fr. Leone e compagni su S. Francesco d'Assisi.* Assisi.

Bonaventure, Saint. 1926–41. *Legenda maior.* In *Analecta Franciscana* 10:555–652.

Brooke, Rosalind B., ed. and trans. 1970. *Scripta Leonis Rufini et Angeli sociorum S. Francisci: The Writings of Leo, Rufino, and Angelo Companions of St. Francis.* Oxford.

Habig, Marion, ed. 1973. *St. Francis of Assisi: Writings and Early Biographies, English Omnibus of the Sources for the Life of St. Francis.* Chicago.

Lemmens, L., ed. 1901–2. *Documenta antiqua Franciscana.* Quaracchi.

Sabatier, Paul, ed. 1928; 1931. *Le Speculum perfectionis ou Mémoires de frère Léon.* 2 vols. In British Society of Franciscan Studies 13;17. Manchester.

Thomas of Celano. 1926–41. *Vita prima Sancti Francisci.* In Analecta Franciscana 10:1–117.

———. 1926–41. *Vita secunda Sancti Francisci.* In *Analecta Franciscana* 10:127–268.

———. 1926–41. *Tractatus de miraculis Beati Francisci.* In *Analecta Franciscana* 10:269–331.

Ugolino di Monte Santa Maria. 1902. *Actus B. Francisci et sociorum eius,* edited by P. Sabatier. Paris.

GALGANO OF CHIUSDINO

Cardini, Franco, ed. 1982. *Leggenda di Santo Galgano confessore.* Siena.

Schneider, Fedor, ed. 1914–21. "Analecta Toscana." *Quellen und Forschungen aus italienischen Archiven und Bibliotheken* 17:61–77.

GERALD OF AURILLAC

Odo of Cluny. *Vita S. Geraldi. PL.* 133:639–704.

GERARDESCA OF PISA

Vita B. Gerardescae. AA.SS., 29 Mai., pp. 162–76.

GERTRUD VAN OOSTEN

Vita Gertrudis ab Oosten. AA.SS., 6 Jan., pp. 349–53.

GODRIC OF FINCHALE

Reginald of Durham. 1847. *Libellus de vita et miraculis S. Godrici,* edited by J. Stevenson. Surtees Society Publications 20.

HELEN OF HUNGARY

Legenda Beatae Helenae de Ungaria. See Fawtier, R. 1913. "La vie de la Bienheureuse Hélène de Hongrie." *Mélanges d'archéologie et d'histoire* 34 (1913): 3–23.

HUGH OF LINCOLN

Adam of Eynsham. 1961. *Magna vita S. Hugonis.* 2 vols. Edited and translated by D. L. Douie and D. H. Farmer. London.

HUMILITAS/UMILTÀ OF FAENZA

Vita S. Humilitatis. AA.SS., 22 Mai., pp. 207–14.

HUMILIANA (UMILIANA DE' CERCHI)

Vito of Cortona. *Vita Humilianae de Cerchis. AA.SS.,* 19 Mai., pp. 385–400.

IDA OF LOUVAIN

Vita Idae Lovaniensis. See Chr. Henriquez, ed. 1630. *Quinque prudentes virgines.* Antwerp.

IDA OF NIVELLES

Vita B. Idae de Nivella. See Chr. Henriquez, ed. 1630. *Quinque prudentes virgines,* pp. 199–297. Antwerp.

JACOBUS DE VORAGINE.

1941. *The Golden Legend.* 2 vols. Translated and adapted by G. Ryan and H. Ripperger. London.

JOHN BONUS

Joannes Bonus. PC of. *AA.SS.,* 22 Oct., pp. 771–885.

JOHN OF CAPISTRANO

Nicholas of Fara. *Vita B. Joannis de Capistrano. AA.SS.,* 23 Oct., pp. 439–83.

JOHN OF MONTMIRAIL

Vita B. Joannis de Monte-Mirabili. AA.SS., 29 Sept. pp. 218–35.

JONATUS OF MARCHIENNES

Hucbald of St Amand. 1886. *Vita S. Jonathi* (prologue). In *Catalogus codicum hagiographicorum bibliothecae regiae bruxellensis,* 2:273. 2 vols. Brussels.

SELECT BIBLIOGRAPHY

JULIANA OF MT. CORNILLON

Vita Julianae Corneliensis. AA.SS., 5 Apr., pp. 442—76.

MARGERY KEMPE

Kempe, Margery. 1940. *The Book of Margery Kempe,* edited by S. B. Meech. Oxford.
————. 1940. *The Book of Margery Kempe: A Modern Version,* edited by W. Butler-Bowdon. London.

LORENZO LORICATO

Processus auctoritate apostolica confectus super vita et miraculis servi Dei Laurentii conversi et eremitae. In Benedict XIV vol. 3, appendix 4, pp. 662– 93.

LUKARDIS OF OBERWEIMAR

Vita venerabilis Lukardis. In *Analecta Bollandiana* 18 (1899): 305–67.

LUTGARD OF AYWIÈRES

Thomas of Cantimpré. *Vita Lutgardis. AA.SS.,* 16 Jun., pp. 189–210.

MALACHY OF ARMAGH

Bernard of Clairvaux. 1963. *Vita S. Malachiae.* In *Opera,* edited by J. Leclercq and H. M. Rochais, 3: 307–78. Rome.

MARCOLINUS OF FORLI

Flaminio Corner, ed. 1749. *Ecclesiae Venetae, antiquis monumentis nunc etiam primum editis illustratae et in decades distributae,* 13 vols., 7: 188– 92. Venice.

MARGARET OF CITTÀ DE CASTELLO

Vita Margaritae de Città de Castello. ed. M H. Laurent in "La plus ancienne légend de la B. Marguerite de Citta di Castello". *Archivum Fratrum Praedicatorum* 10 (1940), 109–31.

MARGARET OF CORTONA

Giunta Bevegnati. *Vita Margaritae de Cortona. AA.SS.,* 22 Feb., pp. 303– 63.
————. 1978. *Leggenda della vita e dei miracoli di Santa Margherita da Cortona,* translated by E. Mariani, in Bibliotheca Franciscana Sanctorum 2 Vicenza.

MARGARET OF FAENZA

Peter of Florence. *Vita B. Margaritae Faventinae. AA.SS.*, 26 Aug., pp. 847–51.

John of Faenza. *Revelationes et miracula [ejusdem]. AA.SS.*, 26 Aug., pp. 851–53.

MARGARET OF YPRES

Thomas of Cantimpré. 1948. *Vita Margarite de Ypris.* In Gilles G. Meersseman, "Frères Prêcheurs et mouvement dévot en Flandre au XIIIᵉ siècle." *Archivum Fratrum Praedicatorum* 18 (1948): 106–30.

MARIA CATERINA BRONDI

Jarcho, Saul. 1944. "Guiseppe Zambeccari: 'Summary of the Life of Maria Caterina Brondi': With the marginalia of an unidentified contemporary." *Bulletin of the History of Medicine* 15 (1944): 400–419.

MARIE D'OGNIES

Jacques de Vitry. *Vita Mariae Oigniacensis. AA.SS.*, 23 Jun., pp. 547–73.

FRA MICHELE DA CALCI

de Luca, G., ed. 1954. *Il supplizio di fra Michele da Calci.* In *Prosatori minori del Trecento,* 2 vols., 1: 213–36. Milan.

NICOLAS OF TOLENTINO

Occhini, N., ed. 1984. *Il processo per la canonizzazione di S. Nicola da Tolentino.* Rome.

ODO OF CLUNY

John of Salerno. *Vita Odonis. PL* 133: 43–86.

ODO OF NOVARA

PC of in "Documenta de B. Odone Novariensi ordinis Carthusiani." *Analecta Bollandina* 1 (1882): 323–54.

PETER DAMIAN

John of Lodi. *Vita B. Petri Damiani. AA.SS.*, 23 Feb., pp. 422–33.

PILINGOTTO OF URBINO

Vita S. Pilingotti Urbinatis. AA.SS., 1 Jun., pp. 149–55.

ROMUALD

Peter Damian. 1957. *Vita B. Romualdi.* In Fonti per la Storia d'Italia, 94, edited by G. Tabacco. Rome.

SELECT BIBLIOGRAPHY

ROSE OF VITERBO

Abate, S. 1952. "S. Rosa da Viterbo." *Miscellanea Francescana* 52 (1952): 113–268. [Includes the vita Ia and IIa.]

SIMON OF COLLAZZONE

Faloci Pulignani, M. 1910. "Il B. Simone da Collazzone e il suo processo nel 1252." *Miscellanea Francescana* 12 (1910): 97–132.

STEPHEN OF GRANDMONT

Gerard of Grandmont. *Vita S. Stephani Grandimontensis. PL* 204: 1006–71.

HENRY SUSO

Suso, Henry. 1952. *The Life of the Servant*, translated by J. M. Clark, London.

THOMAS AQUINAS

Laurent, M. H., ed. "Processus canonizationis S.Thomae Aquinatis." In *Fontes vitae S. Thomae Aquinatis*, pp. 265–532. Toulouse. (Originally published as supplements to *Revue Thomiste* [1911– 34].)

VILLANA DE BOTIS

Hieronimus Joanni [based on Johannes Caroli]. *Vita Villanae Botiae. AA.SS.*, 26 Aug., pp. 864–69.

WERIC

Vita Werici. 1886. In *Catalogus codicum hagiographicorum bibliothecae regiae bruxellensis*, 2 vols., 1: 445–63. Brussels.

WILLIAM OF NORWICH

Thomas of Monmouth. 1896. *The Life and Miracles of St. William of Norwich*, edited and translated by A. Jessop and M. R. James. Cambridge.

Other Sources

Abelard, Peter. 1950. *Historia calamitatum.* Edited by J. T. Muckle, in "Abelard's Letter of Consolation to a Friend *(Historia calamitatum).*" *Medieval Studies* 12: 163–213.

Agnellus of Ravenna. *Liber pontificalis ecclesiae ravennatis*, edited by O. Holder-Egger. *M.G.H.* Scriptores rerum langobardicarum et italicarum saec. VI–IX. pp. 265–391.

Agobard of Lyon. *De grandine et tonituris.* In his *Opera*, edited by L. Van Acker. *C.C.CM* 52: 1–15.

Aigrain, René. 1953. *L'hagiogrphy: ses sources, ses methodes, son histoire.* Paris.

Ambrose of Milan. *De apologia prophetae David ad Theodosium Augustum* PL 14: 854–84.

Amore, Agostino. 1977. "La canonizazzione vescovile." *Antonianum* 52: 231–66.

Asztalos, Monika, ed. 1986. "Les lettres de direction et les sermons épistolaires de Pierre de Dacie." In *The Editing of Theological and Philosophical Texts from the Middle Ages*, pp. 161–84. Stockholm.

Atkinson, Clarissa W. 1983. *Mystic and Pilgrim: The Book and the World of Margery Kemp.* Ithaca NY.

Aurell, Martin. 1986. *Une famille de la noblesse provençal au moyen âge: Les Porcelet.* Avignon.

Barthes, Roland. 1982. "The Reality Effect." In *French Literary Theory Today: A Reader*, edited by T. Todorov, and translated by R. Carter, pp. 11–17. Cambridge, England.

Bäuml, Franz H. 1980. "Varieties and Consequences of Medieval Literacy and Illiteracy." *Speculum* 55: 237–65.

Bell, Rudolph M. 1985. *Holy Anorexia.* Chicago.

Bendix, Reinhard. 1962. *Max Weber: An Intellectual Portrait.* New York.

Benedictus XIV (Prospero Lambertini). 1839–47. *De servorum Dei beatificatione et de beatorum canonizatione*. In *Opera omnia*, vols. 1–7. Prato.

Benz, Ernst. 1969. *Ecclesia spiritualis: Kirchenidee und Geschichtstheologie der franziskanische Reformation.* Darmstadt.

Bibliotheca sanctorum. 1963. 13 vols. Rome.

Bredero, Adriaan H. 1977. "The Canonization of Bernard of Clairvaux." In *St. Bernard of Clairvaus*, edited by M. B. Pennington, pp. 63–100. Cistercian Studies Series 28. Kalamazoo, MI.

———. 1961–62. "Etudes sur la 'vita prima' de Saint Bernard." *Analecta Sacri Ordinis Cisterciensis* 17: 3–27, 215–60; 18: 3–59.

Boas, Franz. 1930. *The Religion of the Kwakiutl Indians.* 2 vols. New York.

Boesch Gajano, Sofia. 1986. "Santità di vita, sacralità dei luoghi: Aspetti della tradizione agiografica di Domenico di Sora." In *Scritti in onore di Filippo Caraffa*, pp. 187–204. Anagni.

Bonaventure, Saint. 1898. *Opera omnia.* Quaracchi.

Bourdieu, Pierre. 1986. *Outline of a Theory of Practice*, translated by R. Nice. Cambridge, England.

Bourke, John G. 1968. *Scatologic Rites of All Nations.* Washington, D.C., 1891; repr. n. loc., 1968.

Brooke, Rosalind B. 1975. *The Coming of the Friars.* London.

———. 1959. *Early Franciscan Government: Elias to Bonaventure.* Cambridge, England.

Brown, Judith C. 1986. *Immodest Acts: The Life of a Lesbian Nun in Renaissance Italy.* Oxford.

Brown, Patricia Fortini. 1988. *Venetian Narrative Painting in the Age of Carpaccio.* New Haven, CT.

Brown, Peter. 1981. *The Cult of the Saints: Its Rise and Function in Latin Christianity.* Chicago.

———. 1983. "The Saint as Examplar in Late Antiquity." *Representations* 2: 1–25.

Brunvand, Jan H. 1981. *The Vanishing Hitchhiker: American Urban Legends and Their Meaning.* New York.

Bryson, Norman. 1985. *Vision and Painting: The Logic of the Gaze.* New Haven, CT.

Bughetti, B. 1927. "Una nuova compilazione di testi intorno alla vita di S. Francesco." *Archivum Franciscanum Historicum* 20: 525–62.

Bullarium Franciscanum 1983. Edited by J. H. Sbaralea. Rome, 1759; repr. Assisi, 1983.

Bullarium romanum pontificum. 1740. Edited by C. Coquelines. Rome.

Bynum, Caroline Walker. 1979. *Docere verbo et exemplo.* Missoula, Montana.

———. 1982. *Jesus as Mother: Studies in the Spirituality of the High Middle Ages.* Berkeley, CA.

———. 1984. "Women's Stories, Women's Symbols: A Critique of Victor Turner's Theory of Liminality." In *Anthropology and the Study of Religion,* edited by R. L. Moore and F. E. Reynolds, pp. 105–24. Chicago.

———. 1985. "Fast, Feast, and Flesh: The Religious Significance of Food to Medieval Women." *Representations* 11: 1–25.

———. 1987. *Holy Feast and Holy Fast.* Berkeley, CA.

———. 1988. "The Female Body and Religious Practice in the Later Middle Ages." In *Fragments for a History of the Human Body,* 3 vols., edited by Michel Faher et al., 1: 160–219. New York.

Carolus-Barré, Louis. 1959. "Consultation du Cardinal Pietro Colonna sur le IIe miracle de S. Louis." *Bibliothèque de l'Ecole des Chartes* 117: 57–72.

Carozzi, Claude. 1976. "Douceline et les autres." *La Religion populaire en Languedoc,* pp. 251–67. Cahiers de Fanjeaux 11 Toulouse.

———. 1975. "Une Béguine Joachimite: Douceline, soeur d'Hugues de Digne." *Franciscaines d'Oc: Les Spiritueles ca. 1280–1324,* pp. 169–201. Cahiers de Fanjeaux 10 Toulouse.

Catherine of Siena, Saint. 1980. *The Dialogue.* Translated by S. Noffke in The Classics of Western Spirituality. New York.

Cazelles, Brigitte. 1982. *Le Corps de saintetté: d'après Jehan Bouche d'Or, Jehan Paulus et quelques vies des XIIe et XIIIe siècles.* Geneva.

Certeau, Michel de. 1975. *L'écriture de l'histoire.* Paris.

Christian, William A., Jr. 1981. *Apparitions in Late Medieval and Renaissance Spain*. Princeton, NJ.

———. 1982. "Provoked Religious Weeping in Early Modern Spain." In *Religious Organization and Religious Experience*, edited by J. Davis, pp. 97–114. A.S.A. Monograph 21. London.

———. 1987. "Tapping and Defining New Power: The First Month of Visions at Ezquioga, July 1931." *American Ethnologist* 14, no. 1 (February): 140–66.

Coakley, John. 1991. "Friars as Confidants of Holy Women in Medieval Dominican Hagiography." In *Images of Sainthood in Medieval Europe*, edited by R. Blumenfeld-Kosinski and T. Szell. Ithaca, NY.

———. 1980. "The Representation of Sanctity in Late Medieval Hagiography: Evidence from Lives of Saints of the Dominican Order." Ph.D. diss. Harvard University.

Corpus iuris canonici. 1959. Edited by Ae. Friedberg. 2 vols. Leipzig, 1879–1881; repr. Graz, 1959.

Craveri, Marcello. 1980. *Sante e streghe: Biografie e documenti dal XIV al XVII secolo*. Milan.

Campagnola, Stanislao da. 1971. *L'Angelo del sesto sigillo e l' "Alter Christus."* Rome.

———. 1981. *Francesco d'Assisi nei suoi scritti e nelle biografie dei secoli XIII– XIV*. Assisi.

———. 1982. "Le prime 'biografie' del santo." In *Francesco d'Assisi: Storia e arte*, edited by Roberto Rusconi, pp. 36–48. Milan.

Davis, Natalie Zemon. 1987. *Fiction in the Archives: Pardon Tales and Their Tellers in Sixteenth-Century France*. Stanford, CA.

Davis, Winston. 1980. *Dojo: Magic and Exorcism in Modern Japan*. Stanford, CA.

De Beer, Francis. 1963. *La conversion de Saint François selon Thomas de Celano: Etude comparative des textes relatifs à la conversion en Vita I et Vita II*. Paris.

Debongnie, Pierre. 1936. "Essai critique sur l'Histoire des Stigmatisations au moyen âge." *Etudes carmélitaines* 21, no. 2: 22–59.

Delehaye, Hippolyte. 1961. *The Legends of the Saints*, translated by V. M. Crawford from the 2d French edition, 1907; repr. London, 1961.

Delooz, Pierre. 1962. "Pour une étude sociologique de la sainteté canonisé dans l'Eglise catholique." *Archives de sociologie des religions* 13: 17–43.

———. 1969. *Sociologie et canonisations*. The Hague.

Deroche, H., J. Maître, and A. Vauchez. 1970. "Sociologie de la sainteté canonisée." *Archives de sociologie des religions* 30: 109–15.

Dinzelbacher, Peter. 1985. "Die 'Vita et Revelationes' der Wiener Begine Agnes Blannbekin (d. 1315) im Rahmen der Viten und Offenbarungsliteratur ihrer Zeit." In *Frauenmystik im Mittelalter*, edited by P.Dinzelbacher and D. R.Bauer, pp. 152–77. Ostfildern.

Drane, Augusta T. 1899. *The History of St. Catherine of Siena and Her Companions*. 2 vols. 3d ed. London.

Elliott, Alison Goddard. 1987. *Roads to Paradise: Reading the Lives of the Early Saints*. Hanover, NH.

Elliott, Dyan H. 1989. "Spiritual Marriage: A Study of Chaste Wedlock in the Middle Ages." Ph.D. diss. University of Toronto.

Esser, Kajetan, ed. 1976. *Die "Opuscula" des hl. Franziskus von Assisi: Neue textkritische Edition*. Grottaferrata.

Evans-Pritchard, E. E. 1937. *Witchcraft, Oracles and Magic Among the Azande*. Oxford.

Favret-Saada, Jeanne. 1980. *Deadly Words: Witchcraft in the Bocage*, translated by C. Cullen. Cambridge, England.

Finucane, Ronald C. 1977. *Miracles and Pilgrimages: Popular Beliefs in Medieval England*. London.

Fleischman, Suzanne. 1983. "On the Representation of History and Fiction in the Middle Ages." *History and Theory* 22: 278–310.

Fontette, Micheline de. 1967. *Les religieuses a l'âge classique du droit canon: Recherches sur les structures juridiques des branches féminines des ordres*. Paris.

Freed, John B. 1977. *The Friars and German Society in the Thirteenth Century*. Cambridge, MA.

Friedberg, Aemilius, ed. 1882. *Quinque compliationes antiquae*. Leipzig.

Frugoni, Chiara. 1982. "Le mistiche, le visioni e l'iconografia: rapporti ed influssi." In *Atti del convegno su "la mistica femminile del trecento,"* pp. 5–45. Todi.

Gaiffier, Baudouin de. 1947. "L'hagiographie et son public au XIe siècle." In *Miscellanea historica in honorem Leonis Van der Essen*, pp. 135–66. Brussels.

Gallén, Jarl. 1946. *La province de Dacie de l'ordre des Frères Prêcheurs*. Rome.

Ganck, Roger de. 1970. "The Cistercian Nuns of Belgium in the Thirteenth Century." *Cistercian Studies* 5: 169–87.

Geary, Patrick J. 1978. *Furta Sacra: Theft of Relics in the Middle Ages*. Princeton, NJ.

———. 1983. "Humiliation of Saints." In *Saints and Their Cults: Studies in Religious Sociology, Folklore, and History*, edited by S. Wilson, pp. 123–40. Cambridge, MA.

Geertz, Clifford. 1983. *Local Knowledge: Furter Essays in Interpretive Anthropology*. New York.

———. 1973. *The Interpretation of Cultures*. New York.

Gellner, Ernest. 1969. *Saints of the Atlas*. London.

Gerard de Frachet (Gerardus de Fracheto). 1896. *Vitae Fratrum Ordinis Praedicatorum.* Edited by B. M. Reichert. In *Monumenta Ordinis Fratrum Praedicatorum Historica* 1 (1896).

Gilsenan, Michael. 1982. *Recognizing Islam: Religion and Society in the Modern Arab World.* New York.

Glaber, Rodulfus. 1989. *Historiarum libri quinque,* edited by N. Bulst and translated by J. France and P. Reynolds. Oxford.

Goffman, Erving. 1959. *The Presentation of Self in Everyday Life.* New York.

———. 1971a. *Relations in Public: Microstudies of the Public Order.* New York.

———. 1971b. *Strategic Interaction.* Philadelphia, PA.

Goffredus of Trani. 1968. *Summa super titulis decretalium.* Lyon, 1519; repr. Darmstadt,

Goodich, Michael. 1985. *"Ancilla Dei:* The Servant as Saint in the Late Middle Ages." In *Women of the Medieval World,* edited by J. Kirshner and S. F. Wemple, pp. 119–36. Oxford.

———. 1983. "The Politics of Canonization in the Thirteenth Century: Lay and Mendicant Saints." In *Saints and Their Cults,* edited by S. Wilson, pp. 169–87. Cambridge, MA.

———. 1982. *Vita perfecta: The Ideal of Sainthood in the Thirteenth Century.* Stuttgart.

Goody, Jack, and Ian Watt. 1968. "The Consequences of Literacy." In *Literature in Traditional Societies,* edited by J. Goody, pp. 27–68. Cambridge, MA.

Guenée, Bernard. 1980. *Histoire et culture historique dans l'Occident médiéval.* Paris.

Guibert of Nogent. *De pignoribus sanctorum.* In *PL* 156: 607–80.

Harding, Susan F. 1987. "Convicted by the Spirit: The Rhetoric of Fundamentalist Baptist Conversion." *American Ethnologist* 14, no. 1 (February): 167–81.

Hart, Herbert L. A. 1948. "The Ascription of Responsibility and Rights." *Proceedings of the Aristotelian Society* 49: 171–94.

Hauck, Karl. 1950. "Geblütsheiligkeit." In *Liber Floridus Paul Lehmann,* pp. 187–240. St. Ottilien.

Hawley, John Stratton, ed. 1987. *Saints and Virtues.* Berkeley, CA.

Head, Thomas. 1990. *Hagiography and the Cult of Saints: The Diocese of Orleans, 800–1200.* Cambridge, England.

Heffernan, Thomas J. 1988. *Sacred Biography: Saints and Their Biographers in the Middle Ages.* Oxford.

Höcht, Johannes M. 1986. *Träger der Wundmale Christi.* Stein am Rhein.

Hofmann, Georg. 1903. *Die Lehre von der Fides Implicita innerhalb der katholischen Kirche.* Leipzig.

Hoffmann, Rudolf. 1976. *Die heroische Tugend: Geschichte und Inhalt eines theologischen Begriffes*. Munich, 1933; repr. Hildesheim, 1976.

Hostiensis (Henricus de Segusio). 1965. *In quinque libros decretalium commentaria*. Venice, 1581; repr. Turin, 1965.

———. 1542. *Summa super titulis decretalium*. *(Summa Aurea)*. Lyon.

Hume, David. 1921. *An Enquiry concerning Human Understanding*. Chicago.

———. 1976. *The Natural History of Religion*, edited by A. W. Colver. Oxford.

Innocent III. 1964. *Die Register Innocenz' III*, edited by O. Hageneder and A. Haidacher, 2 vols. Graz.

Innocent III. 1953. *Selected Letters of Innocent III*, edited by C. R. Cheney and W. H. Semple. London.

Innocent IV (Sinibaldo Fieschi). 1968. *Commentaria in quinque libros decretalium*. Frankfurt, 1570; repr. Frankfurt, 1968.

Iohannes Andreae. 1963. *In quinque decretalium libros novella commentaria*. Venice, 1581; repr. Turin, 1963.

Jancey, M. 1982. *St. Thomas Cantilupe Bishop of Hereford: Essays in His Honour*. Hereford.

Jordan of Giano. 1908. *Chronica fratris Jordani*, edited by H. Boehmer. Paris.

Jordan of Saxony. 1935. *Libellus de principiis Ord. Praedicatorum*, edited by H. C. Scheeben, in *Monumenta Ordinis Fratrum Praedicatorum Historica* 16 no. 2, 1–88.

Kee, Howard C. 1983. *Miracle in the Early Christian World: A Study in Sociohistorical Method*. New Haven, CT.

Kemp, Eric W. 1948. *Canonization and Authority in the Western Church*. London.

Kieckhefer, Richard. 1984. *Unquiet Souls: Fourteenth-Century Saints and Their Religious Milieu*. Chicago.

Kieckhefer, Richard, and George D. Bond, eds. 1988. *Sainthood: Its Manifestations in World Religions*. Berkeley, CA.

Kleinberg, Aviad M. 1987. "*De agone christiano:* The Preacher and His Audience." *Journal of Theological Studies*, NS 38.1: 16–33.

———. 1989. "Proving Sanctity: Selection and Authentication of Saints in the Later Middle Ages." *Viator* 20: 183–205.

Kuttner, Stephan. 1980. "La réserve papal du droit de canonisation." Reprinted in *The History of Ideas and Doctrines of Canon Law in the Middle Ages*, pp. 172–228. London.

Lambert, M. D. 1961. *Franciscan Poverty: The Doctrine of the Absolute Poverty of Christ and the Apostles in the Franciscan Order: 1210–1323*. London.

Lauwers, Michel. 1988. "La mort et le corps des saints: La scène de la mort dans les *vitae* du haut Moyen Age." *Le Moyen Age* 94, no. 1: 21–50.

Lévi-Strauss, Claude. 1967. "The Sorcerer and His Magic." In *Magic, Witchcraft, and Curing,* edited by John Middleton, pp. 23–41. Austin, TX.

Lexikon der christlische Ikonographie. 1968. 8 vols. Rome.

Leyser, Henrietta. 1984. *Hermits and the New Monasticism.* London.

Manselli, Raoul. 1980. *Nos qui cum eo fuimus: Contributo alla questione Francescana.* Rome.

Map, Walter. 1983. *De nugis curialium: Courtiers' Trifles,* edited and translated by M. R. James; revised by C. N. L. Brooke and R. A. B. Mynors. Oxford.

Markus, Gyorgy. 1987. "Why Is There No Hermeneutics of Natural Science: Some Preliminary Theses." *Science in Context* 1, no. 1 (March): 5–54.

Marténe, E., and U. Durand, eds. 1968. *Thesaurus novus anecdotarum.* Paris, 1717; repr., New York.

Martin, G. H. 1976. "Road Travel in the Middle Ages." *Journal of Transportation History.* NS 3, no. 3: 159–78.

McDonnell, Ernest W. 1969. *The Beguines and Beghards in Medieval Culture: With Special Emphasis on the Belgian Scene.* New York.

Moore, Robert I. 1977. *The Origins of European Dissent.* New York.

Moorman, John R. 1968. *A History of the Franciscan Order from Its Origins to the Year 1517.* Oxford.

Morse, Ruth. 1991. *Truth and Convention in the Middle Ages: Rhetoric, Representation, and Reality.* Cambridge, England.

Nelson, William. 1973. *Facts and Fiction: The Dilemma of the Renaissance Storyteller.* Cambridge: MA.

Nessi, Silvestro. 1968. "I processi per la canonizzazione di Santa Chiara da Montefalco." *Bollettino della Deputazione di Storia Patria per l'Umbria* 66, no. 2: 103–60.

Nieveler, Paul. 1975. *Codex Iuliacensis: Christina von Stommeln und Petrus von Dacien, ihr Leben und Nachleben in Geschichte, Kunst und Literatur.* Mönchengladbach.

Nimmo, Duncan. 1987. *Reform and Division in the Franciscan Order: From Saint Francis to the Foundation of the Capuchins.* Rome.

Obeyesekere, Gananath. 1981. *Medusa's Hair.* Chicago.

Petroff, Elizabeth A. 1979. *Consolation of the Blessed.* New York.

———. 1986. *Medieval Women's Visionary Literature.* Oxford.

Poulin, Joseph-Claude. 1975. *L'ideal de sainteté dans l'Aquitaine carolingienne (750–950).* Québec.

Quetif, J., and J. Echard. 1719. *Scriptores Ordinis Praedicatorum.* Paris.

Ratnoff, Oscar D. 1980. "The Psychogenic Purpuras: A Review of Auto-erythrocyte Sensitization, Autosensitization to DNA, 'Hysterical' and Factitial Bleeding, and the Religious Stigmata." *Seminars in Hematology* 17, no. 3 (July): 192–213.

Renan, Ernest. 1884. *Nouvelles études d'histoire religieuse.* Paris.

Roisin, Simone. 1947. *L'hagiographie Cistercienne dans le diocèse de Liège au XIIIe siècle.* Brussels.

Romano V, Octavio Ignacio. 1965. "Charismatic Medicine, Folk-Healing, and Folk-Sainthood." *American Anthropologist* 67.5.1 1151–73.

Sahlins, Marshall. 1985. *Islands of History.* Chicago.

Salimbene de Adam. 1966. *Cronica,* 2 vols., edited by G. Scalia. Bari.

———. 1986. *The Chronicle of Salimbene de Adam,* translated by J. L. Baird, G. Baglivi, and J. R. Kane. Binghamton, New York.

Sallmann, Jean-Michel. 1986. *Chercheurs de trésors et jeteuses de sorts: La quête du surnaturel à Naples au XVIe siècle.* Paris.

———. 1979a. "Il santo e le rappresentazioni della santità: Problemi di metodo." *Quaderni storici* 41: 584–602.

———. 1979b. "Image et fonction du saint dans la région de Naples à la fin du XVIIe et la début du XVIIIe siècle." *Mélanges de l'Ecole Française de Rome: Moyen Age Temps Moderns* 91, no. 2: 827–74.

Schenk, Max. 1965. *Die Unfehlbarkeit des Papstes in der Heiligsprechung.* Freiburg.

Schlafke, Jacobus. 1961. *De competentia in causis sanctorum decernandi a primis post Christum natum saeculis usque ad annum 1234.* Rome.

Schmitt, Jean-Claude. 1984. "La fabrique des saints." *Annales ESC* 39, no. 2: 286–300.

———. 1979a. "La parola addomesticata: San Domenico, il gato e le donne di Fanjeaux." *Quaderni Storici* 41: 416–39.

———. 1979b. *Le saint lévrier: Guinefort, guérisseur d'enfants depuis le XIIIe siècle.* Paris.

Schreiner, Klaus. 1966. "Discrimen veri ac falsi: Ansätze und Formen der Kritik in der Heiligen und Reliquienverherung des Mittelalter." *Archiv für Kulturgeschichte* 48: 1–53.

Sheppard, Lancelot. 1969. *The Saints Who Never Were.* Dayton, OH.

Shorter, Edward. 1986. "Paralysis: The Rise and Fall of a 'Hysterical' Symptom." *Journal of Social History* 19: 549–82.

Sigal, Pierre-André. 1985. *L'homme et le miracle dans la France médiéval (XIe–XIIe siècle).* Paris.

Smalley, Beryl. 1974. *Historians in the Middle Ages.* London.

Soloveitchik, Haym. 1987. "Religious Law and Change: The Medieval Ashkenazic Example." *AJS Review* 12, no. 2: 205–21.

Sperber, Dan. 1985. *On Anthropological Knowledge*. Cambridge, England.
———. 1974. *Le symbolisme en général*. Paris.
Steinen, Wolfram von den. 1959. *Der Kosmos des Mittelalters von Karl dem Grossen zu Bernhard von Clairvaux*. Bern.
Stock, Brian. 1983. *The Implications of Literacy: Written Language and Models of Interpretation in the Eleventh and Twelfth Centuries*. Princeton, NJ.
———. 1976–77. "Literary Discourse and the Social Historian." *New Literary History* 8: 183–94.
Stone, Lawrence. 1981. *The Past and the Present*. London.
Szasz, Thomas S. 1974. *The Myth of Mental Illness: Foundations of a Theory of Personal Conduct*. 2d revised edition. New York.
Thomas of Eccleston. 1951. *Tractatus de adventu Fratrum Minorum in Angliam*, edited by A. G. Little. Manchester.
Thurston, Herbert. 1928. "The Case of Bd. Christina of Stommeln." *The Month* 152: 425–37.
———. 1952. *The Physical Phenomena of Mysticism*. London.
Tierney, Brian. 1972. *Origins of Papal Infallibility 1150–1350: A Study of the Concepts of Infallibility, Sovereignty, and Tradition in the Middle Ages*. Leiden.
Toynbee, Margaret R. 1929. *St. Louis of Toulouse and the Process of Canonization in the Fourteenth Century*. Manchester.
Tubach, Frederic C. 1969. *Index exemplorum: A Handbook of Medieval Religious Tales*. Helsinki.
Van der Essen, Leon. 1923. "Hucbald de Saint-Amand (c. 840–930) et sa place dans le mouvement hagiographique médiéval." *Revue d'histoire ecclésiastique* 19, no. 1: 333–51; 522–52.
Van Uytfanghe, Marc. 1989. "Le culte des saints et l'hagiographie face à l'écriture: Les avatars d'une relation ambiguë." In *Santi e demoni nell' 'alto medioevo occidentale (secoli V–XI)*. 2 vols. Settinmane di Studio del Centro Italiano di Studi sull'Alto Medioevo 36. Spoleto.
Vauchez, André. 1978. "Canonisation et politique au XIVᵉ siècle." In *Miscellanea in onore de Msr. Martino Giusti*, pp. 381–404. Vatican City.
———. 1989. "L'hagiographie entre la critique historique et la dynamic narrative." *La vie spirituelle* 143: 251–60.
———. 1976. "La religion populaire dans la France méridionale au XIV siècle, d'apres les procès de canonisation." In *La religion populaire en Languedoc*, Cahiers de Fanjeaux 11, pp. 91–107. Toulouse. Also see the "Conclusion," pp. 429–44.
———. 1981. *La sainteté en Occident aux derniers siècles du moyen âge, d'après les procès de canonisation et les documents hagiograhiques*. Rome.
———. 1975. *La spiritualité du moyen âge occidental*. Paris.

————. 1968. "Les stigmates de Saint François et leurs détracteurs." *Mélanges d'archeologie et d'histoire Ecole Française de Rome* 80: 595–625.

Veyne, Paul. 1988. *Did the Greeks Believe in Their Myths?: An Essay on the Constitutive Imagination.* Translated by P. Wissing. Chicago.

Wagner, Roy. 1981. *The Invention of Culture: Revised and Expanded Edition.* Chicago.

Wakefield, Walter, and Austin P. Evans. 1969. *Heresies of the High Middle Ages.* New York.

Ward, Benedicta. 1982. *Miracles and the Medieval Mind: Theory, Record, and Event 1000–1215.* London.

Weber, Max. 1947. *The Theory of Social and Economic Organization.* Translated by A. R. Henderson and Talcott Parsons, and edited by Talcott Parsons. London.

Weinstein, Donald, and Rudolph Bell. 1982. *Saints and Society: The Two Worlds of Christendom 1000–1700.* Chicago.

Whitlock, F. A., and J. V. Hynes. 1978. "Religious Stigmatization: An Historical and Psychophysiological Enquiry." *Psychological Medicine* 8: 185–202.

Wilson, Stephen, ed. 1983. *Saints and Their Cults: Studies in Religious Sociology, Folklore and History.* Cambridge, England.

Zanella, Gabriele. 1986. *Itinerari ereticali: Patari e Catari tra Rimini e Verona.* Rome.

Zarri, Gabriella. 1980. "Le sante vive: Per una tipologia della santità femminile nel primo cinquecento." *Annali dell'Istituto Storico Italo Germanico in Trento* 6: 371–445.

Zoepf, Ludwig. 1973. *Das Heiligen-Leben im 10. Jahrhundert.* Leipzig, 1908, repr. Hildesheim, 1973.

INDEX

DATE DUE

GAYLORD   #3523PI   Printed in USA